INTELLECTUALS IN TWENTIETH-CENTURY FRANCE

Intellectuals in Twentieth-Century France

Mandarins and Samurais

Edited and introduced by

Jeremy Jennings
Senior Lecturer in French Political Thought and Government
University of Swansea, Wales

St. Martin's Press

Selection, editorial matter and Introduction © J. R. Jennings 1993
Chapters 2–10 © The Macmillan Press Ltd 1993
Chapter 11 © Stefan Collini 1993

First published in Great Britain 1993 by
THE MACMILLAN PRESS LTD
Houndmills, Basingstoke, Hampshire RG21 2XS
and London
Companies and representatives
throughout the world

This book is published in the St Antony's / Macmillan Series
General Editor: Rosemary Thorp

A catalogue record for this book is available from the British Library.

ISBN 0–333–49889–5

Printed in Great Britain by
Antony Rowe Ltd
Chippenham, Wiltshire

First published in the United States of America 1993 by
Scholarly and Reference Division,
ST. MARTIN'S PRESS, INC.,
175 Fifth Avenue,
New York, N.Y. 10010

ISBN 0–312–08591–5

Library of Congress Cataloging-in-Publication Data
Intellectuals in twentieth-century France: Mandarins and Samurais/
edited and introduced by Jeremy Jennings.
p. cm.
Includes index.
ISBN 0–312–08591–5
1. France—Intellectual life—20th century. 2. Intellectuals–
–France—Political activity—History—20th century. 3. France–
–Politics and government—20th century. 4. Politics and culture–
–France—History—20th century. I. Jennings, Jeremy, 1952– .
DC33.7.I566   1993
001.1'0944—dc20
92–19656
CIP

To my friends in Paris

Contents

Preface

The essays in this volume are intended to be a reflection of the concerns and questions raised in the first, introductory essay and are meant to provide the English reader for the first time with a representative sample of what is in France a growing body of research that spans several different disciplines, most notably history, political science and sociology. The list of topics covered is not exhaustive and other subjects come readily to mind – the intellectual and sport and the intellectual in exile, to take two very different examples[1] – but those covered here illustrate both the methodological issues that are discussed below as well as the broader ethical and historical perspectives that have been raised by the intellectual's prominence in the life and politics of twentieth-century France and by his supposed demise in the last two decades. The articles written by Jacques Julliard and Pierre Nora also give an idea of the contemporary polemic associated with recent discussion of the role of the intellectual. Significantly, none of our authors seem eager to come to a definitive verdict on the intellectual's fate. Finally, all of this – as Pierre Bourdieu has said of his own work[2] – might appear 'very French' but comparisons and equivalences do exist between the world or field of the French intellectual and that of his counterparts in other countries and it is for this reason that the last essay in this collection marks a much-needed beginning to the analysis of the respective positions of the intellectual in Britain and in France.

JEREMY JENNINGS

Notes

1. See P. Balmand, 'Les Ecrivains et le football en France: Une anthologie', *Vingtième siècle*, 26, 1990, pp. 111–26; and the excellent A. Betz, *Exil et Engagement: Les intellectuels allemands et la France 1930–1940* (Paris, 1991).
2. P. Bourdieu, 'Preface to the English-Language Edition', *Distinction* (London, 1984) p. xi.

Acknowledgements

For the editor of this volume its completion was itself a voyage into the French intelligentsia and like all voyages into the unknown it had its moments of pleasure and despair. There is also perhaps something odd about producing a book on intellectuals when one has spent so much of one's past writing about various forms of anti-intellectualism. The original idea to bring together a set of essays written primarily by French scholars came in January 1988, when I attended a conference in Paris on *Jaurès et les intellectuels*. Since then the volume's proposed format has changed considerably and I therefore thank all my contributors for their patience and, in some cases, their willingness to endure my frequent telephone calls. I owe a very special debt to Christophe Prochasson and to Shlomo Sand without whom, it is true to say, the project would never have been completed. Françoise Blum was also there at the very outset and to her is due my appreciation for her always intelligent and critical comments.

More generally I wish to thank the Nuffield Foundation for the award of a grant funding periods of research in France during 1990 and the British Council in Paris (and especially its deputy director, Mr Peter Ellwood) for covering certain travel expenses in 1990–1. I further thank Professor Eugen Weber for allowing me to use his translation of the Pierre Nora article contained in this volume and Stefan Collini for agreeing to write its concluding chapter. The latter resulted from a chance meeting at Jacques Julliard's seminar on intellectuals at the *Ecole des Hautes Etudes en Sciences Sociales* (EHESS).

Finally, the production of this text corresponds to a particular period of my life, an epoch that I associate above all with a group of friends who mean very much to me and it is to them therefore that this volume is gratefully dedicated.

To someone else who never agrees to be cited goes my profound admiration.

JEREMY JENNINGS

Notes on the Contributors

Pascal Balmand is *maître de conférence* at the *Institut d'Etudes politiques de Paris*. He is the author of a series of articles in *Vingtième siècle* and *L'Histoire*. A specialist on intellectual life in inter-war France, he is at present completing a study of Denis de Rougemont. He is shortly to publish a general history of France in the twentieth century and is currently acting as editorial consultant for a dictionary of French intellectuals, to be published by Le Seuil.

Christophe Charle is Professor of Contemporary History at the *Université de Lyon III* and director of research at the *Centre National de la Recherche Scientifique* (CNRS). He is the author of *La Crise littéraire à l'époque du naturalisme: roman, théâtre et politique* (1979), *Les Elites de la République: 1880–1900* (1987), *Naissance des intellectuels, 1880–1900* (1990), *Histoire sociale de la France au XIXe siècle* (1991), several biographical studies of academic élites in France as well as numerous articles, most notably in *Actes de la Recherche en Sciences Sociales*.

Stefan Collini is University Lecturer in English and Fellow of Clare Hall, Cambridge. In 1986 and 1991, he was *directeur d'études associé* at the *Ecole des Hautes Etudes en Sciences Sociales*. He is co-editor of *The Cambridge Review*. His books include *Liberalism and Sociology: LT.Hobhouse and Political Argument in England 1880–1914* (1979), (with Donald Winch and John Burrow) *That Noble Science of Politics: A Study in Nineteenth-Century Intellectual History* (1983), *Arnold* (1988) and *Public Moralists: Political Thought and Intellectual Life in Britain 1850–1930* (1991).

Jeremy Jennings is Senior Lecturer in French Political Thought and Government at the University of Swansea. He is the author of *Georges Sorel: the Character and Development of his Thought* (1985) and of *Syndicalism in France: A History of Ideas* (1990).

Jacques Julliard is *directeur d'études* at the *Ecole des Hautes Etudes en Sciences Sociales* and editorialist at *Le Nouvel Observateur*. He is the author of *Fernand Pelloutier et les origines du syndicalisme d'action* *directe* (1971), *Contre la politique professionnelle* (1977), *La Faute à Rousseau* (1985), *Autonomie ouvrière: études sur le syndicalisme d'action directe* (1988), (with François Furet and Pierre Rosanvallon) *La République du centre: la fin de l'exception française* (1988), *La Génie de la liberté* (1990) and several historical studies of twentieth-century France. A selection of his articles from *Le Nouvel Observateur* covering the period 1981–90 has recently been published under the title *Chroniques du septième jour* (1991).

Daniel Lindenberg is *maître de conférence* at the *Université de Paris VIII*. He is the author of *Le Marxisme introuvable* (1975), (with Pierre-André Meyer) *Lucien Herr, le socialisme et son destin* (1977) and *Les Années souterraines 1937–1947* (1990). He has most recently acted as editorial consultant for a film exploring life in wartime Vichy, *Hotel du Parc*.

Pierre Nora is *directeur d'études* at the EHESS, commissioning editor at the Gallimard publishing house and editor of *Le Débat*. Editor (with Jacques Le Goff) of *Faire de l'histoire* (1974) and of *Essais d'égo-histoire*, he has most recently been responsible for the multi-volumed series exploring the key concepts and institutions of France's cultural and political history, *Les Lieux de mémoire*.

Christophe Prochasson is *maître de conférence* at the EHESS. He is the author of *Les Années électriques 1880–1910* (1991) and a contributor to *Dernières questions aux intellectuels* (1989), edited by Pascal Ory. A revised version of his thesis exploring the role of intellectuals in the French socialist movement between 1900 and 1920 is shortly to be published by Le Seuil.

Shlomo Sand is Senior Lecturer in History at the University of Tel Aviv and visiting *maître de conférence* at the *Ecole des Hautes Etudes en Sciences Sociales* (EHESS). He is the author of *L'Illusion du politique: Georges Sorel et le débat intellectuel 1900* (1985) and (with Jacques Julliard) of *Georges Sorel en son temps* (1985).

Yves Santamaria holds the *agrégation* in history and is a member of the *Centre d'Histoire et de Sociologie du communisme*. The author of a doctoral thesis on the French Communist Party in the 1930s, he has published numerous articles on the subject and is on the editorial board of the review *Communisme*. His most recent publication in

English is 'The French Communist Party and the CGT: Problems of Adaptation', in M. Waller, S. Courtois and M. Lazar (eds), *Comrades and Brothers: Communism and Trade Unions in Europe* (1991).

Jean-François Sirinelli is Professor of Contemporary History at the *Université Charles de Gaulle Lille III*. He is the author of *Génération intellectuelle: Khâgneux et Normaliens dans l'entre-deux-guerres* (1988), *Intellectuels et passions françaises: manifestes et pétitions au XXe siècle* (1990), (with Pascal Ory) *Les Intellectuels en France, de l'Affaire Dreyfus à nos jours* (1986), and (with Jean-Pierre Rioux) editor of *La Guerre d'Algérie et les intellectuels* (1990). He is also the author of numerous articles in historical journals and collections.

Notes on Translation

With the exception of the article by Pierre Nora, translated by Professor Eugen Weber, all the essays in this volume have been written specifically for this collection. Where necessary notes have been added to provide extra information for the English reader or to clarify points of translation. If reference has been made to a text with a readily available English-language version I have endeavoured to cite this in parallel with the original French version in the footnotes. I have not, however, always made use of the available English version in the translated text. I have, of course, always endeavoured to remain as faithful as possible to both the letter and the intention of the original French texts. Any shortcomings that might have escaped the attention of individual authors are entirely my responsibility.

1 Introduction: Mandarins and Samurais: The Intellectual in Modern France

Jeremy Jennings

I

In March 1991, at the very moment when French television was in the process of showing a four-part documentary devoted to the intellectual in France, *The Times* newspaper in England published a wonderfully tongue-in-cheek article entitled 'Dead and Bereted'.[1] The reader was invited to consider the views of the 'identikit intellectual', Jean-Pierre Levy. Levy, we were told, 'sprang from that grand tradition of French thinkers who could think of three new reasons to commit suicide or sign a petition before breakfast. They made their names by sneering more than the average Parisian. Many of them also made their names by picking three, in any permutation, from a list that included Charles, Henri, Paul, Levi, Pierre, Sartre, Bernard, Jean, Claude and Buffy'. No one ever chose Buffy! Even more amusingly the mythical Levy tells us: 'we were never rich – I remember once, soon after everyone thought that Levi-Strauss had licensed his name to a jeans company, that André Gide was so jealous he approached a famous laxative with the idea of marketing a new potion with the slogan, 'Vous serez vide avec une dose de Gide''. Gide, we are led to believe, was spurned and in a huff went off to write *Strait is the Gate*. Such men, however, were happy and there were still plenty of questions to be asked. 'Every day', Levy comments, 'I think of more'.

On the face of it we might reasonably be inclined to locate this piece of Saturday journalism in the long tradition of British anti-intellectualism, a tradition which has its roots in philosophical empiricism and which in its less acceptable form produces such loathsome outpourings as Paul Johnson's abusive *Intellectuals*[2] and is capable of characterising one of Britain's foremost playwrights as a 'Bollinger socialist'.

1

After twelve years of Thatcherite philistinism we too, along with Michael Ignatieff, might ask if this is a country fit to think in.[3]

Yet *The Times* article has its serious side: its subject was the supposed demise of the French intellectual, the disappearance of a figure who for the last forty years or more has been responsible for making Paris one of the undisputed cultural capitals of the world. Moreover, this concern at the passing away of a distinct species – if concern it can be interpreted to be! – is one shared and discussed by the French themselves. And, in truth, the four-part television documentary is emblematic of the whole issue.

Its presenter was none other than the photogenic and fashion-conscious Bernard-Henri Lévy. A former student of Althusser's, so-called 'new philosopher' and self-proclaimed '*intellectuel du troisième type*'[4] Lévy appears equally at ease as author, commisioning editor, director of his own review – *La Règle du jeu* established in 1990 – and media personality. The days of the traditional 'committed' intellectual, he proclaims, are over and in his place is emerging a new model – Lévy himself, of course – dedicated to exploring reality in its full complexity.[5] The keynote is anti-communism and not surprisingly therefore the heroes of Lévy's 'subjective history', *Les Aventures de la liberté*,[6] are Albert Camus and Raymond Aron. The problem is that the whole thing is vacuous, banal, at times factually inaccurate, loosely organised around a liberal pluralism that betrays not an ounce of originality, and even if one agrees with his dismissal of the idea of a 'pure revolution' it is hard not to conclude that here is a man with precious little to say but with a talent for saying it. In short, Lévy himself and his brand of hyped-up presentation tells us much about what has happened: the French intellectual, as Jean Baudrillard remarked, now occupies not the public space but the publicity space.

How did it come to this? The most obvious point is that during the 1980s many of the greatest names of the French intellectual firmament – the 'maîtres à penser' – died: Sartre and Roland Barthes in 1980, Jacques Lacan in 1981, Raymond Aron in 1983, Michel Foucault and Fernand Braudel in 1984, Simone de Beauvoir in 1986 and Louis Althusser, after years of mental illness, in 1990. No one of similar status, it has been argued, has succeeded in replacing them. Less evidently the same period also saw the virtual extinction of a previously numerous specimen, the '*intellectuel de gauche*'. Born with the Popular Front in the 1930s it was after the Second World War and with the immense prestige then enjoyed by the French Communist Party (PCF) that the greater proportion of French intellectuals

situated themselves on the left. '*Existentialo-marxisme*' became the
order of the day and remarkably it remained so until the end of the
1960s. Everything changed, however, in 1974 with the publication in
French of *The Gulag Archipelago*. How so many intelligent people had
for so long been blind to the truth about the Soviet Union is itself an
interesting and important question but the impact of Solzhenitsyn's
book was to jolt France almost overnight into the era of post-
Marxism. To this was then added the death of '*tiers-mondisme*' as
successively China, Cuba, Vietnam and other lesser contenders lost
their status on the left as the embodiments of earthly paradise. For the
left-wing intellectual '*les années orphelines*' were under way and were
still so when, ironically, the Socialist Party in alliance with the PCF
came to power in 1981.

Cast adrift and deprived of ideological certainty the intellectual then
fell prey to a more profound doubt. Was it the case, as some like Alain
Finkelkraut argued in *La Défaite de la pensée*,[7] that we were entering
an age not of universal culture but of mass non-culture, an epoch of
non-literary and even non-verbal expression where the rock star and
the comedian replaced the philosopher as society's guru. Fearful of the
accusation of élitism the intellectual, Finkelkraut contended in *Le
Débat*, remained mute before this cultural infantilism, thus committing
a new form of treason. Other causes of the intellectual's decline were
easily found: the crisis in the French university system, the professionalisation of politics, the emergence of a consumerist consensus in
French society and a corresponding absence of division, the global
decline of French cultural influence, the impact of the mass media. The
economic crisis, beginning in 1973 after twenty years of spectacular
success and continuing well into the 1980s, was sufficient to finish the
job: what need was there for the intellectual's probing critique and
account of society when people had to face up to the daily concerns of
unemployment and inflation?

In short, from the mid-1970s onwards it was not just the personnel
of French intellectual life that changed but its ideological climate, its
mood and atmosphere. The 'New Right' led by Alain de Benoist made
its appearance, the number of 'ex' communists increased dramatically
and in the case of men such as historian François Furet reached
positions of power and eminence, Hannah Arendt was discovered,
Benjamin Constant and Tocqueville re-read, Rousseau and Marx
scorned and vilified. In 1979, Sartre and Raymond Aron, estranged
for over thirty years, symbolically visited the Elysée Palace together to
plead the cause of the boat-people and in the years that followed if

almost everyone was agreed that totalitarianism – frequently re-described as 'barbarism' – was the enemy then by the same token there was near unanimity about the importance of defending democracy and the rights of man. And in all of this the intellectual – or at least those who remained – was obliged to re-assess his role and status.

The clearest example of this came from Michel Foucault during the 1970s. No longer, Foucault argued, could the intellectual be perceived as the bearer of universal values, the spokesman of truth and justice. This model, with Voltaire as its prototype and Sartre as its contemporary representative, was now being superseded by that of the 'specific' intellectual, derived not from the jurist and the writer as had formerly been the case but from the *savant* or expert. No less radical in intention – the ultimate aim was to subvert all forms of power and social control – the intellectual was to intervene in local, specific struggles, challenging power in precisely defined institutional settings, drawing upon his own conditions of life and work. In Foucault's own case this meant, for example, extensive involvement in campaigns for penal reform.[8]

But Foucault's voice was not the only voice to be heard. Jacques Julliard in *Contre la politique professionnelle*,[9] Pierre Nora in the opening editorial of his influential review *Le Débat*,[10] Bernard-Henri Lévy in *Eloge des intellectuels*, article after article in such serious journals as *Commentaire*, *Esprit* and *Le Nouvel Observateur*, plus many more, pursued the issue, in the process meticulously exposing the past follies, errors and doctrinal rigidities of the intellectual in France. No longer was the intellectual seen to be infallible and as such he became the king with no clothes, the grounds of his authority – his supposed superior knowledge and lucidity – unceremoniously taken away. Sartre for one was a casualty, his posthumous reputation overwhelmed by the catalogue of political misjudgements – his support of Maoism and of terrorism, for example – detailed first by Michel-Antoine Burnier and later by such writers as Jeannine Verdès-Leroux.[11] Not even his model relationship with Simone de Beauvoir stood up to the test of close scrutiny. As for Foucault himself he could not escape criticism for his initial enthusiastic support of the Iranian Revolution. The overall conclusion appeared to be that if the intellectual was to survive in what Pierre Nora described as a régime of intellectual democracy then he could no longer pretend to be the legislator of the world. An element of modesty, as Raymond Aron pointed out in 1983, was required.[12]

The impression then was of a community of intellectuals in disarray, unsure of itself and of how it should act, feeling threatened on all sides by a world in which it no longer enjoyed automatic respect. Power and influence seemed to have slipped from its grasp. And not surprisingly there were those prepared to think in terms of reading out its last rites. In the summer of 1983, as France's left-wing government ran into serious economic and political problems, the pages of *Le Monde* were suddenly filled with a series of articles exploring the supposed 'silence of the intellectuals'. Where, asked government spokesman Max Gallo, 'are the Gide, Malraux, Alain and Langevin of today?' The general view was that they were nowhere to be seen.

If this goes some way towards explaining the appearance of Bernard-Henri Lévy on French television – his last two episodes were significantly entitled '*Les Illusions perdues*' and '*La Fin des prophètes*' – then it also provides us with the context for the upsurge of the academic work that has been devoted to intellectuals over the last decade or more. As Jean-François Sirinelli has remarked, it was only when the intellectual began to climb down from the throne which in France he had occupied for approximately seventy years that his history became a proper subject of inquiry.[13] Several questions were immediately posed, although they have to date received far from conclusive answers. Was there anything special or different about the French intelligentsia? Did French intellectuals, for example, exercise greater power or operate in different ways from their British and American counterparts?[14] Secondly, what real impact, if any, had intellectuals had upon events in France? Had they had the influence that they as well as a broader public had sometimes imagined? This in turn opened up the way for a wider discussion of the political responsibility of the intellectual.[15] Could one write and, equally, could one be silent without consequences? This most clearly had a bearing upon the pivotal relationship of the intellectual to the PCF and, in particular, upon the phenomenon of the '*compagnon de route*', the communist fellow traveller. How had it been possible for intellectuals to submit themselves to the authority of a Stalinist party? What sacrifices had been involved? How had the PCF used and exercised its control over a group that it viewed with undisguised suspicion?[16] But similar questions could be asked – and were to be asked – of all forms of collaboration, on the right as well as on the left, with fascism as well as with communism. Where, for example, did collaboration begin and end? What different forms did it take? Should – as, indeed, did happen in the post Second World War purge[17] – a writer, a publisher, a literary critic, pay for his life because of the views he had espoused and the company he had kept? Here a greater willingness and openness in

France as a whole to face up to the years of the Vichy régime played its part. More generally, the intellectual's loss of legitimacy invited reflection upon the diverse, and often forgotten, sources of anti-intellectualism in France. Was it exclusively a bourgeois phenomenon, a right-wing fear of a dangerous sect which would betray the nation and its people in the name of pacifism and internationalism or did it have more varied roots and deeper implications? The reappraisal of the writings of Georges Sorel, for so long neglected in his own country, and the creation, by Jacques Julliard and others, of the *Cahiers Georges Sorel* made sense, for example, in the context of an increasingly negative assessment of the impact of the intellectual upon the working-class movement as a whole. But even more fundamentally the realisation that the days of the 'committed' intellectual, born with the Dreyfus Affair and sanctified by Sartre in the very first issue of *Les Temps modernes* in 1945, were at an end raised the issue of exactly who or what was the intellectual. Was the intellectual always the disinterested person he claimed to be? Was he in reality the unconsolable critic of bourgeois society? Was he without exception antagonistic towards those in power? Did he have to have a moral mission?

There were also other factors which contributed towards this growth of scholarly interest in the intellectual, factors which had their genesis in developments within related academic disciplines. At its most simple level, as France entered its self-proclaimed period of post-Marxism the enthusiasm – in particular amongst publishers – for working-class history, for studies of the masses, declined dramatically and the way was suddenly clear for a closer examination of élites. More seriously, a lessening of the power of structuralism in its various forms and of the strictures imposed upon the writing of history by the *Annales* school made possible a greater attention to recent political history, to events and to the individual as subject.[18]

Nowhere perhaps has this been more evident than in the renewed respectability accorded to the writing of biography, for so long despised as one of the worst forms of *'histoire événementielle'*.[19] The sceptic could argue that this too was due to the mediatisation of French culture, pointing to the enormous impact and popularity of Bernard Pivot's television programme *Apostrophes* – *'l'effet Pivot'* – and its obsession with the author, the personality behind the work, but when even Jacques Le Goff, one of the leading representatives of the *Annales* school, set out to write a life of Saint Louis – admittedly avoiding a return to what he regarded as 'the traditionally superficial, anecdotal, straightforwardly chronological biography'[20] – it was a sign that the 'history of mentalities' had been subject to considerable revision. Paradoxically, one of the first victims of this new-found enthusiasm for the genre of biography was none other than Michel Foucault himself, the denouncer of the sovereignty of the subject treated as an autonomous agent.[21] But this trend has not been restricted either to the study of the great and the famous or to the itineraries of individuals. Significant gaps undoubtedly remain but a figure such as Paul Nizan was explored in two books published in 1980[22] and to this can be added the names of others, for example that of André Bellessort, teacher at the Lycée Louis le Grand and member of the *Académie française*.[23] Similarly, the project of prosopography – a form of truncated biography – made possible the accumulation of data about many of the lesser personalities of French intellectual life, especially those whose careers had been in higher education. In the same vein autobiography – although at times in less than conventional form[24] – has also made something of a comeback and this in particular has provided valuable information about former communist intellectuals.[25]

But what sort of history was the history of intellectuals to be? What was to be its methodology, its evidence, its subject? Having escaped from the perils of 'structuralist terrorism' was it simply to be a form of the history of ideas?[26] One of the first attempts at an answer came from the pen of Régis Debray in *Le Pouvoir intellectuel en France* and then, a year later, *Le Scribe*.[27] Viewed as part of a broader *traité de médiologie* Debray's enthusiasm for zoological imagery disclosed not just his scientific pretensions but his desire to dissect the activities of France's *haute intelligentsia*, its teachers, writers and intellectual celebrities. According to Debray the history of twentieth-century French intellectuals could be divided into three ages: the university cycle (1880–1930); the publishing cycle (1920–1960); and the media cycle (1968–?); each age having its archetypal figure, the academic, the writer in the literary review, and the television personality. But the real purpose of Debray's account was first of all to evoke a golden age – in effect, the days of the *Nouvelle Revue Française* in the 1930s – and then to contrast it with the corrupted, degraded and mediocre present. Of the media-dominated post-1968 cycle he writes: 'An Americanised intelligentsia in a Europeanised France puts the emphasis on smiles, good teeth, nice hair and the adolescent stupidity known as petulance.' Debray then was in truth into the business of moral indignation and outrage, his pseudo-scientific analysis being primarily designed to unmask the petty jealousies and careerism of today's intellectual media superstars and the debasement and trivia-lisation of French culture which has occurred as a consequence. Far from being serious history it was another tale of the French intellectual in crisis.

Curiously the underlying moral tone to be found in the writings of sociologist Pierre Bourdieu is not that dissimilar. Intellectuals are portrayed as an 'aristocracy of culture' eager to preserve their titles to cultural nobility – and its power and privileges – through the development of an ideology of 'distinction'. They are, to use Bourdieu's own language, 'a dominated fraction of the dominant class', dominated in their relations with those who hold economic and political power yet occupying a place within the dominant class. Placed in a precariously balanced position, any sympathies they might have with the dominated are at best fragile and uncertain. 'Despite their revolt against those they call 'bourgeois' ', Bourdieu has argued, 'they remain loyal to the bourgeois order, as can be seen in all periods of crisis in which their specific capital and their position in the social order are really threatened'.[28] Paradoxically however – and this perhaps provides a clue to part of the argument developed by Shlomo Sand in this volume – Bourdieu concedes that 'cultural producers' can transcend personal interest 'in the ordinary sense', thus leading them 'to political or intellectual actions that can be called universal'.

Yet it is in the range of concepts and the related methodology that Bourdieu has developed that he has had the greatest influence. Bourdieu's own account of his work emphasises that in his view it is a means of escaping from the choice between a structuralism without a subject – most notably Althusserian Marxism – and the methodolo-gical individualism of the philosophy of the subject that has now become so fashionable. Despite modification over time Bourdieu's abiding concern has been to explore what he regards as patterns of educational *reproduction* and symbolic *domination* in French society, thus producing what as early as 1971 he referred to as 'a rigorous science of intellectual and artistic facts'.[29] His key concepts are those of the field or *champ* and the *habitus*. The concept of the field has been applied and elaborated by Bourdieu to cover a wide range of areas – religion, education, science, literature, art, etc – but one of its primary functions is as a means of avoiding such relatively vague references to the social world as 'milieu', 'context' or 'social background'. As such the field, each of which is deemed to be partially autonomous, is said to be constituted by a field of forces defined by a system of objective relations of power and the struggle within it to transform or maintain those relationships. For example, in the field of cultural production Bourdieu has in mind, amongst many other things, the power to publish or to refuse publication. Everyone entering the field feels the full force of those power relations, especially new entrants such as the unpublished author. By contrast to the specific logic of each of these fields of competition Bourdieu defines the *habitus* as 'a system of durable, transposable dispositions' entertained by each of the protagonists. Less prosaically it is seen as 'the virtue made of necesity', the incorporation – either consciously or unconsciously – of objective necessity by the agent to produce strategies and practices adjusted to the situation. The point is that as positions within the field change so too do the dispositions of the protagonists, the *habitus* being essentially a form of mediation between objective conditions and the realm of practice. Equally on this view there are only certain possibilities inherent in the field.[30]

In truth Bourdieu's work has been subject to exhaustive critical scrutiny and to those brought up on the Anglo-American models of sociology and philosophy it might seem especially fraught with problems; but in this context its importance lies in the fact that Bourdieu himself – for example, in *Homo Academicus*[31] and *La Noblesse d'Etat*[32] – has applied his own methodology to the study of the intellectual and of intellectual élites and that his ideas have been taken up and employed by other researchers in related areas. In his inaugural lecture to the *Collège de France* in 1982, Bourdieu made the point that each of the particular fields had to be examined 'in the most singular detail, in the manner of the most painstaking historians'.[33] It is this, for example, that has been undertaken by Christophe Charle in his meticulous examination of the emergence of a self-conscious intellectual élite at the end of the nineteenth century.[34] Given both its indebtedness to Bourdieu and its general relevance to the theme of this volume Charle's analysis is briefly worth looking at in closer detail.

Prefaced by an account of the displacement of the traditional leading class – *les grands notables* – at the summit of French society, *Les Elites de la République* focuses its attention upon the emergence within the dominant class, drawn essentially from the bourgeoisie, of three separate élites: politico-administrative, academic and business. Committed in principle to the replacement of the method of social reproduction and dominance based upon the family – lineage – by one based upon ability and merit – competition – for the new dominant class the primary function of the republican ideology of a meritocracy was as an instrument of legitimation. It created, in other words, the impression of opportunity, even if the reality was one of restricted access.

What follows is a detailed and fascinating examination of the career and social strategies which served to ensure the ascendency of these new élites in the period between 1880 and 1900. It would be impossible to do justice to the richness and volume of information Charle deploys to support his argument: education, selection and recruitment, career moves, marriage, family size, finance and investment, styles of life, leisure and tastes; these and other aspects of the strategies of the three élites are utilised to disclose the alliances and divisions within and between élites and to demonstrate their unequal capacity to influence government.

Charle's conclusions are both original and far-reaching. Firstly, the distance separating the political and administrative élites from one another was only minimal. This applied especially to the upper levels of government administration where an unwillingness fully to implement the principles of meritocracy meant that those in charge recruited men of similar background, education and interests to themselves. Secondly, there was no significant gap between the political and administrative élites and the élite constituted by the leaders of big business. There was, Charle writes, 'a constant exchange of personnel and services at the highest level of the State and industry' and these links were further strengthened by similar social strategies and preoccupations. Out of this emerged a pattern of shared values built around moderation and the search for consensus which had a fundamental impact upon the political and economic evolution of the Third Republic. Thirdly, therefore, Charle concludes that it is possible to discern the growing isolation from other élites of the intellectual élite in general and the university élite in particular. In the practice of marriage, for example, matrimonial choices served to strengthen the relative turning inwards upon itself of the intellectual community. More significantly, not only was the intellectual élite progressively distanced from the sphere of political power but its members were thus obliged to choose between adopting either the attitude of the expert (which made possible contacts with other élites) or that of the pure *savant* (which accorded with the pretension to autonomy and independence). This, he believes, is one of the major characteristics of the period under investigation and provides 'one of the objective foundations of the birth of 'intellectuals' and of the continuance of their role in the field of power during the different crises of the nation's history since the Dreyfus Affair'.[35] It was, in other words, out of this process that emerged the model of the intellectual. Charle's second volume, *Naissance des «intellectuels»: 1880–1900*, presents what is in effect a re-reading of the Dreyfus Affair, the different political positions adopted by the Dreyfusard and anti-Dreyfusard intellectuals being explained not so much by reference to their adherence to competing ideologies and values – the rights of the individual versus the superior claims of the nation – but in terms of divisions within the 'intellectual field' and the dissimilar relationship of each group with the dominant class. If both sides were in relative agreement about the legitimacy of the intellectual's intervention in public affairs, where they diverged was in their appreciation of whether they saw themselves as part of that élite and from this derived their contrasting stances.

It would be wrong, however, to suggest that the influence of Bourdieu has been all-pervasive – frequently his impact is restricted to terminological usage, the key words being 'dominant' and 'dominated' – but he is nonetheless representative of a broad body of opinion in France which believes that the history of intellectuals should not be seen purely, or perhaps even primarily, as a history of ideas. If we move beyond the moralistic critique offered by Debray and the sociological unmasking performed by Bourdieu and his followers then what we find is a series of attempts – most notably by such people as Jean-François Sirinelli – not merely to formulate the conceptual apparatus thought appropriate to the study of the intellectual but also to begin the detailed empirical investigation of the mechanisms and practices of intellectual life. Sirinelli's richly documented *Génération intellectuelle*[36] is a study of the uniquely French institution of the *khâgne*, the preparatory classes for entry into the *Ecole normale supérieure*, and through it the reconstruction of the cultural and political world of what he has identified as 'the generation of 1905'. Elsewhere Sirinelli has analysed the role of the petition and the manifesto as a means of observing 'the field of forces which structures and polarises French intellectual society'[37] and to this can be added the work of others designed to illuminate the structures or networks of intellectual 'sociability' constituted by the salon or café, the publishing house,[38] the review,[39] the international congress,[40] literary institutions such as the *Académie Goncourt* and the *Comité national des écrivains*[41] and personal correspondence[42]. Ideas, as Jacques Julliard has expressed it, do not run naked in the street.

II

In the late summer of 1941 Simone Weil, dismissed from her post as a philosophy teacher and now working as a farm hand in the Ardèche, wrote to the Vichy Commissioner for Jewish Affairs in order 'to express the sincere gratitude I feel toward the government for having removed me from the social category of intellectuals and given me the land and, with it, all of nature'. Pleased with her life amongst those who endured 'the daily suffering of their limbs', she concluded: 'these people . . . live through each day, they do not dream it'.[43] Five years earlier Julien Benda, in his autobiographical *La Jeunesse d'un clerc*, expressed a rather different sentiment. 'Our teachers', he wrote, 'brought us up to value only the scholar (and, to a lesser extent, the statesman) and to have no respect for the manual worker, the peasant, the labourer. This was the attitude of the mandarin and it is one to which I have always remained deeply attached and so much so that I always have to make an effort to remember that the people exist.'[44] For Benda it was not life in the fields but the life of study that represented 'the supreme mode of existence'. It was also the same Julien Benda who admitted that it had been the Dreyfus Affair that had enabled him to move from high-minded intellectualism to intellectual action and, moreover, to learn that he was capable of 'ideological fanaticism'.[45] Of course, in contrast to Weil, who had been deeply moved at first hand by the plight of the factory worker, he had not been influenced by the personal suffering of Dreyfus himself but by the desire to see truth – abstract truth – defended.

Who then is this figure of the intellectual–mandarin? And how, to use Simone Weil's phrase, has he dreamed life? By common consent the category of intellectual is open to a wide range of definition. The intellectual, for example, exists as a socio-economic category and thus in its broadest sense can be taken to include all those professions and occupations not involved in manual labour. In France – a country where the intellect is traditionally highly prized – there is ample evidence to suggest that there have been many people prepared to embrace this description. It is, however, so extensive as to be virtually meaningless. A second definition gives the intellectual a predominantly ethical personality, portraying him in terms of a moral, even pseudo-religious, mission. He is reason, truth or justice made flesh, a powerful voice of protest and criticism. The problem here is that in many cases it is simply not an accurate description of the way intellectuals have behaved. Nor does it necessarily fit the conception that intellectuals have had of themselves. More narrowly, the intellectual as intellectual, as opposed to the intellectual as philosopher, novelist, film director and so on, becomes an intellectual precisely at the point where he enters that area of public space or civic life known under the general title of the world of politics. The intellectual, as Pascal Ory has noted, is defined not by what he is but by what he does.[46] The emphasis – to borrow Benda's words – falls upon intellectual *action*. It does, therefore, make no sense to ask if the intellectual should be committed – '*engagé*' – because it is part of his very definition that he should be so. The mistake has only been not to recognise the diverse forms that that commitment can take and to perceive it solely in its prevalent post-1945 guise, as membership or support of the PCF or other left-wing groupings. Moreover, if the intellectual has pre-modern ancestors, he is very much a twentieth-century phenomenon.

The intellectual's origins can with ease be traced back to the eighteenth-century *philosophe* or man of letters[47] and if, with the French Revolution, the prestige accorded to this figure diminished considerably he was subsequently revived in the form of the artist-poet, the historian and then the *savant* or scientist. The latter, as Christophe Charle has argued,[48] enjoyed immense status derived in large part from public esteem of his professional expertise and it was this which allowed him to pass judgement on issues strictly beyond his technical competence. He was adjudged to possess a certain moral authority or capital. Yet if the grounds for intervention into the wider field of politics had been established it still remained the case that, as the end of the nineteenth century approached, both the category of intellectual and his manner of intervention remained largely undisclosed. The word itself began to be used in avant-garde literary circles in the early 1890s but it is interesting to note that when in 1895 the Marxist journal *Le Devenir social* published a translation of an article by Karl Kautsky exploring the relationship between socialism and the liberal professions it could find no French equivalent of the word '*Intelligenz*' and was therefore obliged to use the German original. By 1898, however, it had hit the headlines. In January of that year Emile Zola published his famous open letter to the President of the French Republic, '*J'accuse*', an act of provocation designed to bring a disgraceful miscarriage of justice to the nation's attention, and with that he ceased to be a detached observer to become an active participant in the drama surrounding Captain Dreyfus. The following day the second of two petitions calling for a re-trial appeared in the pages of *L'Aurore* and to it was appended not just the names of Zola and Anatole France but those of André Gide, Marcel Proust, Lucien Herr, Charles Andler and Célestin Bouglé as well as those of hundreds of lesser known academics and literary personalities, their profession and qualifications proudly proclaimed.[49] It was this petition that shortly afterwards became known as the manifesto of the intellectuals and which set the pattern for later participation in the political debates of twentieth-century France.

The circumstances surrounding this sudden explosion of truth are themselves significant. At its most profound level it marked the culmination of a long process which had seen the intellectual professions progressively disentangle themselves from the tutelage and patronage of, first, the Church and then the State. In this they were greatly aided by their own expansion in numbers (especially in higher education), the increased power and wider audience of the press, journalism and publishing in general, and also the democracy of France's Third Republic. The tactics of the open letter and of the petition had both already been used (Jean-François Sirinelli cites a petition signed as early as 1887 by 'writers, painters, sculptors, architects and art lovers' protesting against the building of the Eiffel tower) but never before had the appearance of the intellectual upon the public stage taken on such a self-conscious and collective form. The implicit, but clear, assumption was that they as a group were under an obligation to express an opinion. A new name seemed appropriate to a new style and mode of action.

It was arguably from this point onwards that intellectuals in France occupied a place in the deliberations of the nation's politics that far outweighed their numerical importance. Periods of relative inactivity contrast with epochs of great agitation (the 1930s, for example) and even moments of notoriety and scandal (the publication of the '*Manifeste des 343*' in 1971 calling for the legalisation of abortion) but until recently there appears to have been no shortage of writers, university professors, actors and actresses, cinema directors, and so on, prepared to append their names to petitions and manifestoes, stand on public platforms, demonstrate in the streets, join and launch various associations and parties of one sort or another, and even endorse political candidates, and thus take on the role of the intellectual. If certain figures have appeared with depressing frequency – Sartre and Simone de Beauvoir come near the top of the list – then those less eminent and less visible have still made their contribution. What is also clear is that despite the appearance of new ideas, events and movements and the definite periodisation of French intellectual life the battle fought over the Dreyfus Affair has to an extent been re-staged and re-enacted. There have been Dreyfus Affairs.[50]

It is frequently asserted that in their defence of a man unjustly condemned the Dreyfusards established that the task of the intellectual was not merely to act as the guarantor of public morality but also to speak in the name of universal principles. This was certainly how Julien Benda interpreted it in *La Trahison des clercs*. It is, however, incorrect. If the Dreyfus Affair brought into existence the *Ligue des Droits de l'Homme* then so too it produced its opposite, the *Ligue de la Patrie française*. No sooner had Zola made his stand than he and those who lined up behind him were roundly condemned. By what right, Ferdinand Brunetière asked, could a professor of Tibetan claim to instruct his fellow citizens about politics?[51] The autonomous intellectual found himself face to face with the self-proclaimed '*parti de l'intelligence*'. The point is that at this level the Dreyfus Affair saw not just disagreement about what were taken to be the proper obligations of the intellectual but also the emergence of a battle of ideas that at its heart revolved around two competing systems of values. It is this, as Michel Winock has argued, that gives the Dreyfus Affair its symbolic power and its paradigmatic quality.[52]

Crudely stated, that battle saw the advocates of the rights of man pitted against the defenders of the nation and its twin institutions, the army and the Church. The claims of truth, justice and reason were counterposed to those of hierarchy, order and homeland. It was, as both Emile Durkheim and Ferdinand Brunetière made explicitly clear,[53] a clash over the respective prerogatives of the individual and of society. Raymond Aron has since argued that for the intellectual the Dreyfus Affair was a unique and exceptional case not subsequently repeated, an issue without moral ambivalence where the correct course of action was unmistakably apparent.[54] This, unfortunately, accords with neither the sentiments of those involved at the time (when many agonised over the decisions to be taken) nor with the later experiences of intellectuals and the examples of commitment that they provide.

The great moments and periods where the intellectual felt most keenly the responsibility to act and to be heard can be easily listed. After the Dreyfus Affair came 1914, the era of the Popular Front, the period of the Vichy régime and post-war liberation, the war in Algeria and, finally, May 1968. Each, in differing ways and in different contexts, rehearsed the same arguments and each saw intellectuals reverting to patterns of behaviour established at the turn of the century. The outbreak of the First World War, for example, saw a variety of responses.[55] One, the most obvious, was enlistment, the neo-nationalist generation of Agathon's famous 1912 inquiry rallying to the *union sacrée*.[56] Amongst the casualties were to be Charles Péguy, Ernest Psichari and Alain-Fournier. Another, sometimes under constraint although often voluntarily, was silence or even exile. But the predominant response – especially from the older generation – was support for the war effort and the attempt, in the manner of the anti-Dreyfusards, to defend the nation from its enemies, be they Germans or defeatists. Barrès, Maurras, Bourget and Daudet, not surprisingly, took this course but so too did former anti-patriot Gustave Hervé and philosopher Henri Bergson. Bergson, who had remained silent throughout the Dreyfus Affair, announced to the *Académie des sciences morales et politiques* that their 'scientific' duty was to expose the cynicism and brutality of Germany and then, in 1917 and 1918, made two diplomatic missions to the United States, the first to encourage American involvement in the war and the second to secure allied intervention in Russia.[57] Curiously the Dreyfusard concern with defending the rights of the innocent and with the claims of universal justice found itself momentarily alongside the nationalism of the extreme right. But as outrage at the plight of Belgium and a hatred of militarism slid into an active support for the humanitarian peace proposals of Woodrow Wilson this same current of opinion gave voice to pacifism (Barbusse), internationalism (Romain Rolland) and outright opposition to imperialism and an unjust war (Alfred Rosmer and Pierre Monatte). For the latter group the innocent victims were the soldiers being slaughtered daily at the front.

In a sense, however, such was the prevalence of nationalist sentiment amongst intellectuals that the First World War represented the revenge of the anti-Dreyfusards. As the Vichy régime demonstrated it was not to be their last. The inter-war years marked a period of intense political and cultural ferment, the initial dominance of the right-wing *Action française* being matched by a growth in support for communism and then, as the economic crisis deepened, a wave of 'non-conformism'.[58] It was, however, the rise of fascism and with it the threat posed to the democracy of the Third Republic that saw intellectuals re-draw the battle lines of 1898. As the right, in a manifesto entitled *Pour la défense de l'Occident et la paix en Europe*, rallied behind Mussolini's conquest of Ethiopia, condemned the corruption and decadence of the parliamentary régime, and launched a vitriolic personal attack against the Jewish Léon Blum the left responded with the formation of the *Comité de vigilance des intellectuels antifascistes*,[59] the creation of its own journals (*Vigilance*, *Vendredi*) and petitions defending republican Spain (*Déclaration des intellectuels républicains au sujet des événements d'Espagne*). This bipolarisation of opinion was only confirmed by the election of the first Popular Front government. 'The false revolution of 1936', wrote Robert Brasillach in 1941, 'was truly an intellectuals' revolution'.[60]

From then on the debate gravitated around the themes of anti-fascism, anti-communism and the desire, in various forms, to avoid war. The left found itself torn between the conflicting demands of pacifism and opposition to Hitler (hence the profound divisions over the Munich agreement) whilst on the right nationalism was increasingly tinged with defeatism as disenchantment with the régime – 'Rather Hitler than Blum' ran the famous slogan – paved the way for later collaboration. Once again intellectuals on all sides mobilised themselves around opposing values in an effort to influence public opinion and government policy. But to little effect. No amount of meetings, petitions, manifestoes or journal articles could prevent the catastophe that befell France in the summer of 1940 and with that the world of the intellectual was turned completely upside down.

The list of those intellectuals prepared to lend their support either to the occupying Germans or to Pétain's 'national revolution' was truly impressive. Maurras, Drieu la Rochelle, Céline, Brasillach, Henry de Montherlant, Pierre Andreu, Alphonse de Châteaubriant, and many more, had little difficulty publishing their work in any one of a number of reviews or publishing houses that either openly endorsed or, at worse, came to terms with the new situation. Xenophobia, anti-semitism (here again Blum played the role of *bouc émissaire*), racism, plus, in some cases, an admiration for virile young German soldiers flourished as expressions of the Dreyfusard values of democracy and the rights of man were silenced by censorship and persecution. Yet intellectual resistance was not long in forthcoming. If some, like Paul Nizan, did not survive the fall of France and others, like Sartre, were at the outset confined to the prisoner of war camp then there were also those, like Aron and André Malraux, who joined the resistance abroad and still others who were prepared to embrace the dangerous, and sometimes fatal, path of internal resistance. Perhaps even more remarkably a normal intellectual life of sorts continued in existence. Camus, for example, saw both *L'Etranger* and *Le Mythe de Sisyphe* published during the Occupation whilst Sartre published the existentialist classic *L'Etre et le Néant* in 1943. Both writers had plays performed on the Paris stage during the same period. But the overall impression – confirmed by Simone de Beauvoir's recently published letters to Sartre[61] – was that for those who remained behind in Paris life was, if only for once, dominated by the daily concerns of food and physical survival. The years 1940–4 also present us with one of the very few occasions when the French intelligentsia found itself dispersed throughout the entire country. Many of its members, especially those of Jewish parentage, were simply in hiding. Worse, in the eyes of some (and as Gisèle Sapiro has shown), the name of the winner of the *Prix Goncourt* was almost announced in Lyons!

Liberation brought with it yet another re-drawing of the French intellectual map. The right emerged discredited and many of its leading members were to be amongst the principal victims of the post-war purge. It was, proclaimed Charles Maurras at the end of his trial, 'the revenge of Dreyfus'. The *Comité national des ecrivains* saw to it that few escaped retribution. The Resistance, on the other hand, not only gave birth to France's first serious and sustained movement of left-wing catholicism (with Emmanuel Mounier's review *Esprit* as its quintessential mouthpiece) but also confirmed the growing ascendency of the PCF amongst her intellectuals. In the 1930s increasing numbers had been drawn to the party but the revelations (and controversy) of Gide's *Retour de l'URSS*,[62] the treatment meted out to Victor Serge[63] and Moscow show trials had been sufficient to invite caution. Now, after Stalingrad, the attraction of the Soviet Union for many seemed irresistible. And, moreover, the PCF was determined to make maximum use of its new converts in the struggle to displace bourgeois cultural hegemony. With its journal *Lettres françaises* at the centre the PCF set up a series of publishing ventures and front organisations designed to spread the influence of the communist intellectual into all sectors of literary and artistic life.[64] The same structures could be, and were to be, used to vilify its opponents.

But the immediate post-war years were, above all, to be the years of the *compagnon de route* and of intellectual commitment *par excellence*. Defined by Simone de Beauvoir as the 'writer's total presence in what he has written'[65] commitment in this sense was translated into Sartre's charge that both Flaubert and Goncourt were responsible for the repression that followed the fall of the Paris Commune because they wrote not a single line to prevent it. As the Cold War intensified Sartre, along with other non-communist left intellectuals, founded the *Rassemblement démocratique révolutionnaire* as a grouping of those that believed that a neutral Europe could serve as a mediating force between the two superpowers. Nevertheless the Soviet Union was identified with the cause of peace and the United States – the America of McCarthyism, the trial and execution of the Rosenbergs for espionage, and Coca-Cola – with imperialism and nuclear destruction. Famously, on his return from Moscow in 1954, Sartre could declare that in Russia the freedom to criticise was absolute.[66]

Not everyone, however, was prepared to adopt the *esprit de parti* demanded by Laurent Casanova in his *Le Parti communiste, les intellectuels et la nation*.[67] If Paul Claudel, Raymond Aron and André Malraux took the unusual step of allying themselves with the nascent Gaullist movement, then so too the likes of Arthur Koestler, Maurice Merleau-Ponty and Albert Camus found it impossible to remain silent before the cult of Stalin and continuing revelations about Soviet labour camps. The conviviality of days and nights spent together in left-bank cafés and jazz clubs was replaced by bitter internecine quarrels as, first, Moscow's break with Tito and then the combined effect of intervention in Hungary and Khrushchev's report to the XXth Congress of the CPSU served to drive a wedge between the PCF and many intellectuals of the progressive left.

It was at this point that demands from the indigenous Muslim population for Algerian independence became the new focus of attention for France's intellectuals.[68] The issues at stake – the use of torture by the French army and the merits or otherwise of decolonisation – were never as clear-cut as at a distance they now might seem. Those who supported the calls for independence and who protested at the army's brutal tactics had to contend with the *Front de Libération Nationale* (FLN)'s own use of indiscriminate terror whilst the cause of a French Algeria was itself undermined by the growing awareness amongst its supporters that as the war dragged on the prestige and international status of France was being damaged immeasurably. Albert Camus, of course, was reduced to silence by the tragedy befalling his own *pied noir* community but for the not inconsiderable number of intellectuals who did become involved the continuities (as well as discontinuities) with the Dreyfus Affair were, as Jean-Pierre Rioux has argued, all too evident.[69] Apart from the methods employed in an effort to mobilise public opinion – petitions, press campaigns and open meetings – France was once again portrayed by her intellectuals as a country whose own fate, and salvation, depended upon the outcome of a struggle between competing moral principles. The innocent victim (of torture) and the innocent nation (the dispossessed and colonised) stood locked in combat with the sanctity of the army (and hence the nation), fear of the outsider (in this case the Arab), the defence of the West (against Islam), anti-communism and *raison d'état*. The discontinuity lay in the fact that here, as opposed to 1898, the intellectuals of neither side were ever able to exercise a decisive influence upon events. This privilege went to General de Gaulle.

It was, however, the war in Algeria that provided intellectuals with their last all-out mutual confrontation. Not since have circumstances furnished them with such a fine occasion to display their differences. It also had a decisive impact upon later developments and upon the formation of subsequent intellectual generations.[70] It did, for example, play a key role in moulding the opinions of many of the intellectuals who later became associated with the New Right and with Alain de Benoist's *Groupement de Recherche et d'Etudes sur la civilisation européenne*.[71] Conversely, if, as Jeannine Verdès-Leroux has argued,[72] the Algerian war did little to shake the faith of intellectuals within the PCF – the key moments of disillusionment, she argues, were 1956, the crushing of the Prague spring in 1968 and the breakdown of the Union of the Left in 1978 – then it is nevertheless the case that, amongst the student population especially, it did give rise to the emergence of a new generation of political activists, operating outside the PCF, who were to form the backbone of the *gauchisme* of the 1960s. The same people are now in many cases members of the academic and political establishment.[73] The Algerian war, according to Jacques Julliard,[74] also ironically marked the beginning of a process of political disengagement for intellectuals and therefore the end of the particular form of treason they had committed since the days of post-war liberation. The campaign against the use of torture in particular again re-defined the intellectual, as in the Dreyfus Affair, as being above all the defender of the rights of man. On this view the involvement of intellectuals in the events of May 1968 was nothing more than a 'neo-Marxist, neo-revolutionary parenthesis'.[75]

If then, by common consent, it was in the mid-1970s that France's intellectual community found itself obliged to re-think its position and role within French society the roots of that crisis of identity go back to the early 1960s. After Algeria came Vietnam and an enthusiasm for the liberation movements of the Third World but this, like the demonstrations and strikes of the summer of 1968, proved to be a short-lived release from disillusionment. Marxism still retained its position as a dominant mode of discourse but a refusal to play the part of *chien de garde* to either the bourgeoisie or a State educational system in deep crisis was now matched by a growing distance from communist orthodoxy. Foucault's 'specific' intellectual of the 1970s was prefigured in increased involvement in the politics of the personal as intellectuals on the left retreated into the struggles for gay and women's rights and the legalisation of abortion. This is not to say that those struggles were without significance. Far from it. But it was small consolation for both a loss of inner certainty and a general decline of prestige and status.

But was this necessarily a bad thing? Was it entirely appropriate that intellectuals should have had such a significant voice in France during the twentieth century? One response, enunciated by Julien Benda in his *La Trahison des clercs*, was of course that intellectuals had abused their position and, after the Dreyfus Affair, had ceased properly to perform their function as the conscience of society. This criticism, in different forms, has been voiced by liberals ever since. Another, that appeared at the very moment of the intellectual's birth and which has been above all associated with the name of Maurice Barrès, has been to argue that intelligence and logic – the supposed qualities of the intellectual – do not constitute a complete description of mankind and therefore, by the same token, they should not claim to be the sole forces governing the world. The intellectual was the very embodiment of the *déraciné*, the uprooted. But this criticism did not only come from the nationalist right. The Dreyfus Affair, through the institution of the *Universités populaires* in particular, brought about a significant intrusion of intellectuals into the working-class and socialist movement, which was initially welcomed, with a few exceptions, as a sign of strength; however, this favourable attitude quickly turned to hostility with the recognition that these same people were seeking to turn the Dreyfusard victory to their own advantage. Georges Sorel, Edouard Berth, Hubert Lagardelle, Daniel Halévy and Charles Péguy pilloried what they saw as a *'parti intellectuel'* that was both hierarchical and dictatorial in aspiration. The workers had no need of the sons of the well-to-do to tell them how to act. Moreover, the intellectuals would prove to be ruthless masters.[76]

What drew these last two lines of criticism together was a profound distrust of a body of people that Brunetière defined as an 'intellectual aristocracy'.[77] If Lagardelle, for example, pinpointed the scorn which most intellectuals felt for the manual worker and their belief in their own capacity 'to understand everything', to be 'the most capable of governing' then Barrès highlighted the contempt felt by the 'aristocracy of thought' for the 'stinking mass'. Their objection, in other words, was precisely to Benda's conception of the intellectual as mandarin.

It is, moreover, this semi-scholarly notion of the mandarin that has come in many respects to characterise the intellectual in twentieth-century France. The story goes, for example, that it was Pierre Bost who provided Simone de Beauvoir with the title of her famous book recounting in a loosely autobiographical fashion the quarrels, passions and lives of her group of friends in the immediate post-1945 period. His argument was that he, Sartre and de Beauvoir, as intellectuals, represented the only remaining nobility in France and thus could be compared with the mandarin class in pre-communist China.[78] When discussing *Les Mandarins* in her own memoirs Simone de Beauvoir herself refers to intellectuals as 'a race apart'. More recently, and presumably in self-conscious imitation, the feminist writer Julia Kristeva updated the image of the intellectual as a being obsessed by his own set of intricate rules and self-consuming games in her novel *Les Samouraïs*.[79] The latter, far more than de Beauvoir's original text, is a piece of sacrilege, an analysis of the progressive disintegration of the post-1968 *haute intelligentsia*, a disintegration that comes complete with the obligatory visit to China and in which the thinly disguised figures of Foucault, Althusser, Barthes and others make their appearance. The reader can only feel sorry for the character of Edward Dalloway, the American Professor of Government '*plutôt britannique*', when faced with such dauntingly complex and self-absorbed figures. Simone de Beauvoir's real life Nelson Algren did not fare much better.

Seen in this light – and Julien Benda's comments in *La Jeunesse d'un clerc* illustrate this – the intellectual is the victim of his own contradictions. Drawn by definition and by obligation towards the expression of commitment and involvement in public affairs his own 'aristocratic' demeanour puts the emphasis upon independence and distance. This contradiction is perhaps at its most glaring in the case of the figure of the *compagnon de route*. Why, Jeannine Verdès-Leroux asks in her magisterial *Au service du Parti: Le parti communiste, les intellectuels et la culture*[80], had intellectuals been prepared to forgo their own autonomy when as a category their evolution had been largely defined by the attempt to free themselves from all religious and political control? Part of her answer lies in what she describes as 'the search for a superior authority before which they are ready to sacrifice everything'.[81] However, even here the aristocratic dimension of their position is by no means absent, as the same author reveals in *La Lune et le Caudillo: Le rêve des intellectuels et le régime cubain*.[82] The Cuban régime, she argues, gave French intellectuals on the left the two things for which they most craved: the certitude of revolution and, through Castro's enthusiatic welcome, proximity to power. Yet, as Verdès-Leroux shows in meticulous detail, endorsement of that régime entailed support for a system which denied all the values for which those intellectuals supposedly stood. There was no recognition of formal liberties, no right to strike, there was press censorship, frequent use of the death penalty, homosexuality was illegal, and so on. This was possible in part because of the sheer physical distance separating Paris from Havana – and here it is hard not to conclude that what was operating here was an element of cultural élitism which stipulated that what might not be all right for the Parisian intellectual was fine for the Third World peasant – but also because intellectuals, as they themselves could testify, appeared to be being offered a privileged status in the new order. As Sartre rather sententiously put it, he considered Castro to be one of his friends. The régime's fall from favour occurred not when the Cuban Revolution's failures and abuse of the people were exposed but when one of their own – the poet Heberto Padilla – was arrested in 1971. Only then – in a signed letter to *Le Monde*, of course – did they express their 'shame' and 'anger'.

But the life of the intellectual as mandarin has other dimensions, most notably confinement to a very specific and narrowly concentrated geographical space: the Left Bank of Paris. It is here that the intellectual lives, works and socialises. He exists cheek-by-jowl with government ministries and is separated from the capital's business community and middle class by the impassable barrier of the river Seine. It is in this small area that are located the headquarters of France's publishing houses, its literary magazines, its reviews and periodicals. Its cafés and restaurants provide the setting for informal (if sometimes expensive) conversation. And, when the need arises, the *Palais de la Mutualité* serves to house the public meeting of protest. For those not willing to contemplate the final journey to Père Lachaise the Left Bank even has its own cemetery at Montparnasse. The intellectual establishment is represented in the shape of the *Académie française*. More than this, however, it is off the Latin Quarter's narrow streets that are to be found France's most prestiguous institutions of higher learning.

The French educational system has unashamedly set out to produce a State-created élite and if the manner in which this has been achieved has been the source of controversy there is no doubt that at its heart lies the institution of the *grande école*. Of these it has been the *Ecole normale supérieure*, situated in the Rue d'Ulm just to the south of the Panthéon, that has reigned supreme.[83] 'One is', Georges Pompidou commented, 'a *normalien* as one is a prince of the blood'.[84] Raymond Aron's opinion was similarly unequivocal. Upon arrival at the ENS his first impression was one of astonishment. Not since, he wrote, 'have I ever met so many intelligent people brought together in such a small area'.[85] And, as befits a group of people blessed with extraordinary intelligence, the impact of the former students of the ENS upon France's intellectual and political life has been enormous. But it is not just this that explains their pre-eminence. Whether he enjoyed or despised his time at the Rue d'Ulm, whether he emerged on the left (like Nizan) or the right (like Brasillach) of the political spectrum, the *normalien* is tied to his fellows by an intense bond of friendship. Often these bonds can last a lifetime and can span enormous differences of opinion. It is this, for example, that enabled Raymond Aron at the end of his life still to refer to Sartre as 'mon petit camarade'.

The ENS is not alone, however, on the Left Bank as a home to the intellectual élite. More recently, as the French university system has lurched ever deeper into crisis touching even to the heart of the Sorbonne, the *Ecole des Hautes Etudes en Sciences Sociales* has emerged as a bastion of educational power and privilege. To this can be added its near-neighbour, *Sciences-po*: the *Fondation nationale des sciences politiques*. But at the summit of prestige and influence comes the *Collège de France*, election to which for the scholar – Foucault, for example – constitutes the most sought-after and the most cherished of all academic prizes.

The environment of the French intellectual is therefore characterised by excessive centralisation and hierachical organisation. On the Left Bank are concentrated not just the personnel of intellectual life but also its principal institutions and sources of power. The remainder of the country is, to all intents and purposes, *le désert français*. Few are the members of the intellectual élite who, with the exception of *les vacances*, flourish in the provinces, and with the development of the TGV, France's high-speed train, and the consequent emergence of the '*turbo-prof*' it is likely that the situation will only get worse.

Certainly there is little that is new in this. The roots of this singularly French aspect of intellectual life go back to at least the seventeenth and eighteenth centuries, if not before. It was, however, further accentuated in the nineteenth century and especially so after the creation of the Third Republic. Moreover, as one of the enduring traits of French intellectual life it provides the objective context for that process described by Benda as the transition from intellectualism to intellectual action. As the inhabitants of the Left Bank live an intensely public existence dominated by a series of intricate and tightly-knit social and professional networks the very physical proximity of political power almost invites their participation. And this is how it has operated in the twentieth century. The students and staff of the ENS played a key role in the Dreyfusard cause[86] and, as Christophe Charle shows in this volume, the professors of the University of Paris were predominant in accepting the role of the academic as intellectual. The evidence could be extended almost indefinitely. Suffice to say that when Sartre chose to distribute the Maoist *La Cause du peuple* he did so not on the streets of Belleville, still less on those of Lille, but in the Latin Quarter.

The argument is, however, that this long-established pattern of Parisian, and more specifically Left-Bank, dominance has of late become further accentuated. It surfaces, for example, in what is in effect another version of the picture of the intellectual as mandarin. There now exists, it is suggested, a group of people who can best be described as *intellocrates*.[87] They do, of course, live in Paris but this is by no means their defining characteristic. What distinguishes them is precisely that the power they possess is not limited to one area of intellectual production but spreads across several such areas, from the world of higher education into publishing and then into journalism and television. They are, to use the phrase deployed by Hervé Haman and Patrick Rotman, *cumulards*, people who occupy a series of different, but complementary, positions, the greatest power going to those who control the posts of greatest strategic importance. Amongst the *intellocrates* themselves – between whom, of course, there is intense rivalry – the spoils are distributed according to something akin to a barter system. Literary prizes are a clear case in point.

The objection to this development is two-fold. Firstly, and here there are definite echoes of Debray's critique, that the substance of intellectual life, that of thought and ideas, is being sacrificed to an increasingly depoliticised and conformist pattern of expression. The mass media – and their seductive attractions – are again cast as the principal culprits. Secondly, and perhaps more importantly, that the control of the intellectual and, more broadly, cultural life of France is in the hands of a very small number of intermediaries. So, for example, it is pointed out that academic and literary bookselling is controlled by three or four major publishing houses (Le Seuil, Gallimard, Grasset and Editions du Minuit), that these in turn are directed by editors usually occupying powerful academic posts, that until its recent demise sales were heavily influenced by Pivot's television programme *Apostrophes*, and that certain book reviewers (Bernard Poirot-Delpech in *Le Monde*, for example) have an almost official status. The critic would no doubt add that it is from the members of this very small world that are drawn the very people who are deciding the controversial fate of France's much-discussed new national library. The *intellocrates* are then the intellectual establishment.

One response to these complaints has been to argue that much the same has been said about French intellectual life and French intellectuals from the eighteenth century onwards. We need, for example, only to think of Rousseau's fulminations against the salons of Paris to realise that the charges of careerism and corruption are not new and that networks of influence and power have for long existed. Balzac's *Les Illusions perdues*, published at the end of the 1830s, paints a similarly depressing picture of the cynical and self-seeking world of the Parisian *literati*. What today is said of the damaging impact of television was formerly said with equal conviction of the book shop, the press and then radio. Similarly the 'crisis' of the 1970–80s was not the first to be suffered by France's intelligentsia. Others periods of self-doubt can quite easily be found.

So if then there was never a golden age for France's intellectuals what, if anything, has now changed? On the surface it would have to be said very little. Intellectuals in France – although admittedly in fewer numbers – are still prepared to append their names to manifestoes and in times of national crisis their opinions and advice are still sought. *Le Monde*, for example, continues to give space to *manifestes d'intellectuels*, be they in defence of the right of Jews to leave the Soviet Union or to protect a history professor against the charge of collaboration with the enemy during the Indo-China war.[88] At the height of the war against Iraq, *Libération*, in a touching act of faith in the power of the word, filled its pages with the views of those intellectuals for and against the conflict.[89] The Socialist Party, mindful of its earlier criticism of their silence, has again tried to rally intellectuals to its side.[90] So too the abuse of the intellectual continues much as before and from some surprising quarters. Prime Minister Edith Cresson, in the course of her controversial interview in July 1991 calling for the forceful repatriation of illegal immigrants, also denounced what she termed the '*classe intellectualo-médiatique*' and their enthusiasm for '*grandes théories*'.[91] In short, for the cynic there seems little to suggest that the comment of the South African exile

Breyten Breytenbach to the effect that 'You could wake up a Parisian intellectual any time of the day or night and ask him a question and they'd give you a thesis' no longer applies.[92]

Yet the style and mood of the intellectual has undoubtedly been subject to revision. What marks out this crisis from those that have apparently occurred before is not just the level of political disengagement that has taken place but the attempt to re-fashion the relationship that exists between the intellectual and the society in which he lives. The key phrase – frequently repeated – when talking about the intervention of the intellectual in public affairs now appears to be that of *'engagements ponctuels'*, intervention on specific issues that are relatively devoid of ideological content and which bear immediately upon the present. It is this project, for example, that Pierre Nora had in mind when in 1980 he launched *Le Débat* and which he re-affirmed at the time of its tenth anniversary issue in 1990. The intellectual, he argued, had to be seen as *'un éclaireur compétent'*. His job was quite definitely not to speak in the name of those who could not speak but was rather to utilise his 'critical capacities' and his 'judgement' to enlighten and to inform. 'To be an intellectual today,' Nora writes, 'has no other meaning'. Moreover, the list of 'essential questions' cited by Nora as appropriate to discussion by the intellectual is itself revealing. To the burning issue of the new national library are added constitutional reform, immigration, university teaching, the reform of public television, and so on. The point is that the intellectual is no longer entitled to play the role of prophet or hero. He is there to demystify and not to preach.[93] The intellectual – despite the criticisms of Régis Debray and Pierre Bourdieu amongst others – becomes a high-class journalist, something which, as Jacques Julliard here argues, he has often been since the time of Chateaubriand, if not before.

The implications of this re-appraisal should not be underestimated. In effect, it implies and denotes the death of the intellectual as mandarin. There is a view, recently re-stated by Alan Montefiore but contested by Ernest Gellner, that stipulates that intellectuals by the very nature of their work have a responsibility for truthfulness and towards truth.[94] The radical element of this argument – forcefully stated by Julien Benda – is that this responsibility can only be exercised if the intellectual stands apart and is detached from the society in which he lives. It is from afar and from the vantage point of abstract and universal principles that society must be judged. Nora's conception, whilst it clearly retains the obligation towards truth, reduces the distance which separates the intellectual from society to a minimum and firmly places him within this world. The question then arises as to what extent meaningful social criticism of a radical nature is still possible.[95] It is this that represents the most decisive challenge facing the intellectual in contemporary France. Significantly, at the end of *Les Samouraïs*, Julia Kristeva's heroine, after two decades of personal exploration and travel, sits tending her infant in the Luxembourg gardens.

Notes

1. *The Times Saturday Review*, 2 March 1991, pp. 4–6.
2. P. Johnson, *Intellectuals* (London, 1988).
3. M. Ignatieff, 'A country fit to think in', *The Observer*, 25 February 1990, p. 17.
4. B-H. Lévy, *Eloge des intellectuels* (Paris, 1987).
5. See 'BHL: la nouvelle règle du jeu', *Le Point*, 14 May 1990, pp. 12–13.
6. B-H. Lévy, *Les Aventures de la liberté* (Paris, 1991).
7. A. Finkelkraut, *La Défaite de la pensée* (Paris, 1987). This work has been translated as *The Undoing of Thought* (London, 1988).
8. See in particular M. Foucault, 'Truth and Power', in C. Gordon (ed.), *Michel Foucault: Power/Knowledge: Selected Interviews and Other Writings 1972–77* (Brighton, 1980) pp. 109–33. First published in Italian, the French version of this interview appeared in *L'Arc*, 70, 1977.
9. J. Julliard, *Contre la politique professionnelle* (Paris, 1977).
10. P. Nora, 'Que peuvent les intellectuels?', *Le Débat*, 1, 1980, pp. 1–19. See below, pp. 187–98.
11. M-A. Burnier, *Le Testament de Sartre* (Paris, 1982) and J. Verdès-Leroux, *La Lune et le Caudillo: le rêve des intellectuels et le régime cubain* (Paris, 1989).
12. R. Aron, 'Les intellectuels et la politique', *Commentaire*, 22, 1983, pp. 259–63. For a wider discussion of Aron's position see R. Aron, *Le Spectateur engagé: entretiens avec Jean-Marie Missika et Dominique Walton* (Paris, 1981). On broader developments in this period see K. M. Reader, *Intellectuals and the Left in France since 1968* (London, 1987).
13. J. F. Sirinelli, 'Les intellectuels', in R. Rémond (ed.), *Pour une histoire politique* (Paris, 1988) p. 208.
14. See F. Bourricaud, *Le Bricolage idéologique: essai sur les intellectuels et les passions démocratiques* (Paris, 1980) and D. Lindenberg, 'L'intellectuel est-il une spécialité française?', in P. Ory (ed.), *Dernières questions aux intellectuels* (Paris, 1990) pp. 155–205.
15. See J. M. Goulemot, 'L'intellectuel est-il responsable (et de quoi)?', in P. Ory (ed), *Dernières questions* , pp. 51–105. For a broader discussion of

this issue in English see Ian Maclean *et al.* (eds), *The Political Responsibility of Intellectuals* (Cambridge, 1990).

16. The first serious study of these issues was published by D. Caute, *Communism and the French Intellectuals* (London, 1964) but in French see especially J.Verdès-Leroux, *Au Service du Parti: le parti communiste, les intellectuels et la culture (1944–1956)* (Paris, 1983) and *Le Réveil des Somnambules: Le PC, les intellectuels, et la culture, 1956–1985* (Paris, 1987); P. Grémion, *Paris/Prague: la gauche face au renouveau et à la régression tchécoslovaques* (Paris, 1985); and B. Legendre, *Le Stalinisme français: qui a dit quoi? (1944–1956)* (Paris, 1980). For an excellent analysis of the wider phenomenon of French perceptions of the Soviet Union see R. Desjardins, *The Soviet Union through French eyes, 1945–85* (London, 1988). But see especially S. Hazareesingh, *Intellectuals and the French Communist Party: Disillusion and Decline* (Oxford, 1991).

17. See, for example, P. Assouline, *L'Epuration des intellectuels* (Brussels, 1985).

18. For a discussion of these developments see R. Chartier, 'Intellectual History or Sociocultural History? The French Trajectories', in D. La Capra and S.L. Kaplan (eds), *Modern European Intellectual History* (Cornell, 1982).

19. J. Lacarne and B. Vercier, 'Premières personnes', *Le Débat*, 54, 1989, pp. 54–67. See also D. Madelenat, 'La biographie aujourd'hui', *Mesure*, 1, 1989, pp. 47–58 and F. Torres, 'Du champ des Annales à la biographie', *Sources. Histoire au présent*, 3–4, 1985, pp. 141–51. For a word of extreme caution see P. Bourdieu, 'L'Illusion biographique', *Actes de la Recherche en sciences sociales*, 62/63, 1986, pp. 69–72.

20. J. Le Goff, 'Comment écrire une biographie historique aujourd'hui?', *Le Débat*, 54, 1989, 48–53. For Pivot's response to the criticisms directed against him see 'L'Esprit d'Apostrophes', *Le Débat*, 60, 1990, pp. 157–87.

21. D. Eribon, *Michel Foucault* (Paris, 1989).

22. A. Cohen-Solal, *Paul Nizan, communiste impossible* (Paris, 1989) and P. Ory, *Nizan. Destin d'un révolté 1905–1940* (Paris, 1980).

23. J-F. Sirinelli, 'Biographie et histoire des intellectuels: le cas des «éveilleurs» et l'example d'André Bellessort', *Sources. Histoire au présent*, 3–4, 1985, pp. 61–73.

24. See for example N. Sarraute, *Enfance* (Paris, 1983).

25. The classic intellectual's autobiography is, of course, Simone de Beauvoir's monumental, and not always truthful, account of her own life, but see R. Aron, *Mémoires: 50 ans de réflexion politique* (Paris, 1983) and E. Le Roy Ladurie, *Paris–Montpellier* (Paris, 1982).

26. See J-F. Sirinelli, 'Le hasard ou la nécessité? Une histoire en chantier: l'histoire des intellectuels', *Vingtième siècle*, 9, 1986, pp. 97–108. See also T. Judt, 'The judgements of Paris', *Times Literary Supplement*, 28 June, 1991, pp. 3–5.

27. R. Debray, *Le Pouvoir intellectuel en France* (Paris, 1979) and *Le Scribe* (Paris, 1980). *Le Pouvoir intellectuel en France* has been translated as *Teachers, Writers, Celebrities: The Intellectuals of Modern France* (London, 1981).

28. P. Bourdieu, *Choses dites* (Paris, 1983); translated as *In Other Words* (Oxford, 1990) p. 145. For the most recent statement by Bourdieu on the role of intellectuals see 'Un entretien avec Pierre Bourdieu', *Le Monde*, 14 January 1992.
29. P. Bourdieu, 'Champ du pouvoir, champ intellectuel, et habitus de classe', *Scolies*, I, 1971, pp. 7–86.
30. For a discussion of these and related issues see R.Harker *et al.* (eds), *An Introduction to the Work of Pierre Bourdieu: The Practice of Theory* (London, 1990).
31. P. Bourdieu, *Homo Academicus* (Paris, 1984); translated as *Homo Academicus* (Oxford, 1988).
32. P. Bourdieu, *La Noblesse d'Etat* (Paris, 1990).
33. P. Bourdieu. *In Other Words*, p. 191. See here the journal *Actes de la Recherche en sciences sociales*.
34. C. Charle, *Les Elites de la République 1880–1900* (Paris, 1987) and *Naissance des «intellectuels» 1880–1900* (Paris, 1990). For an example of the way Bourdieu has been used in the English-speaking world see F. Ringer, *Fields of Knowledge: French Academic Culture in Comparative Perspective 1890–1920* (Cambridge/Paris, 1992).
35. C. Charle, *Naissance des «intellectuels»*, p. 13.
36. J-F. Sirinelli, *Génération intellectuelle: Khâgneux et Normaliens dans l'entre-deux-guerres* (Paris, 1988).
37. J-F. Sirinelli, *Intellectuels et passions françaises: Manifestes et pétitions au XXe siècle* (Paris, 1990).
38. See C. Prochasson, *Les années électriques 1880–1910* (Paris, 1991), pp. 15–82; A. Simonin, 'Les Editions de Minuit et les Editions du Seuil: deux stratégies éditoriales face à la guerre d'Algérie', in J.P. Rioux and J-F. Sirinelli (eds), *La Guerre d'Algérie et les intellectuels français* (Brussels, 1991) pp. 219–45; L. Pinto, *L'Intelligence en action: le Nouvel Observateur* (Paris, 1984) and A. Boschetti, *Sartre et 'Les Temps modernes': une enterprise intellectuelle* (Paris, 1985).
39. *Cahiers Georges Sorel*, 5, 1987: special issue, 'Les revues dans la vie intellectuelle'. See also the recently established *La Revue des revues*.
40. *Mil neuf cent: revue d'histoire intellectuelle*, 7, 1989: special issue, 'Les congrès lieux de l'échange intellectuel 1850–1914'.
41. G. Sapiro, *Institutions littéraires et crise nationale: Académie Française, Académie Goncourt et Comité national des écrivains dans les années quarante*, DEA thesis, Ecole des Hautes Etudes en sciences sociales (Paris, 1991).
42. *Mil neuf cent: revue d'histoire intellectuelle*, 8, 1990: special issue, 'Les correspondances dans la vie intellectuelle'.
43. Quoted in D. McLellan, *Simone Weil: Utopian Pessimist* (London, 1989) p. 178.
44. J. Benda, *La Jeunesse d'un clerc* (Paris, 1936) p. 89.
45. Ibid., p. 201.
46. P. Ory, 'Qu'est-ce qu'un intellectuel?', in P. Ory (ed.), *Dernières questions*, p. 27.
47. See below, pp. 35–8.
48. See C. Charle, *Naissance des «intellectuels»*, pp. 20–38.

49. See below p. 103 and M. Rebérioux, 'Zola, Jaurès et France: trois intellectuels devant l'Affaire', *Cahiers naturalistes*, 54, 1980, pp. 266–81 and 'Histoire, historiens et dreyfusisme', *Revue historique*, 518, 1976, pp. 407–32.

50. M. Winock, 'Les Affaires Dreyfus', *Vingtième Siècle*, 5, 1985, pp. 19–37.

51. F. Brunetière, *Après le procès: Réponse à quelques «intellectuels»* (Paris, 1898) p. 93.

52. M. Winock, 'Les Affaires Dreyfus', p. 26.

53. See E. Durkheim, 'L'individualisme et les intellectuels', *La Revue bleue*, 10, 1898, pp. 7–13 and F. Brunetière, *Après le procès*. Durkheim's article has been translated as 'Individualism and the Intellectuals', *Political Studies*, 17, 1969, pp. 14–30.

54. R. Aron, 'Les intellectuels et la politique'.

55. G. Colin and J-J.Becker, 'Les écrivains, la guerre de 1914 et l'opinion publique', *Relations internationales*, 24, 1980, pp. 425–42.

56. See R. Wohl, *The Generation of 1914* (Cambridge, Mass., 1979) pp. 5–41.

57. P. Soulez, *Bergson politique* (Paris, 1989).

58. See especially J-F. Sirinelli, *Génération intellectuelle*, and J-L. Loubet del Bayle, *Les non-conformistes des années 30* (Paris, 1969).

59. See N. Racine-Furlaud, 'Le Comité de vigilance des intellectuelles antifascistes (1934–1939): Antifascisme et pacifisme', *Le Mouvement social*, 101, 1977, pp. 87–113.

60. R. Brasillach, *Notre avant-guerre* (Paris, 1972) p. 236.

61. S. de Beauvoir, *Lettres à Sartre 1940–1963* (Paris, 1990).

62. A. Gide, *Retour de l'URSS* (Paris, 1936).

63. See J-L. Panné, 'L'affaire Victor Serge et la gauche française', *Communisme*, 5, 1984, pp. 89–104.

64. For an interesting discussion of one aspect of this strategy see M. Lazar, 'Les «Batailles du livre» du Parti Communiste Français (1950–1952)', *Vingtième siècle*, 10, 1986, pp. 37–50.

65. S. de Beauvoir, *Force of circumstance* (Harmondsworth, 1968) p. 49. For an extended discussion of this whole period see A. Chebel d'Appollonia, *Histoire politique des intellectuels en France 1944–1954* (Brussels, 1991) 2 vols.

66. See M. Poster, *Existentialist Marxism in Post-war France* (Princeton, 1975).

67. L. Casanova, *Le Parti communiste, les intellectuels et la nation* (Paris, 1949).

68. See especially J-P. Rioux and J-F.Sirinelli (eds), *La Guerre d'Algérie et les intellectuels français* (Paris, 1991).

69. J-P. Rioux, 'La guerre d'Algérie dans l'histoire des intellectuels français', in J-P. Rioux and J-F. Sirinelli (eds), *La Guerre d'Algérie*, pp. 33–55.

70. See P. Thibaud, 'Génération algérienne', *Esprit*, 161, 1990, pp. 46–60.

71. A.M. Duranton-Crabol, 'Le GRECE dans le chantier de l'histoire des intellectuels (1968–1984)' *Les Cahiers de l'Institut d'histoire du temps présent*, 6, 1987, pp. 95–104.

72. J. Verdès-Leroux, 'La guerre d'Algérie dans la trajectoire des intellectuels communistes', in J-P. Rioux and J-F. Sirinelli, *La Guerre d'Algérie*, pp. 307–26.

73. See H. Hamon and P. Rotman, *Génération*, 2 vols (Paris, 1990).
74. J. Julliard, 'La réparation des clercs', in J-P. Rioux and J-F. Sirinelli, *La Guerre d'Algérie*, pp. 387–95.
75. For a broader discussion of the 1968 events see D.Bertaux *et al.*, 'Mai 68 et la formation de générations politiques en France', *Le Mouvement social*, 143, 1988, pp. 75–88.
76. See C. Prochasson, *Place et rôle des intellectuels dans le mouvement socialiste français 1900–1920* (doctoral thesis, Université Paris 1, 1989). A revised version of this thesis is shortly to be published by Le Seuil.
77. F. Brunetière, *Après le procès*, p. 92.
78. D. Bair, *Simone de Beauvoir* (London, 1990) p. 427.
79. J. Kristeva, *Les Samouraïs* (Paris, 1990).
80. J. Verdès-Leroux, *Au service du Parti: Le Parti communiste, les intellectuels et la culture* (Paris, 1983).
81. Ibid., p. 15.
82. J. Verdès-Leroux, *La Lune et le Caudillo*.
83. See J-F. Sirinelli, *Génération intellectuelle*.
84. G. Pompidou, 'Préface' to A. Peyrefitte, *La Rue d'Ulm: chroniques de la vie normalienne* (Paris, 1963) p. 9.
85. R. Aron, *Mémoires*, p. 31.
86. See R. Smith, 'L'Atmosphère politique à l'Ecole normale supérieure', *Revue d'histoire moderne et contemporaine*, XX, 1973, pp. 248–68.
87. H. Hamon and P. Rotman, *Les Intellocrates: expédition en haute intelligentsia* (Paris, 1981).
88. See 'Un appel d'intellectuels en faveur des juifs d'URSS émigrant en Israël', *Le Monde*, 6 April 1990 and 'Deux manifestes intellectuels', *Le Monde*, 12 February 1991. Other examples could be cited.
89. *Libération*, 12 February 1990.
90. 'Le grand retour des clercs', *Le Monde*, 1 December 1990.
91. 'Mme Cresson approuvée par le Front national', *Le Monde*, 10 July 1991.
92. M. Camber-Porter, *Through Parisian Eyes* (Oxford, 1986) pp. 54–5.
93. See P. Nora, 'Dix Ans de Débat', *Le Débat*, 60, 1990, pp. 5–11 and 'Un entretien avec Pierre Nora', *Le Monde*, 1 June 1990.
94. See E. Gellner, 'La trahison de la trahison des clercs' and A. Montefiore, 'The political responsibility of intellectuals', in I. Maclean *et al.*, *Political Responsibility*, pp. 17–28 and 201–29.
95. For an extended discussion of these themes see M. Walzer, *The Company of Critics: Social Criticism and Political Commitment in the Twentieth Century* (London, 1989).

2 Mirror, Mirror on the Wall, Who is the True Intellectual of Them All? Self-images of the Intellectual in France

Shlomo Sand

It is necessary to think of the political problem of intellectuals not in terms of 'science/ideology' but in terms of 'truth/power'. (Michel Foucault, 'Vérité et pouvoir', *L'Arc*, 70, 1977)

The celebrated historian D. W. Brogan once remarked that 'We in Britain do not take our intellectuals that seriously.' It is difficult to be sure if the 'average' French citizen accords greater importance to intellectuals than his British counterpart but it is absolutely certain that French intellectuals take themselves very seriously indeed. Moreover, this has very little to do with either the fact that the noun 'intellectual' is a French product or the substantial number of Parisian publications that have explored the subject (a figure that in recent years has increased in inverse proportion to those devoted to the working class). Even a cursory glance through the writings of France's most well-known intellectuals of the last two centuries (philosophers, sociologists or publicists) shows to what extent the latter have been preoccupied by the desire to define their own image.

The origin of the term 'intellectual' is now well-known: it dates from the end of the nineteenth century and came into existence in a specific social and political context. Equally, the history of intellectuals as a social group possessing its own peculiar political role begins with the Dreyfus Affair. However, it is easy to see that the modern intellectual has, from the eighteenth century onwards, a series of distinguished ancestors, known variously, according to the period, as either *philosophes* or as men of letters. Clearly in an article such as this it would be impossible to examine the literature devoted to these figures

33

in any great detail but it is hoped that we will at least be able to highlight some important aspects of what intellectuals have said and thought about themselves.

Two broad pictures arise out of this discourse: one is favourable towards, even enthusiastic about, intellectuals, whilst the other is largely critical, if not openly hostile. The two have co-existed, at various times either challenging or ignoring each other, but both have always attributed greater influence and interest to intellectuals than that normally found in other cultures.

What is it then that determines either the positive or negative character of the intellectual's own discourse about intellectuals? Answers of various kinds can be found. It is possible, for example, to examine the political positions embraced by different writers. To what extent can they be placed on the right or on the left? Are they conservative or progressive? An effort can also be made to locate their discourse within the context of the 'general attitude' towards intellectuals as it has existed over time and, of course, by reference to their position within the social structure at any given moment. Furthermore, there is also the possibility of seeing this discourse in terms of either a favourable or an unfavourable attitude towards political power.

Clearly, all of these factors play a role, however indirect, in the formulation of all theoretical discourse but in this particular case and in so far as it concerns the self-image of the intellectual we want to suggest that the positive or negative response which the intellectual bears towards the group to which he himself belongs is determined above all else by the relationship of this discourse to the dominant ideology operating within the intellectual milieu and/or by the place of the speaker within the social hierarchy of this milieu.

Obviously, to extract the dominant ideology from a particular intellectual universe located in a defined time and space is not an easy task and would require a very different type of enterprise from that being undertaken here. We also have to recognise that the ideology which is dominant within the world of the intellectual is not necessarily always identical to that which is dominant in the world of political power. Indeed, there are moments, however brief, when they can be diametrically opposed. Moreover, the dominant ideologies operating within the different spheres of the intellectual milieu are frequently at odds. Dominance within the university, for example, does not always mean dominance in the world of literature or the media. Despite these obstacles and reservations it is our intention in this chapter to examine some of the most important aspects of the positive and negative self-images of intellectuals in France and their relationship to the dominant ideologies of their day. In order to do so we have chosen a series of well-known intellectuals, two per epoch (with the exception of the last case), in whose writings the image of the intellectual (or the *philosophe* or the man of letters) is extensively considered and discussed. Whilst to an extent these choices are arbitrary the dialogue that they will enable us construct will allow us to perceive what might be regarded as the 'ideal-type' self-image of the intellectual in France.

THE MAN OF LETTERS AND THE *PHILOSOPHE*

As our first pair of modern intellectuals we have chosen the two most famous philosophers of the eighteenth century: Voltaire and Rousseau. The authors of *Candide* and of *Du Contrat social* typify two very different patterns of thinking in the century of enlightenment, the first representing a form of liberalism that was dominant in the early half of the eighteenth century whilst the second was one of the original theorists of democracy in an age when the concept still remained virtually unknown. There is, in fact, no more typical representative of the enlightened optimism of the eighteenth century than Voltaire. Respected and sollicited by the court, scornful of received ideas and of all narrow-mindedness, it was he, who in three entries of his *Dictionnaire philosophique* (1764) – 'Philosophes', 'Gens de lettres' and 'Lettres, Gens de lettres, ou lettrés' – first outlined a portrait of what would later be seen as the modern intellectual. In effect, what Voltaire paints is a collective self-portrait of the generation of *philosophes*.[1]

Who then has the right to regard himself as a man of letters? Certainly it was not sufficient that one should have only written and published books. The man of letters must, by definition, be the master not of one but of several disciplines. Moreover, according to Voltaire, he possessed a 'double character', at one and the same time disclosing truth by virtue of his reason and preaching the lessons of a superior morality. Equally, it seems that for Voltaire the concepts of *philosophe* and of man of letters were virtually interchangeable. 'It is this philosophical spirit,' Voltaire wrote, 'which appears to define the character of the man of letters, and when it is combined with good taste it produces a formidable literature.'[2]

Thus for Voltaire it was the bringing together of different qualities, a range of diverse activities and a special combination of aesthetics, ethics and politics which served to define the *philosophe* of the eighteenth century and which also, on this view, made him superior to his predecessors. However the one thing he had in common with his forebears was that he, like them, was the object of persecution. Being neither a member of the Academy nor of the University he was the victim of the prejudices of his contemporaries. And so as to emphasise this point Voltaire draws the comparison – of long-term significance in the evolution of the self-image of the modern intellectual – between the persecuted man of letters, the *philosophe*, and the prophet: 'Descartes,' Voltaire wrote, 'was obliged to leave his country, Gassendi was calumniated, Arnauld dragged out his days in exile. Every *philosophe* is treated as were the prophets by the Jews.'[3]

A further characteristic of the *philosophe* was his 'independence of mind'. Here it is especially interesting to note the relationship that Voltaire establishes between this quality and the material conditions enjoyed by the man of letters. 'Normally,' Voltaire argued, 'they have more independence of mind than other men; and those born without money can now easily find sufficient from the funds of Louis XIV to strengthen their independence. Gone are the days of those dedications offered to vanity out of self-interest and baseness.'[4] Moreover, it seems clear that these reflections upon the socio-economic status of the man of letters were derived from 'lessons' drawn from Voltaire's own ascent through society. Throughout his life Voltaire greatly envied the situation of his British counterparts who, he believed, enjoyed far greater recognition than their French equivalents. The brilliant philosopher of progress was constantly seeking ways of resolving his ever-increasing financial problems (a fact which explains his accep-tance in 1750 of Frederick II's invitation). However, his praise of Louis XIV's role in transforming aristocratic patronage into mon-archical patronage accorded with his royalist liberalism and was perhaps also an expression of a widely-held feeling among authors of the day grateful for their newly-found autonomy. Conversely, there can be no doubt that this process greatly reinforced the links between intellectual élites and political power in modern France.

But had this patronage really made the eighteenth-century man of letters more independent? In his second article devoted to the man of letters Voltaire, in fact, seems to forget what he had previously said about his economic independence and complains about his difficult and precarious existence when compared to that of the bourgeoisie.[5]

One could for a moment mistakenly believe that Voltaire belonged to the literary underground of the old régime described by Robert Darnton. It was, however, rather his philosophical opponent, Jean-Jacques Rousseau, who *at times* came to occupy the position of a writer excluded from the spheres of privilege.

Rousseau, in marked contrast to Voltaire, was never able to – and perhaps never wanted to – gain acceptance into the intellectual élites that frequented the salons of Paris. Virtually throughout his entire life he scorned and loathed them and it is therefore perhaps possible to read his influential essay *De l'inégalité parmi les hommes* (1755) as a philosophical reaction to the worldly intellectualism of the capital.

In this discourse Rousseau sets out to emphasise that what separates man from the beast is not his reason but rather his liberty. His anthropological portrait of primitive man is thus meant to operate as a theoretical model which allows him to criticise the condition of modernity that arises out of the division of labour and the ever-increasing intellectualisation of life. It is, Rousseau believes, precisely this division of labour and the consequent existence of leisure that gave birth to philosophy and this 'product' of human progress, in his opinion, was indicative of a definite decline when compared with the morality of the people. In fact, it is reason, according to Rousseau, that engenders *amour-propre* and that turns man's mind back upon itself, dividing him from everything that might disturb him:

> Nothing but such general evils as threaten the whole community can disturb the tranquil sleep of the philosopher, or tear him from his bed. A murder may with impunity be committed under his window; he has only to put his hands to his ears and argue a little with himself, to prevent nature, which is shocked within him, from identifying itself with the unfortunate sufferer. Uncivilised man has not this admirable talent; and for want of reason and wisdom, is always ready to obey the promptings of humanity.[6]

It is significant that this serious charge levelled against the philosopher draws upon a moral and not an intellectual argument. For Rousseau, as for Voltaire, the *philosophe* was above all to be judged in terms of his moral and social role. And it goes without saying that, in contrast to Voltaire, Rousseau did not identify himself with the description of the man of letters that he had sketched out. The model of the *philosophe* as courtier horrified him. The question then is whether there lies hidden in the writings of Rousseau another image of the intellectual.

Perhaps if anywhere it is to be found in the mythical figure of the lawgiver described by Rousseau in Book II of *Du Contrat social*. Despite the emphasis placed upon the general will and upon egalitarianism in Rousseau's project it is nevertheless the case that society, at its inception, is deemed to require the intervention of a lawgiver, an intellectual of exceptional quality. 'To discover the rules of society that are best suited to nations,' Rousseau writes, 'there would need to exist a superior intelligence who could understand the passions of men.'[7] Moreover, in his later works on Poland and Corsica, does not Rousseau to a certain extent see himself in the role of Solon and of Lycurgus? In short, is it not perhaps the case that the first man to denounce intellectuals himself secretly aspired to possess spiritual power? Certainly in *Du Contrat social* the lawgiver always exists apart from the citizens who make up society and it is clear that for Rousseau spiritual power must always be an integral part of political power.

SPIRITUAL POWER AND REVOLUTIONARY WRITERS

Less than a hundred years later and in the aftermath of the great revolution of 1789 Auguste Comte dedicated the whole of his life to answering one question: how could a new spiritual power be brought into existence? At the same time his contemporary, Alexis de Tocqueville, for his part was concerned to understand by what misfortune had it been the case that *philosophes* and men of letters had been able to seize temporal power!

Looked at from a distance the respective biographies of these two great nineteenth-century figures would lead us to conclude that the career of the former was marked by total defeat whilst that of the latter – especially in political terms – was overwhelmingly successful. In vain Comte tried repeatedly to gain entry into the world of university (witness, for example, the petition he sent to Guizot in an effort to secure a chair at the *Collège de France*) whilst Tocqueville was not only a parliamentary deputy for many years but also for a brief period minister of foreign affairs under the Second Republic. Nevertheless, within the world of the Parisian intellectual it was to be the name of Comte that came to occupy an increasingly important place and so much so that by the time of his death there was already in existence a school of thought devoted to propagating his ideas. By contrast Tocqueville, despite the success of his book on America, saw interest in his work decline and after his death he was for many years forgotten by those who represented French culture.

Despite what might be called his institutional marginality Comte considered himself to be the representative of a new science that was progressively gaining ground in the world of ideas. Tocqueville, by comparison, saw his own work as a 'defeatist' reaction to the course which events had taken. Comte, for example, was enthusiatic about the impact of industrialisation whilst Tocqueville was fearful of its social consequences. In short, Comte represented a certain ideological optimism typical of the nineteenth century and which in political terms expressed itself in cautious approval of the Republic whilst Tocqueville embodied an aristocratic pessimism that found itself ready to accept with resignation the existence of some form of democracy.

As has already been indicated, Comte's central preoccupation was the absence of spiritual power in the post-revolutionary world in which he lived. The decline of the church in the eighteenth century combined with the challenge to its spiritual authority during the Revolution had brought into existence a dangerous vacuum that made it impossible to establish a new and stable social order. Henceforth, therefore, the function of philosophy was to outline a plan that would permit the creation of a new spiritual power and in accordance with this from his earliest writings onwards – for example, *Les sciences et les savants* and *Considérations sur le pouvoir social*, published in the 1820s – Comte set out an initial programme that varied only very slightly during the remainder of his life. At the outset, and in accordance with the views of his acknowledged master, Saint-Simon, Comte allotted spiritual power to the *savant*. And to the *savant* rather than the man of letters because 'the *savants* in our day possess, to the exclusion of all other classes, the two fundamental elements of spiritual government, capacity and authority in matters of theory'.[8] Elsewhere the term *savant* was replaced by that of 'intellects' and much later Comte used the expression 'the contemplative class' to describe society's new spiritual leaders. This class, Comte wrote, is 'absorbed by speculative labours, constantly and exclusively occupied in furnishing all the others with the general rules of conduct which they can no more dispense with than create'.[9]

Thus the spiritual power of the 'contemplative class' was not to be limited to the inculcation of knowledge or to intellectual education: in effect, its primary function was to offer moral guidance and this for the transparent reason that 'men would need a moral government, because no one could of his own accord confine his personal dispositions within limits suitable to his own condition'.[10] The development of civilisation, the growth of industrialisation, the intensification of the division of labour and the accentuation of class conflict were such as to require, according to Comte, an extension of spiritual–intellectual authority in a world where it had been lacking since 1789. On its own temporal power could not survive for any length of time. 'In truth,' Comte argued, 'temporal repression has never been, and never will be, anything but the complement of spiritual repression, which, at no time, can wholly suffice for social necessities. If, by the natural progress of civilisation, the former increasingly diminishes, this diminution unavoidably presupposes a proportional increase of the latter.'[11]

The revolution of 1848 combined with the role that the workers had played in it was sufficient to convince Comte of the important political role that the proletariat would play in the future temporal order. Nevertheless, he still remained convinced of the necessity of a spiritual power and it is this which explains why in the year of the revolution he established the *Société positiviste* and why it was Comte in person who wrote its manifesto. This new society of spiritual Jacobinism was to have an entirely intellectual function, that of completing the revolution, and this was to be achieved through the re-fashioning of opinions and morals.[12] Moreover, this new spiritual authority would not be French but European (France, of course, would be at its centre) and at its head, without question, would be the source of its inspiration, Auguste Comte himself. 'In order to ensure the unity of purpose that is indispensable to the *Société positiviste*,' Comte proclaimed, 'I will remain the sole judge of the intellectual aptitude of all those who ask to join'.[13] In short, it is in the writings of the precursor of modern sociology that is most clearly expressed the unsatisfied desire of the intellectual to control an institutionalised spiritual power that, in the modern age, would replace the lost authority of the Church.

We do not know whether Tocqueville ever read Comte's manifesto establishing the *Société positiviste*. Given his political activities at the time it seems highly unlikely. But if he had read it we can be sure that he would have been terror-stricken, especially by the parallel drawn between the Jacobins and the *Société positiviste*. As far as Tocqueville was concerned the desire of philosophers to change the world was never anything else but a danger.

It was the consequences of the revolution of 1848 that led Tocqueville to write his famous work *L'Ancien régime et la révolution*, and in which is to be found an important chapter entitled 'How towards the middle of the eighteenth century men of letters took the lead in politics and the consequences of this new development'. Tocqueville, as is well known, never disguised his lack of respect for the authors of the century of Enlightenment but what we want to emphasise here is that it was precisely that dimension which turned the man of letters into an 'intellectual', namely his relationship to politics, that most inspired his distrust.

In line with his usual form of argument, Tocqueville analysed the character of the French man of letters by way of a comparison with his English and German counterparts. Unlike his colleagues in England the French man of letters remained separated from political power and to such an extent that 'they did not play an active part in public affairs'. And in effect, therefore, the absence of free political institutions and of an active political life in France deprived the man of letters of the possibility of understanding the complexity of the world of politics. Nevertheless, and in contrast to his German contemporaries, he did not completely turn his back on politics in order to retire to the world of pure philosophy. Whatever their differences, Tocqueville argued, all of them believed 'that what was wanted was to replace the complex of traditional customs governing the social order of the day by simple, elementary rules deriving from the exercise of human reason and natural law'.[14]

From this – and in a style reminiscent of Edmund Burke – Tocqueville then establishes what amounts to a quasi-sociology of intellectuals. Their abstract political and literary thought, he argues, derives from the socio-economic position of the man of letters. 'Their very way of living,' he writes, 'led these writers to indulge in abstract theories and generalisations regarding the nature of government and to place blind confidence in these. For living as they did, quite out of touch with practical realities, they lacked the experience which might have tempered their enthusiasms'.[15] Moreover, even if these writers did not play an active part in politics the general ideas that they expounded in their works had an enormous impact upon events and this for the reason that this same abstract approach ignoring the complexities of political life became a model which the people themselves were to follow. The result, according to Tocqueville, was that the whole nation became imbued with 'the instincts, the turn of mind, the tastes, and even the eccentricities characteristic of the literary man. And when the time came for action these literary propensities were imported into the political arena'.[16] The *philosophes* were, in other words, responsible, if only in part, for France's later misfortunes during the Revolution.

The idea then which arises out of this chapter, although clearly it was not expressed in these precise terms – the vocabularly itself was lacking – was that it had been intellectuals, deprived of any sense of reality, who had seized power during the Revolution. As such Tocqueville is surely one of the first to comprehend the role of intellectuals in modern revolutions.

As has already been mentioned, Tocqueville wrote his famous work after the revolution of 1848. Was he thinking about Danton, Robespierre and Saint-Just or such other 'intellectuals' as Lamartine, Ledru-Rollin and Louis Blanc? Whatever the case it is clear that he always regarded the attraction of poets, journalists and historians in France to politics as a potential source of disaster. But did this mean that Tocqueville thought that intellectuals should be entirely removed from political action? His writings as well as his own political activities indicate otherwise, revealing an undisclosed model of another type of 'political intellectual': like his British counterpart the French man of letters must resign himself to being a modest 'civil servant' and must free himself from the image of being the bearer of universal truth.

THE *SAVANT* AND SOCIALIST MANDARINS

Amongst the numerous descendents of the founder of the *Société positiviste* living at the end of the nineteenth century, one of the most brilliant was undoubtedly the sociologist Emile Durkheim. A matter of months after the publication of Emile Zola's famous article 'J'accuse' in 1898 he rallied to the Dreyfusard cause. We are, then, here concerned with the period – that of the Dreyfus Affair – when the word 'intellectual' itself begins to come into common usage. It was, in other words, a political event that transformed the man of letters into 'a man of the intellect' and this because in the first place it was men of letters who turned a judicial case into that political event.

In 1898, Durkheim was not yet the famous Sorbonne professor who would one day succeed in introducing a new discipline into the world of the French university. But he already possessed a considerable reputation and his review, *L'Année sociologique*, had begun to appear. Despite the fact that he did not sign the manifesto in support of Zola (known immediately as the 'manifesto of the intellectuals') he nevertheless replied to the article 'Après le procès' published by the anti-

Dreyfusard literary critic Ferdinand Brunetière. The title of Durkheim's article – 'L'individualisme et les intellectuels'[17] – is itself indicative of its content. Durkheim's intention was to analyse the significance of modern individualism, a phenomenon which, according to him, was not anti-social. But it is the defence of the involvement of intellectuals in the Dreyfus Affair contained within this argument that gives this article its particular interest and which we will therefore quote at length:

> If, therefore, in these recent times a certain number of artists, but above all *savants*, have believed that they ought to refuse to assent to a judgement whose legality appeared to them to be suspect, it is not because, as chemists or philogists, philosophers or historians, they attribute to themselves any special privileges, or any exclusive right of exercising control over the case in question. It is rather that, being men, they seek to exercise their entire right as men and to keep before them a matter which concerns reason alone. It is true that they have shown themselves more jealous of this right than the rest of society; but that is simply because, as a result of their professional activities, they have it nearer to heart. Accustomed by the practice of scientific method to reserve judgement when they are not fully aware of the facts, it is natural that they give in less readily to the enthusiasms of the crowd and to the prestige of authority.[18]

Even at a time when many artists considered themselves to be men of science and when Zola regarded himself as a surgeon dissecting society's ills, it is nevertheless something of an exaggeration to regard those of the earliest Dreyfusards such as Bernard-Lazare and Charles Péguy as 'above all *savants*' but what, in effect, we are witnessing here is an expression of the then dominance of scientism in the French intellectual world, a dominance which manifested itself in the consecration of the *savant* (as opposed to the man of letters or the *philosophe*) as a cultural hero and which, because of the prestige accorded to science, offered the intellectual an entry into politics. In a sense, therefore, Durkheim's argument echoes that of Voltaire and is in line with the analysis offered by Comte. Furthermore, it is worth noting that Durkheim's position is indicative of the degree of relative autonomy enjoyed by French intellectuals in their relationship with political authority.

Durkheim was later to continue in his defence of the right of intellectuals to intervene in the political arena, believing that in order that the interests of science and of art should be protected it was appropriate that they should have representation in parliament. Intellectuals, without actually governing, should be the advisers and the educators of their contemporaries, keeping an ever-watchful eye on political and moral issues because, in his words, 'the critical period begun by the end of the ancien régime has not yet come to a close'.[19]

Georges Sorel – one of Durkheim's most important critics at the turn of the century – would no doubt also have recognised, albeit in different terms, that he lived in a critical period. It was also the case that at one point he even accepted the definition of intellectuals as advisers. However he steadfastly rejected the role attributed to them by Durkheim as educators, preferring rather – to use Marx's phrase - to recommend the education of the 'educators', the education of those intellectuals who were divorced from the modern world of industrial production.

This retired government engineer, Marxist fellow-traveller at a time when Marxism was virtually unknown in France and, later, 'theoretician' of revolutionary syndicalism quickly rallied to the Dreyfusard cause, unlike Durkheim, signing the second of the so-called manifestoes of the intellectuals. Yet in parallel to this classically 'intellectual' act he also, rather curiously, in 1898 published his important essay *L'Avenir socialiste des syndicats*, a work which just as easily could have been entitled *L'Avenir étatique des intellectuels*. Here, in essence, was a study which, in terms of theory, acted as a point of transition from the acerbic criticism of intellectuals voiced by such representatives of official Marxism as Karl Kautsky and Paul Lafargue to the virulent anti-intellectualism of the future 'intellectuals' of revolutionary syndicalism.

Setting out from the assumptions of orthodox Marxism Sorel reached the novel conclusion that 'the contemporary hierarchy has as its principal basis the division of labour into intellectual and manual categories'.[20] And, contrary to what had been generally thought, bourgeois democracy tended not to restrain the development of this hierarchy but to accentuate it. It strives, Sorel commented, 'to utilise the people's superstitious respect for learning; it uses the most unscrupulous means to heighten its prestige; it multiplies diplomas and strives to transform the slightly educated person into a mandarin'.[21]

This, in short, was Sorel's response to the dominant intellectual ideology formulated, as we have already seen, by Durkheim. The modern intellectual made use of the prestige accorded to science in order to strengthen his social and economic status as well as – and this was even worse as far as Sorel was concerned – their political position.

If for Durkheim in 1898 the term 'intellectual' was synonymous with *'savant'* then for Sorel it was equivalent to 'politician'. It was the member of the liberal professions, the lawyer, the journalist and the university academic who was about to take his place as the parliamentary representative of democracy and of socialism. 'The true vocation of intellectuals,' Sorel argued, 'is the exploitation of politics. The role of the politician is very like that of the courtier and does not require any industrial aptitude. We need not try speaking to them of eliminating the traditional forms of the State'.[22]

For Sorel, therefore, the future of socialism lay in the conquest of the workshop and not in that of the parliamentary forum of democracy where the word reigned supreme and where the intellectual was able to hold sway over the worker. The intellectual élite, Sorel believed, kept silent about the enduring problem of the distance that existed between the representative and the represented and thus was able to turn itself into a virtual 'representative dictatorship of the proletariat'.[23] Moreover, it is perhaps not entirely accidental if in this context Sorel cites Tocqueville by the side of Marx. The aristocratic pessimism of the mid-nineteenth century which dreaded the revolutionary intellectual had, at the end of the century, been transmuted into a syndicalist pessimism whose fear and loathing was directed towards the newly-emerging class of socialist intellectuals.

The outcome of the Dreyfus Affair only served to heighten Sorel's hostility towards intellectuals and their involvement in politics, a fact amply demonstrated in his classic work *Réflexions sur la violence*. Sorel believed that the intellectual who supported the syndicalist movement had no right either to control or to direct it. His sole task was to destroy the dominant culture from the inside without the least pretence of contributing towards the creation of the new proletarian culture, and it was in line with this that, at the end of his life, he identified himself with Proudhon and with the latter's definition of the role of the intellectual as a 'disinterested servant of the proletariat'. Again the discourse of the intellectual on intellectuals reveals another hidden model of his role.

CLERCS AND WATCHDOGS

When Julien Benda painted his portrait gallery of the great traitors of his day it was not perhaps surprising that Sorel should find a place amongst this distinguished company! The period between the two wars did, in fact, see the publication of two classic books that addressed the question of the role of intellectuals: Benda's own *La Trahison des clercs* (published in 1927) and Paul Nizan's *Les Chiens de garde* (published in 1932), the latter being an indirect reply to Benda's earlier polemic. Both consider the question of the relationship of the intellectual to politics to be of central importance and both, moreover, tend to substitute the term 'clerc' for that of intellectual. However while Benda, despite the title of his work and the impression given by a hasty reading of its contents, idealised the spiritual function of the intellectual, Nizan viewed him only with scorn and mistrust.

Benda was always a man of independent means and by the 1920s he had already achieved a certain notoriety as a writer. According to him the *clercs* were 'all those whose activity is not the pursuit of practical aims, all those who seek their joy in the practice of an art or a science or metaphysical speculation, in short in the possession of non-material advantages, and hence in a certain manner say: 'My kingdom is not of this world' '.[24] From this one could conclude that Benda's aim was to deny totally the legitimacy of the intellectual's involvement in politics but as the text unfolds it is clear that his position is less clear-cut. It is not necessarily the case, Benda writes, that 'when the *clerc* descends to the market place he is failing to perform his functions'. In the past such committed intellectuals as Gerson, Spinoza, Voltaire and Zola were 'carrying out their functions as *clercs* in the fullest and noblest manner. They were the officiants of abstract justice and were sullied with no passion for a worldly object.'[25]

At the end of the century Benda had himself been a young Dreyfusard and later, in the 1930s, he would lend his support to the French left. The problem was that in the 1920s commitment to the left did not seem to be an option. According to Benda those *clercs* who had been Dreyfusards had fought in the name of universal justice and had, at the same time, kept faith with their moral mission. Likewise, those *clercs* who had rallied to the defence of France during the First World War had also defended universal values. By contrast a pacifism of the sort displayed by Romain Rolland was adjudged to be reprehensible. But the real traitors, according to Benda, were to be found elsewhere. It must be admitted, Benda wrote, 'that the German *clercs* led the way . . . most of the moral and political attitudes adopted by the *clercs* of Europe in the past fifty years are of German origin'.[26]

However, the heart of the great betrayal lay in the enthusiasm with which modern intellectuals had embraced political passions and it is this idea which is the key to understanding Benda's text. Of these passions there were two principal kinds: those associated with 'the realist passions of the nation' and those with the 'passions of class'. From Fichte to Marx, from Barrès to Maurras and on to Sorel these traitors had admired only the particular and the temporal and therefore, in contrast to the great tradition which had existed from Socrates to Renan and to Taine and which had embodied universal values and a message of spiritual humanism, had betrayed their name as intellectuals, had betrayed their vocation and their traditional social function. 'This prodigious decline of morality, this kind of (very Germanic) intellectual sadism,' Benda argued, 'is usually and quite openly accompanied by a huge contempt for the true *clerc*.'[27]

There were then, according to Benda, true and false *clercs*, with a whole series of factors – social and ideological – explaining why the latter had so recently come into existence. The modern age, Benda believed, was 'the age of politics' and its attractions had proved to be very strong and seductive but it was above all the socio-economic situation that had been primarily responsible for the politicisation of the false *clerc*. In the past the *clerc* had been independent but he had progressively become more and more economically dependent and concerned with the necessities of earning a living. 'The real evil to deplore,' Benda contended, 'is perhaps not so much the great betrayal of the *clercs* but the disappearance of the *clercs*, the impossibility of leading the life of the *clerc* in the world of today. One of the gravest responsibilities of the State is that it has not maintained (but could it do so?) a class of men exempt from civic duties, men whose sole function is to maintain non-practical values.'[28]

In short, Benda in his turn reproduces Voltaire's dream. But there is more to it than that. Whilst without doubt he considered himself to be one of the last of the true *clercs* (in his text Benda does not cite a single one of his contemporaries as a true *clerc*) and while he also considered himself to be a non-conformist, Benda was, in fact, not only a representative of the dominant moderate and republican nationalism that loathed political extremes but also illustrative of the very strong affinities, specific to France, between the intellectual and the State.

It was precisely this charge that Paul Nizan, the former student of the *Ecole normale supérieure* and member of the Communist Party, levelled against the 'watchdogs' of the modern State. 'Through a series of intricate maneuvers, carried out under the watchful eye of our forefathers,' Nizan argued, 'the secular clergy was promoted to the position formerly held by its ecclesiastical counterpart. But this new clergy has discharged exactly the same functions as its predecessor; that is, it has borne the chief responsibility for all the forms of moral suasion, all the spiritual propaganda, which the State might require.'[29] Like Benda, Nizan scarcely uses the term 'intellectual', preferring either *philosophe* or sociologist and, at times, *clerc*, but the target of his attack is those thinkers who believe that they deal with abstract issues and promote universal values whilst in reality they serve the State and defend bourgeois rule. 'It is especially noteworthy,' Nizan remarked, 'that, generally speaking, our professional thinkers are salaried employers of the State, that the weightiest opinions in this country are produced in exchange for public monies and are backed by government sanctions.'[30]

Nizan's aim, therefore, was to unmask 'the myth of the clerisy', to expose a class which, believing itself to be a universal class, considered itself to be devoid of all material interests. The reality was that those thinkers who made up this class aspired to live only in peace in order that they might produce their ideas in the same way that an industrialist produced merchandise. In Nizan's view the refusal to accept the political realism that Benda had condemned was itself an act of hypocrisy because to adopt neutrality before the struggles of everyday life was implicitly to embrace a political position. 'The desire to be a *clerc* and nothing but a *clerc*,' he argued, 'is less a choice made by Eternal Man than the decision of a partisan.'[31]

However, if Nizan scorned the apolitical philosopher and sociologist his deepest bitterness was reserved for those intellectuals who had supported the First World War, those very same intellectuals that Benda had praised and to whom he had belonged. 'These *clercs*,' he raged, 'simply followed the crowd and obeyed the orders of the generals and the politicians. These men, most of whom were not subject to mobilization, meekly went along with the forces of ignorance and exhorted those who had been mobilized to give up their lives. Every one of their students who died in battle was a martyr to their philosophy. They pointed with pride to the dead men as so many proofs of their virtue. These dead men were their dead.'[32] And if Benda criticised and condemned what he saw as the treason perpetrated by intellectuals towards their own class, Nizan concluded his book with an impassioned call for just such an act of betrayal. 'It is no longer a question,' he wrote, 'of doing something for the workers, but of doing something with them, in response to their demands, of being one voice amongst many and not the voice of the Mind.'[33]

This rejection of the spiritual function of the intellectual was, for Nizan, all part of a broader desire to see the disappearance of the traditional forms of the division of labour. But this did not mean that in the meantime the intellectual–traitor had no role to play. As with those of his predecessors who had been critical of the intellectual it is possible in Nizan to find an 'alternative' model of the intellectual, of the intellectual who 'henceforth will be nothing other than a specialist in the privations and indignities borne by the exploited'.[34] It was, according to Nizan, a modest function but one which would entail membership of the political party of the oppressed and which would require the transformation of the *clerc* into a 'technician'.

AUTHENTICITY AND OPIUM

It is interesting to note that the term 'technician', used by Nizan at the end of his book but in an altogether different sense, provided the point of departure for Jean-Paul Sartre's analysis of intellectuals. Presented as a series of lectures in Japan in 1965, *Plaidoyer pour les intellectuels* further advanced a line of argument set out originally in the very first issue of *Temps modernes* in 1945 and, at first sight, looks very much to be located within the radical tradition inhabited by Nizan, Sartre's former friend from his student days in the 1930s. In truth, viewed from the perspective of the discourse about intellectuals, Sartre's text is the very opposite of Nizan's.

In contrast to the two decades prior to the war, the so-called 'Sartre years' which followed the liberation of France were characterised by the ideological hegemony not just of the left but specifically of Marxism. The attitude of the now-famous existentialist philosopher was full of self-confidence and this was reflected in his positive assessment of the intellectual. In the beginning there was the *clerc*, the servant of the Church who knew how to read – 'Reading,' Sartre commented, 'was the province of the cleric' – and who therefore was the possessor of knowledge. His modern successor was the technician, the specialist in the field of practical knowledge, who first appeared with the emergence of the bourgeoisie. But these technicians were not yet intellectuals and it is this question – by what means does the technician become an intellectual? – that Sartre addressed in the first two of his lectures. The technician, Sartre argued, as the possessor of practical knowledge and because of the goals of his work – what is useful without specification or limits – will always adopt a universalist perspective and thus every technician is a potential intellectual. However, the technician is always torn by an inner contradiction which arises from the conflict between the universalism entailed in his search for truth and the ideological particularism and extra-scientific limits to which he is subjected. Sartre's point, however, is that as soon as the technician applies the universalist techniques of science to the society in which he lives, then he becomes an intellectual. 'In a certain sense,' Sartre writes, he 'becomes a guardian of fundamental ends (the emancipation, universalisation and hence humanisation of man).'[35]

Thus, if Durkheim chose to emphasise that it was the rationalism characteristic of the *savant* which conferred an advantage when he entered the spheres of morality and of politics, according to Sartre it was the implicit and fundamental universalism of the technician that enabled him to become an intellectual. Moreover, and despite their numerous differences, Sartre, like Benda, had a conception of the 'true intellectual' – who is necessarily a radical thinker[36] – and the 'false intellectual' – whose habit it was to say 'No, but . . . '.[37] And it was this universalist logic that obliged the true intellectual – either as a fellow traveller or as an organic intellectual – to line up beside the working class, but the crucial dimension was the role that he was to play. 'It is by applying the dialectical method, by grasping the particular in the demands of the universal and reducing the universal to the movement of a singularity towards universalisation,' Sartre wrote, 'that the intellectual – defined as a man who has achieved consciousness of his own constituent contradiction – can help the proletariat to achieve its own self-consciousness.'[38]

Certainly Sartre, unlike Comte, rejected any idea that intellectuals should possess spiritual power and he was consistent in his praise of the proletariat but almost imperceptibly he transformed them into a universal class, the 'true' intellectual – and not the bureaucracy or the proletariat as Hegel and Marx had in turn believed – being the embodiment of a 'true' universalism. The truth was universal and it was through their work that the technician became aware of that truth.

Nevertheless, for Sartre there remained a serious problem. Neither he nor the great majority of committed intellectuals in the 1950s or 1960s were by origin even remotely technicians of practical knowledge. How then, for example, was it possible for a writer to become a universal intellectual? It was this difficulty which Sartre addressed in the third and last of his lectures in Japan and it is in his conclusion that can be discerned his own most explicit attempt to define himself as an intellectual. 'Whereas other intellectuals,' Sartre commented, 'see their function arise from a contradiction between the universalist demands of their profession and the particularist demands of the dominant class, the inner task of the writer is to remain on the plane of lived experience while suggesting universalisation as the affirmation of life on its horizon. In this sense, the writer is not an intellectual accidentally, like others, but essentially.'[39]

Was it then the writer who was the authentic intellectual? Nothing in fact irritated Raymond Aron more than the pretension of the novelist or the philosopher to occupy centre stage in France and to cast themselves in the role of political prophets. 'The political ambitions of bestselling novelists,' he wrote, 'clash with the literary ambitions of statesmen. The latter dream of writing a novel whilst the former dream of becoming government ministers.'[40] It was in these terms, taken from *L'Opium des intellectuels*, that in the 1950s the opponent of Sartre defined the relationship of intellectuals and politics in France. Ten years before Sartre's lectures in Japan, in other words, Aron published a work entirely devoted to criticising Sartrean intellectualism and its taste for revolutionary opium!

Without doubt this line of criticism had little impact in intellectual circles during the 1950s, whilst Aron himself, despite his then brilliant university career, remained remarkably isolated within French political culture. Moreover, the presuppositions of the 'committed spectator' were not only anti-Sartrean but also opposed to the whole tradition exemplified by Voltaire, Comte, Durkheim and even Benda. Aron was categorical in his judgement. When, he argued, one observed the political opinions of intellectuals the first impression was that they were akin to those of non-intellectuals: 'the same mixture of half-truths, outdated prejudices, aesthetic as opposed to rational preferences appear'.[41] Certainly Aron, in contrast to Sorel and Nizan, made an effort to preserve the appropriate distance of the sociologist but as his text proceeds his remarks in criticism of intellectuals become more and more acerbic and wide-ranging.

His first question, therefore, was why was it that in France, the paradise of intellectuals, the latter considered themselves to be revolutionary? His answer was almost identical to that provided by Tocqueville a hundred years earlier: 'The majority of intellectuals who are interested in politics,' Aron contended, 'are embittered because they feel denied of something which is theirs by right. Whether rebellious or well-behaved, they feel that they are preaching in the desert . . . In a way, the intelligentsia in France is less involved in day-to-day affairs than it is elsewhere.'[42]

It was this distance from the world of politics that engendered both an intellectual messianism and a desire to speak in the name of all mankind. Lacking any grasp of political realities the French intellectual presumed to speak out against every crime wherever it was committed in the world. And as such, and in imitation of the clerisy, he displayed a nostalgia for universal ideas. However, if Aron accepted that the messianic religion associated with the humanism of the intellectual was born in France he recognised that it was not specific to his home country and he was in general severely critical of the role played by the intellectual in the twentieth century. In his view it was intellectuals who had conceived and led the revolutions of our century. What is more: 'In Russia, it is intellectuals who exercise supreme authority. Communism is the first religion purveyed by intellectuals to have succeeded.'[43]

It clearly follows from this that one cannot entirely understand Aron's vision of the contemporary intellectual if it is not seen in the wider context of his attitude to communism in general. In the Soviet Union, in his view, there had occurred a dangerous development that happily had been avoided in the West. 'All of those – capitalists, bankers and elected representatives – who in a parliamentary democracy bar the way of the intellectual to the summits of power,' he argued, 'have disappeared.'[44] Not only Lenin, in other words, but also Stalin had to be seen as a type of intellectual.

From Sartre to Stalin, therefore, Aron was not sparing in his criticism. His tone was always harsh and the overall picture was a negative one. Yet throughout his analysis Aron was careful not to condemn each and every intellectual. And just like those critics of the intellectual who had preceded him (although this time it was not hidden) Aron himself possessed a positive model of what the intellectual should be. Writing in the 1950s this representative of French liberalism – like many French liberals before him – found in the moderate and reformist British intellectual an example that he felt could be followed. Thus the function of the intellectual was important but modest. He had to restrict himself to the role of adviser, respecting the institutions of government and always accepting the politics of the possible.

What undoubtedly annoyed Aron, however, about the dominant discourse of the intellectual was the extent of its pretentiousness and hypocrisy. And in one particular passage of his text where he could no longer contain his anger this is all too evident: 'Why,' he asks, 'cannot intellectuals admit that they are less interested in the standard of living of the working class than they are in the refinement of life and of work? Why do they cling on to democratic jargon when, against the intrusions of mass man and of mass production, they strive to defend authentically aristocratic values?'[45]

THE RETURN OF THE UNIVERSAL?

There can be no doubt that Raymond Aron's analysis of intellectuals was at times more 'materialist' than that of many of his opponents who considered themselves to be experts in historical materialism but it was another sociologist who, a few years later, took it upon himself to dispel the illusions that intellectuals had about their own image and the myths that they had created about their cultural universe. In an interview given in 1978, Pierre Bourdieu stated: 'What I have done is questioned what had previously been unquestioned: intellectuals are always in agreement that their own affairs and activities should be left alone.'[46] And thus in contrast to the leftist intellectuals of the 1960s and 1970s who viewed their own role in society with such enthusiasm the author of *Homo Academicus* and of *Distinction* produced a perceptive and rigorous analysis, all the time attempting to define the relationship of what he described as the intellectual field to the field of power and to disclose the power relationships constituted by it. Moreover, it has been above all the work of Bourdieu which in the area of cultural studies has been responsible for re-directing university research in France and which has made possible a non-normative approach to the study of intellectuals.

Bourdieu's initial definition of the intellectual has remained unchanged over time. 'Intellectuals, as the possessors of cultural capital,' he wrote, 'represent a dominated fraction within the dominant class and many of the positions they adopt, in politics for example, arise from the ambiguity of their position as the dominated amongst the dominant.'[47] The title of intellectual itself could, according to the circumstances, be claimed by *savants*, university professors, writers, artists, publicists and journalists but even as early as the 1970s Bourdieu had developed a critical position towards the last two categories, a development which reflected the broader view that all the intellectual professions – even those of the sociologist and of sociology – were properly the subjects of research.

Certainly Bourdieu himself recognised that he did not feel at ease in the role of the (socially privileged) intellectual but he nevertheless denied the accusations of anti-intellectualism that were levelled against him. However, whilst it is clear that he did not share Sorel's and Nizan's scorn for the *clerc*, nor Aron's secret aversion, his response to the tradition begun with Voltaire and continuing via Durkheim was unambiguous. 'It occurs only too frequently,' he commented, 'that intellectuals make use of the competence (in a quasi-judicial sense of the term) that society recognises in them in order to speak with authority about things well beyond the limits of their technical competence, especially in the area of politics.'[48] Bourdieu, as this makes clear, did in other words completely reject the Sartrean model of the universal intellectual as well as the version of it which became popular in the 1970s, that of Foucault's 'specific' intellectual.[49] Any intellectual supremacy in areas where the intellectual intervened as a citizen was denied and Bourdieu for one did not forget that in political and economic terms the 'dominated' intellectual belonged to the dominant class.

Nevertheless, in the 1980s, after the death of Sartre and of Foucault, with the decline of radical leftism in university and intellectual circles as well as important changes in Bourdieu's own intellectual and university position, significant modifications in the tone of his argument can be discerned. It was, in fact, precisely in an article dedicated to the memory of Michel Foucault that this more positive and more normative approach towards intellectuals first became visible. 'They are not,' Bourdieu remarked, 'the spokesmen of the universal, even less a 'universal class' but it is the case that, for historical reasons, they are often interested in the universal . . . Today we need to create an international of artists and of *savants* capable of putting forward ideas and recommendations and of imposing them upon the political and economic powers that be . . . It is in the most complete autonomy *vis-à-vis* all other powers that resides the sole possible foundation of a properly intellectual power which is intellectually legitimate.'[50] We hesitate to go so far as to say that Auguste Comte has here found a descendant at the end of the twentieth century – Bourdieu would undoubtedly be annoyed by the comparison and it is true that, officially at least, he has not modified his initial stance – but his writings show that, little by little, he has sought to extend the power of the dominated within the dominant class.

Moreover, the political changes in eastern Europe and the role that intellectuals played in these events further encouraged Bourdieu to develop the idea of a new international of intellectuals.[51] Thus on the occasion of the bicentenary of the French Revolution Bourdieu, like

Sartre before him, gave a series of lectures in Japan, one of which was entitled 'Le corporatisme de l'universel: le rôle des intellectuels dans le monde moderne'.[52] Its subject was the strategic bases that informed the new commitment of 'cultural producers' and the lecture itself was committed and designed to inspire action, with Bourdieu, as sociologist, intent on outlining the means which would make possible new forms of political intervention. The objective of the intellectuals' struggle was two-fold: in the first place, 'to establish their autonomy' in respect of all other powers; secondly, 'to keep the most autonomous cultural producers from the temptation of the ivory tower by creating appropriate institutions to enable them to intervene collectively in politics under their own specific authority'.[53]

In the past organic intellectuals or fellow travellers had always favoured universal struggles to the detriment of the protection of their own interests and it was in this way, Bourdieu argued, they had forgotten 'that the defence of the universal presupposes the defence of the defenders of the universal'.[54] Henceforth it was above all the fight for the defence of the republic of *savants* and of artists and the defence of the methods and conditions of intellectual production that needed to be fought. But against whom? Against the journalists, the publicists and 'the second-rate sociologists,'[55] who, in Bourdieu's eyes, represented forces exterior to the intellectual field. In other words, Bourdieu's old apprehensions about publicists and journalists had worsened and so much so that he now believed that the autonomy of the intellectual field was threatened by a Trojan horse led by public opinion and market forces. It was this which explained why 'first-rate' sociologists must organise themselves alongside other *savants* as part of an organised international form of action.

How can this shift of emphasis be explained? Placed at the dominant pole of the (international) university field, Bourdieu nevertheless remains ill at ease in his relationship with the national field of the mass media and it is this, perhaps, which lies at the origin of his desire, henceforth, to champion a greater area of autonomy for a fraction of the intelligentsia rather than to unmask its activities. It is, furthermore, significant that it is not against the encroachments of political power that the autonomy of the field needs to be protected.

The activity of intellectuals could not, however, be restricted solely to the defence of their own interests. The emergence of a technocracy, the new nobility of the State, had effectively excluded intellectuals from political debate and Bourdieu, concerned about this decline in their political and spiritual power, was eager to articulate a strategy that would once again place them at centre stage. Upon this occasion the model was not that propounded by either Sartre or Foucault but rather that of the eighteenth-century intellectual. 'Excellent models for this already exist in the past,' Bourdieu remarked, 'for example, the Encyclopedists.'[56]

An international network of *encyclopédistes*? The circle is complete and our survey of the self-image of intellectuals, begun with Voltaire, comes to an end with Bourdieu. And as with Voltaire, so with the professor of the *Collège de France*, one finds a deep historical awareness of the position endured by the intellectual in the past. 'Plato somewhere says of Socrates,' Bourdieu comments, 'that he was rootless, excluded, displaced, in disequilibrium, without hearth or home . . . I also quite frequently feel in disequilibrium, off-balance, in an unstable situation.'[57] If one puts oneself at the very top of the hierarchy constituted by the intellectual world then the reflection of the Parisian intellectual given back by the magic mirror is not a very modest one!

The object of this chapter has not been to argue that in every case the social position of the intellectual or the position of his discourse in relation to the dominant ideology of the intellectual field determines directly and in a mechanical way the whole range of self-images articulated by the *clerc*. The self-image of the intellectual, his assessment of his peers and of himself, is no less complicated, for example, than that of the peasant. But what we have sought to establish is that as part of any analysis of the discourse of intellectuals on intellectuals we need to take into consideration the position, at the moment of enunciation, of the speaker in the cultural and ideological world, given that the situation from which he speaks is always a situation where power relationships are at play and that this necessarily has an impact upon the character of the discourse.

Of course, the same rule applies to the author of this chapter. Honesty demands that we acknowledge that a text which examines the discourse of the intellectual and which puts forward the hypothesis that the position of that discourse in relation to the dominant ideology determines its character is itself part of a discourse critical of intellectuals. From this it follows, without question, that this chapter belongs to the second of the two traditions we have outlined and that, therefore, its origin lies in the inferior position occupied by the author within the intellectual field!

Notes

1. *Oeuvres complètes de Voltaire* (Paris, 1897) III, pp. 250–2, 575–7; IV, pp. 195–6.
2. Ibid., III, p. 251.
3. Ibid., p. 576.
4. Ibid., p. 252.
5. Ibid., pp. 576–7.
6. J. J. Rousseau, *De l'inégalité parmi les hommes* (Paris, 1971) p. 98: see 'A Discourse on the Origin of Inequality', in J. J. Rousseau, *The Social Contract and Discourses* (London, 1973) p. 68.
7. J. J. Rousseau, *Du Contrat social* (Paris, 1923) p. 277: see *The Social Contract* (Harmondsworth, 1971) p. 84.
8. A. Comte, 'Plan des travaux scientifiques nécessaires pour réorganiser la société', in *Du Pouvoir spirituel* (Paris, 1978) p. 122: see 'Plan of the Scientific Operations Necessary for Reorganizing Society', in R. Fletcher (ed.), *The Crisis of Industrial Civilization: The Early Essays of Auguste Comte* (London, 1974) p. 131.
9. A. Comte, 'Considérations sur le pouvoir spirituel', in *Du Pouvoir spirituel*, p. 316; see 'Considerations on the Spiritual Power', in R. Fletcher, *Crises*, pp. 235–6.
10. A. Comte, 'Considérations', p. 317: R. Fletcher, *Crises*, p. 236.
11. A. Comte, 'Considérations', p. 318: R. Fletcher, *Crises*, p. 237.
12. A. Comte, 'Le Fondateur de la société positiviste', in A. Comte, *Du Pouvoir spirituel*, p. 340.
13. Ibid., p. 344.
14. A. de Tocqueville, *L'Ancien régime et la Révolution* (Paris, 1967), p. 230: see *The Ancien Régime and the French Revolution* (London, 1969) p. 161.
15. *L'Ancien régime et la Révolution*, p. 232: *The Ancien Régime and the French Revolution*, p. 162.
16. *L'Ancien régime et la Révolution*, p. 240: *The Ancien Régime and the French Revolution*, p. 168.
17. E. Durkheim, 'L'individualisme et les intellectuels', *La Revue bleue*, 10, 1898, pp. 7–13: see S. Lukes (ed.), 'Durkheim's 'Individualism and the Intellectuals'', *Political Studies*, 17, 1969, pp. 14–30.
18. E. Durkheim, 'L'individualisme et les intellectuels', in *La Science sociale et l'action* (Paris, 1970) pp. 269–70.
19. E. Durkheim, 'L'Elite intellectuelle et la démocratie' (1904) in *La Science sociale et l'action* p. 281.
20. G. Sorel, 'L'Avenir socialiste des syndicats' (1898) in G. Sorel, *Matériaux d'une théorie du prolétariat* (Paris, 1981) p. 89: see 'The Socialist Future of the Syndicates', in J. Stanley (ed.), *From Georges Sorel: Essays in Socialism and Philosophy* (New York, 1976) p. 76.
21. 'L'Avenir socialiste', p. 90: J. Stanley (ed.), p. 76.
22. 'L'Avenir socialiste', p. 98: J. Stanley (ed.), p. 79.
23. 'L'Avenir socialiste', p. 94: J. Stanley (ed.), p. 78.
24. J. Benda, *La Trahison des clercs* (Paris, 1927) p. 54: see J. Benda, *The Betrayal of the Intellectuals* (Boston, 1955) p. 30.
25. *Trahison*, pp. 62–3: *Betrayal*, p. 36.

26. *Trahison*, p. 71: *Betrayal*, p. 42.
27. *Trahison*, p. 216: *Betrayal*, p. 141.
28. *Trahison*, p. 197: *Betrayal*, p. 128.
29. P. Nizan, *Les Chiens de garde* (Paris, 1960), pp. 104–5: see P. Nizan, *The Watchdogs* (London, 1971) p. 103.
30. *Chiens*, p. 103: *Watchdogs*, p. 101.
31. *Chiens*, p. 49: *Watchdogs*, p. 43.
32. *Chiens*, pp. 41–2: *Watchdogs*, p. 37.
33. *Chiens*, p. 132: *Watchdogs*, p. 137.
34. *Chiens*, p. 135: *Watchdogs*, p. 139.
35. J-P. Sartre, *Plaidoyer pour les intellectuels* (Paris, 1972) p. 80: see 'A Plea for Intellectuals', in J-P. Sartre, *Between Existentialism and Marxism* (London, 1983) p. 266.
36. *Plaidoyer*, p. 58: 'A Plea', p. 254.
37. *Plaidoyer*, p. 54: 'A Plea', p. 252.
38. *Plaidoyer*, p. 70: 'A Plea', p. 260.
39. *Plaidoyer*, pp. 116–17: 'A Plea', p. 284.
40. R. Aron, *L'Opium des intellectuels* (Paris, 1955) p. 229: see R. Aron, *The Opium of the Intellectuals* (London, 1957) p. 219.
41. *L'Opium*, p. 223: *The Opium*, p. 213.
42. *L'Opium*, pp. 230–1: *The Opium*, p. 220.
43. *L'Opium*, p. 287: *The Opium*, p. 279.
44. *L'Opium*, p. 299: *The Opium*, p. 290.
45. *L'Opium*, p. 238: *The Opium*, p. 228.
46. P. Bourdieu, 'Les intellectuels sont-ils hors jeu?', in P. Bourdieu, *Questions de sociologie* (Paris, 1984) p. 62.
47. P. Bourdieu, 'Comment libérer les intellectuels libres?', in Ibid., p. 70.
48. Ibid., pp. 72–3.
49. See M. Foucault, 'Truth and Power', in C.Gordan (ed.), *Michel Foucault:Power/Knowledge: Selected Interviews and Other Writings 1972–1977* (Brighton, 1980) pp. 109–33.
50. P. Bourdieu, 'Les intellectuels et les pouvoirs', *Michel Foucault – Une histoire de la vérité* (Paris, 1985) p. 94.
51. P. Bourdieu, 'L'Histoire se lève à l'Est', *Liber*, December 1989, p. 3.
52. This lecture was delivered on 6 October 1989. In English it has appeared as 'The Corporatism of the Universal: The Role of Intellectuals in the Modern World', *Telos*, 81, Fall 1989, pp. 99–110.
53. Ibid., p. 103
54. Ibid., p. 103
55. Ibid., p. 105
56. Ibid., p. 108
57. P. Bourdieu, 'Que faire de la sociologie? Entretien avec Pierre Bourdieu', in *CFDT aujourd'hui*, 100, March 1991, pp. 123–4.

3 Intellectuals as Actors: Image and Reality

Christophe Prochasson

There is hardly a single work devoted to intellectuals or to their history which does not at some stage attempt to provide a preliminary definition of what the intellectual is. In effect, the word 'intellectual' has been given two quite distinct meanings.[1] One is negative and overtly venomous in intention. Intellectuals, it is argued, are depraved individuals who spread lies and who abuse their moral authority. Authentic products of bourgeois democracy, it is intellectuals themselves who are the first to profit from this régime and who do so to the detriment of the nation (the extreme right-wing version) or of the working class (the extreme left-wing version). The second definition takes an opposite position. Intellectuals are perceived as the teachers of the people, are deemed to preserve them from the errors towards which they are sometimes led – here the Dreyfus Affair remains the classic point of reference – and are thought to honour the nation by the quality of their work. For some time now French historians have attempted to thread their way between these opposed conceptions and, broadly speaking, today they are divided into two different schools of thought, each of which apparently deploys a different approach. Some put the emphasis upon a sociology of intellectuals. Others emphasise the political and intellectual statements of a social group whose primary interest lies precisely in the fact that they are the producers of texts and of cultural artefacts. It is assumed that these two different perspectives are incompatible with each other. The argument of this article is that a history of intellectuals cannot be written if it excludes either an element of social history (the history of individuals located within a particular social environment, the history of their practices and, as we hope to show, the history of their behaviour) or a history of their ideas. A history of intellectuals, as we envisage it, would consist of a combination of these two types of history . In short, it is only by placing intellectuals in their context that we will fully understand their place and their role in French society as well as the genesis of their work.

THREE HISTORIES

A Political History of Intellectuals

Of all the possible approaches to the subject, that which draws upon political history is undoubtedly the most popular.[2] And not without good reason. No one can be ignorant of the ties that bind the French intellectual to politics, to the Republic and to the nation. The Dreyfus Affair, which sanctioned the very existence of the intellectual, was itself nothing else than the moment when these three elements came together. And subsequently each important occasion in the intellectual's history has been intimately linked to these factors.. The ups and downs of political life and of ideological conflict have undoubtedly had an enormous impact upon the intellectual and upon what he has produced. For the historian, therefore, the idea of appending the history of the intellectual to that of the State and to the destiny of the nation has its undoubted merits and attractions. Indeed, the very first history of French intellectuals, a synthesis of their achievements and their actions over the past century, took precisely this approach.[3] In terms of its content it faithfully follows the lineaments of France's political history, with the authors not ceasing to analyse the reactions and the foresight of their subjects. Such an approach, however, rests upon two assumptions: intellectuals are taken above all to be political agents (their strictly intellectual activity is therefore deliberately ignored); they are furthermore entrusted with a particular responsibility which derives from an assumed especially perceptive form of lucidity. Thus the claim, either implicitly or explicitly formulated, of intellectuals to constitute a separate group, blessed with greater understanding and armed with outstanding powers of analysis, is taken as given. The profoundly aristocratic dimension of the behaviour and the language of French intellectuals, to which we will return, is not analysed. It is simply accepted, only occasionally to be turned against them when they are found to be in flagrant error. And, as we know, there has been no shortage of this!

However, despite its obvious relevance, it is by no means clear that it is only political history that affords the best understanding of what an intellectual is in France. The very special character of his place and role within society as a whole easily extends beyond the privileged relationship he enjoys with politics. What, for example, are we to do with those not infrequent periods in the twentieth century when, either under duress or by choice, his voice was stifled and his actions constrained? Must we cease to regard him as an agent of history as soon as he moves into the background? Did, for example, socialist intellectuals cease to exist after 1905 when so many of them refused to join the newly-created socialist party? Does not their withdrawal from politics merit as much attention as their commitment to the Dreyfusard cause? Must we ignore the indisposition of left-wing intellectuals during the 1920s when at the very same time those on the right were very active? Is there nothing else to be said of the political silence of intellectuals in the 1980s than that it represents their final death?[4] We would surely be mistaken if we were to be satisfied with this. Would it not be utterly absurd, for example, to remember Léon Blum only for his commitment as a socialist, to abandon the work for the theatre that Sartre completed during the Occupation or to forgo seeking to understand the way in which the philosophical work of Michel Foucault overlapped with the society of his day in order to concentrate exclusively upon his left-wing enthusiasms? The intellectual, in short, has to be seen as a whole and as such his political face is thus only one amongst many. And, moreover, its visibility varies according to the moment. Therefore the history of intellectuals must examine their seclusion and withdrawal from public view as much as it does the controversy associated with their political commitments. The problem with an exclusively political history of intellectuals, in other words, is precisely that in seeing everything in political terms it is unable to grasp the whole being. It deliberately concentrates upon the world of public utterance, thereby forsaking the person in preference for the actor.

A Sociological History of Intellectuals

In order to escape from this problem and thereby to elaborate a method of explanation capable of making sense of the behaviour peculiar to intellectuals, another approach has endeavoured to portray the latter as straightforward social actors employing sophisticated strategies and sharing common ambitions. Here the intellectual dimension of the intellectual yields its place not to politics – which itself is scarcely taken seriously – but to a series of social profiles which are studied with particular care and precision and in which the intellectual is subjected to a purely quantitative analysis. The first theoretical framework for this kind of study was provided by Pierre Bourdieu who, armed with a range of concepts which today have been accepted by many historians of intellectuals, undertook a detailed study of French academics during the 1960s.[5] Prosopography – the accumulation of social data for each individual – has since been the basis for a series of studies devoted to élites and to intellectuals, two terms frequently associated with one another. Christophe Charle, for example, made use of Bourdieu's concepts in his in-depth investigation of social élites at the end of the nineteenth century.[6] Minutely examined are the school backgrounds, careers, family fortunes, matrimonial strategies and styles of living characteristic of lawyers, civil servants, the liberal professions and academics at the time of the Belle Epoque. Other studies claiming to delineate systems of shared social dispositions (or *habitus*) and their evolution have also adopted this methodology. Each choice made by an individual, it is argued, relates to a place occupied within a field of power (or *champ*) characterised by dominant and dominated poles.[7] Moreover, in reaction against the kind of descriptive history which accepts literally the statements and actions of the intellectual this school introduces an element of distrust into its analysis. We must, it is held, look *beyond* and *behind* the phenomenon and not be misled by the system of values that the intellectuals themselves deploy to justify their actions. Amongst intellectuals, it seems, there is no such thing as innocence. In fact, the debate is an old one and echoes of it are to be found in expressions of anti-intellectualism of all kinds. Charles Péguy, for example, never ceased to denounce as a form of treason the ambition which he believed consumed the intellectual. Surreptitiously, they made use of the aura of personal selflessness which surrounded all cultural activity in order to attain less respectable goals.

It is not the intention, however, to reduce this approach to intellectuals to that of the strong anti-intellectualist tradition that exists in France. Pierre Bourdieu is after all today a vigorous defender of intellectuals.[8] Rather its primary interest lies in the fact that it seeks to root the history of intellectuals in a social history from which it is inconceivable that it could escape. Moreover, the rigour of these investigations has been such that it has enabled us to quantify certain previously suspected but unproven phenomena. We all know the extent to which intellectuals in France have given rise to works full of passion, emotional excess and the settling of accounts and it is therefore to be welcomed that a form of positivist reaction should have put an end (however provisional) to this sometimes dubious literature. One simple statistical truth can be sufficient to make us abandon a whole series of widely-held misconceptions. However, it is striking to note the extent to which this legitimate desire to decipher history without resorting to a purely ideological or conceptual analysis tends inevitably to reduce the principal activity of intellectuals to that of a simple game of words and the pursuit of influence. That this dimension exists no one would deny, except perhaps those intellectuals lost in their own illusions. But whether it is such as to deny all autonomy to intellectual work appears more doubtful. More seriously this approach has the added drawback that it can find no place for the analysis of texts and is therefore forced to disregard them. Opinion and content fit uneasily into the categories offered by prosopography, as dictionaries devoted to intellectuals frequently reveal. How, for example, can the relationship of the intellectual to religion, to ideology and ideas be summarised in a few words?[9]

An Intellectual History of Intellectuals

Recognising this weakness, a purely intellectual history has come into existence which sets itself against any form of sociological explanation. The idea, in fact, is an old one and the aim has been to ascertain the genealogy of ideas by reference to forms of explanation that assume that resemblance establishes influence and even kinship. To connect one text to another or to compare an author to his counterpart allows us, so the argument runs, to assume some sort of deep relationship. Yet frequently the connections asserted have more to do with appearances and with word play than they do with an authentic intellectual reality. What in effect has one shown when one has established an affinity between two texts, two authors, two bodies of philosophical doctrine, two works of art? Nothing else perhaps than straightforward resemblance! In short, if we really want to understand how the mechanism of influence operates then these connections must be explained in their historical context. For example, the manner in which ideas are received never occurs without misinterpretation and rarely takes the most obvious route.[10] Texts are read and re-read, handled and re-handled, betrayed and turned upside down, without the author necessarily giving his approval. The history of the way ideas are received constitutes an entire section of intellectual history and, therefore, also of the history of intellectuals.

So, for example, the fact that different works occupy the same intellectual space is amenable to many different types of explanation. It could simply be a matter of pure chance, a misunderstanding or a false resemblance. Nevertheless, there are many occasions when the history of ideas quite properly speaks of what it regards as influences.

The point is that an intellectual history worthy of the name needs to get beyond this reality. Can it grasp the substance of this influence? Were the intellectuals under consideration in contact with one another? Are there letters or archives which allow us to establish the existence of these contacts? How did the latter operate? For example, if one cannot help but be struck by the similarity between the analyses of socialism developed in France by the disciples of Durkheim and in Britain by the Fabians their actual contacts appear to have been quite slight. There is little evidence of correspondence by letter, that they read each other's works or even that they referred to one another. What then can we make of this probable influence if we cannot establish its veracity? A more complicated form of explanation might therefore be necessary.

Intellectuals all operate within a social and political context and, especially those more closely connected with academic work, also within a common intellectual frame of reference, what Foucault called an *episteme*.[11] To deny the impact of these factors in the name of the autonomy of ideological superstructures, as for example has been the case from the mid-1970s onwards, is nothing else than a passing fashion which has obviously had Marxism as its first casualty. Foucault, who cannot be accused either of having used or misused Marxism, himself analysed his own way of working in these simple terms:

> Every time that I set out to produce a theoretical piece of work the starting point was always drawn from my own experience and from the processes that I saw unfolding around me. It was precisely because I believed that in the things I was seeing, the institutions that I was dealing with, the relations I had with other people, I recognised breaks, upheavals, dysfunctions that I undertook the work I did: it was a sort of autobiographical sketch.

Thus the analysis of the actual relationship of intellectual production to history must be a top priority. The latter, quite simply, arises out of the encounter between an individual (an intellectual or an artist) and his time.

For example, the debate which has seen French historians in disagreement with the Israeli historian Zeev Sternhell in many respects summarises the disagreements which issue from these two conceptions of intellectual history.[12] Sternhell's approach is descriptive and sets out to find in the writings of French intellectuals in the twentieth century the slightest trace of fascism capable of sustaining his thesis that it is in France that fascism has its origins. The problem is that, in taking everything out of context, by disembodying ideas and detaching them from their author, Sternhell falls into the worst kind of errors. Not a few of the French intellectuals that Sternhell regards as the 'theoreticians' of French fascism found their way into the Resistance! And what are we to make of the alliance forged, according to the same author, between revolutionary syndicalism and anti-semitic nationalism when we realise that the contacts were limited to just a few individuals? What we have in effect is an abbreviated account which never gets beyond the surface of things.

The best solution on offer, therefore, is to construct a history of intellectuals which combines a history of ideas, a history of contexts and a history of their behaviour. In short, the place which intellectuals occupy in French society is not unconnected with what they actually do in real life and this explains why these three different approaches are indissociable. As we have seen, the first two types of history have not been in short supply in France: the third remains to be tried.

A BEHAVIOURAL HISTORY OF INTELLECTUALS?

Determining Practices and Behaviour

It would be incorrect to say either that the public or the private behaviour of intellectuals, artists and academics has never been an object of attention. It has, however, never been systematically regarded as one of the principal means which allow us to ascertain the place of intellectuals in society, even less as one of the keys which unlock a work. Writers have, without doubt, often resorted to anecdote and, of course, to the malevolent gossip that is itself frequently inspired by anti-intellectualism. As we all know, accounts of the world of the intellectual have always flourished on rumour and on trivia. However, another more serious and less voyeuristic approach has been successful in recognising the importance of those biographical details usually relegated by the history of ideas to the level of useless extras. Again the reference is to Pierre Bourdieu and his school whose concern it has been to decipher the ensemble of practices and socially acquired patterns of behaviour, the *habitus*, which enable us to define an individual and the *field* to which he belongs.[13] Patterns of behaviour, tastes, enthusiasms as well as political commitments are subjected to the painstaking scrutiny of the sociologist. The problem is, however, that this method, when it comes to the analysis of intellectuals, often limits itself to bringing to light the complex mechanisms via which conscious or unconscious factors come into operation. In other words, this intermediary path between biographical anecdote and macro-sociology, with its reliance upon numerical analysis, is not entirely satisfactory and, it could be argued, is unable to discuss many of the most central aspects which relate to the history of intellectuals. What we want to emphasise here is the importance of the relationship that exists between what an intellectual produces and the context within which he works.

The contention is then that a history of the social, political, intellectual, professional and even private practices of the intellectual would improve our understanding of what an intellectual is in France and of what sense we are to attach to his work. For example, the conditions, place and environment in which an intellectual works cannot fail but to have an impact upon him. We could not possibly put on the same level a work undertaken for money and produced under the pressure of need and a work completed in conditions of serenity, or a university textbook and a journalistic pamphlet, a scientific article and a propagandist text. The conditions surrounding the formulation of a work, in short, undoubtedly have a bearing upon its internal structure. Sartre, for example, said that he always wrote against someone. More recently, in his biography of Roland Barthes, Jean-Louis Calvert asserted that it was possible to discern a relationship between the body and what it produces.[14] This was clearly especially relevant in the case of Barthes, whose homosexuality was never explicitly stated but which found its way discreetly and silently to the very heart of his work. But the most obvious proof of this – is it even necessary to cite the evidence? – is provided by those moments in history when politics intruded to an absurd degree into the world of the intellectual. Because in France – and this too does not need re-stating – the intellectual has also involved himself in affairs of State. Indeed, it was from this involvement that he derived his name.

Intellectuals and Politics

Since the end of the nineteenth century intellectuals have performed as actors in the world of politics. This was by no means unconnected with the establishment of the Republic: the Dreyfus Affair served to finish the job. And after this it was acknowledged that politics, as well as the two broader areas of the nation and society, were fields into which the intellectual was to intervene. Indeed, these three subjects – politics, nation and society – came to preoccupy a large number of intellectuals, guided their every step and were to become the principal inspiration behind their work in the twentieth century. The great nationalist intellectual Charles Maurras was in no way mistaken when he launched his rallying cry as 'Politics first'. Moreover, this extensive involvement in politics did not occur without exciting both the irony and the anger of those who believed that in this commitment they saw either the signs of a betrayal or the traces of a malady inherent to democracy. For example, in the same year, 1927, and with the same publisher, two authors criticised the intellectuals of their day: one, Albert Thibaudet, resorted to irony;[15] the other, Julien Benda, to a tone of rage.[16] In effect, the period between the wars seems to have turned upside down the relationship that had earlier been established between politics and the intellectual. During the Dreyfus Affair the intellectuals had subordinated politics to values. The appearance of what can be seen as modern politics coupled with the emergence of fascism and of communism reversed the terms of this equation. Henceforth it was the intellectual who had to accept the logic of politics. The pre-war liberal model of the intellectual tended to disappear, to be replaced by that of the intellectual as militant.

What this meant was that, having entered politics as educators and as a form of moral conscience, artists, academics, scientists and scholars were obliged to transform themselves into experts and into political activists. The cultural hegemony of the French Communist Party (PCF) after the Second World War, symbolised in the fascination it exercised over a significant number of intellectuals, was undoubtedly the high point of this process. The PCF in this period effectively sought to reduce the autonomy of the intellectual to an absolute minimum. In 1947, for example, at the Strasbourg congress of the Communist Party its general secretary, Maurice Thorez, made a speech the contents of which would have been absolutely inconceivable to the pre-1914 Dreyfusard intellectual:

We advocate an optimistic literature, looking towards the future, praising effort, solidarity, the march towards a better society that we have ourselves to build and that we will build. To those intellectuals who are disorientated and who are lost in a labyrinth of doubt we offer certainty and the possibility of limitless progress. We therefore call upon them to turn away from the false problems of individualism, pessimism and a decadent aesthetics in order to give a meaning to their lives by allying themselves with the lives of others. We appeal to them to draw the inspiration and strength which alone makes lasting achievements possible from contact with the popular masses.[17]

After so many years of servitude, years moreover which compelled those most articulate and most cynical to adopt a veritable form of double-speak as the only means of preserving their independence, it is not surprising to find that from the mid-1970s onwards French intellectuals have renewed their attachment to the practices and the discursive paradigms of the Dreyfusard years. Henceforth the priority was to safeguard freedom of thought and not to comply with the instructions of politics, and in line with this a series of essays written in the 1980s went out of their way to defend the independence of the intellectual and to display open contempt for all forms of partisan commitment.[18] Only great humanitarian causes of universal significance, for example those where the rights of man were at stake, were now to have the good fortune to interest our contemporary intellectuals. Thus it is entirely typical that Alain Finkelkraut should have placed his work, *La Défaite de la pensée*,[19] under the auspices of Julien Benda as in part he re-works the theses found in the latter's *La Trahison des clercs*: the intellectual should break with the particularistic commitments demanded by the mentality of party politics in order more properly to defend 'great causes'. Of late, therefore, intellectuals have again dreamt of becoming once more the teachers of the nation, just as they were at the turn of the century when, at the height of the Dreyfus Affair, the *Universités populaires*[20] were established and where intellectuals taught philosophy, history, literature, the sciences and mathematics to a working class eager to learn from them. In the imagination of the French intelligentsia it is this era – an era which symbolises their dominance through the possession of knowledge – which remains the golden age.[21]

Intellectuals and Money

Amongst intellectuals the glaring contradiction between what they say in public and what they do in practice has frequently been remarked upon. This is, after all, part of a long-established anti-intellectual tradition that has existed for over a hundred years. However, the relationship that exists between an individual and money is part of a much broader cultural question that is not restricted solely to the French intellectual. Until recently, it could be argued, money remained something that was adjudged to be obscene, a value that was to be rejected. French intellectuals themselves fostered a discourse that was openly hostile to money and which drove them, no matter to what ideological persuasion they belonged, towards a visceral hatred of the bourgeoisie, a hatred that finds its roots in Flaubert and beyond. The intellectual has as his primary enemy the bourgeois. The bourgeois has as his implacable opponent the intellectual. The bourgeois is on the side of work and of avarice. The intellectual and his Dionysian double, the artist, stands for laziness and extravagence. Such at least are the stereotypes that inform a whole body of literature.

In order to survive socially intellectuals have had of necessity to promote a series of values that are hostile to the logic of the commercial world. Their work cannot be measured by the criterion of profit because it is understood that the commercial value of a work of art or a scientific discovery tells us nothing about its real value. Intellectuals thereby escape from the universe of the bourgeoisie which in any case is incapable of seeing them as anything other than parasites. The violence of the intellectual's scorn for money, in other words, is part and parcel of their wish to define themselves differently. Georges Bernanos wrote:

> As far as I am concerned, I would prefer to sit every day at table with old monks or with young officers in love with their trade. Nor does the conversation of a good peasant farmer displease me, because I like dogs, hunting, the stalking of woodcock in the spring. But as for the leaders of big business discussing the last automobile exhibition or the world economic situation, they make me laugh. Keep away! Keep away! What people regard as a distinguished man today is precisely someone who is distinguished in nothing he does. How can they be told apart?[22]

It is therefore thought preferable to be associated with those who are socially undistinguished rather than with those who believe themselves to be distinguished. And it is this which in part explains the unlikely marriage between the intelligentsia and the proletariat. Even for such right-wing intellectuals as Bernanos, as indeed was also the case for certain monarchists at the turn of the century, it was thought far better to mix with and to support those adjudged to be ignoble but who possessed a noble soul and who defended a worthy cause than the

louts who had usurped the place of traditional élites. Amongst
intellectuals the preference has always been for the ways of the
aristocratic Guermantes family rather than those of the bourgeois
Verdurin.[23]

In a short study such as this there is perhaps no need to give
innumerable examples of this mentality. The point is that hostility
towards the bourgeoisie has been a permanent reaction. Philippe
Soupault, for example, begins his *Mémoires de l'Oubli* with a virulent
diatribe against the bourgeois world which in many respects is a model
of the style of argument. 'My family,' he wrote, 'was a good example
of that bourgeoisie which was supposed to represent the strength of
France. I had only contempt for this social class and was only too
pleased to contribute to its slow disintegration. It believed itself to rest
on two principles: religion and morality. In truth it only really
respected one thing: money.'[24] The entire work of Barthes is informed
by this same hatred for the bourgeoisie, although even this class is
thought to be less distasteful than the narrow-minded spirit of the
petit-bourgeoisie, which is itself seen as a sort of social monster
inspired by disreputable and shabby desires. The text that he devoted
to Pierre Poujade, a small shopkeeper who came to sudden political
prominence in the 1950s as the defender of France's tradesmen, is
rooted in this context.[25]

It is therefore all the more remarkable to realise that the actual
relationship between the intellectual and money has not always
mirrored this stance. It is quite simply a fact, as the works of
Christophe Charle have so clearly shown, that the greater majority
of intellectuals are the products of the relatively well-off sections of
society or, put another way, precisely the bourgeois and petit-
bourgeois world that they detest. There is perhaps nothing too
surprising about that. However, what we do need to understand is
the real relationship that the intellectual has entertained with money.
The truth of the matter is that, as they are very often connected to the
élite of society whose purchasing power is simply superior to theirs,
intellectuals are forced to live beyond their means. In short, the
intellectual of today who indulges himself in this world is forced to
find several different jobs, be it as a journalist, an editor, and so on.[26]
At the same time it is vitally important that no one realises the extent
of the steps that are being taken to earn a living! Sartre, for example,
cultivated an aristocratic attitude towards money. 'All things considered,' he told Simone de Beauvoir, 'for a very long time, if not for
almost my entire life, I never knew what money was.'[27] Spending

without a second thought, leaving big tips for waiters, doling out money to friends and to young students in need was all part of affecting to live with a disregard for money-making. Many other examples could be given which disclose the same disposition.

Intellectuals and Morality

In 1895, Victorian England condemned Oscar Wilde, convicted of homosexuality, to two years in prison with hard labour. The verdict was accompanied by a widespread explosion of joy. The entire British press attacked Wilde.[28] A dissolute intellectual, who for years had been the subject of scandal, had fallen, the victim of established morality. In attacking the moral code of his day it was as if he had threatened the entire social order. By contrast, republican France seemed unconcerned by a form of behaviour that in England was thought to be intolerable. Yet at the time of the Wilde affair French intellectuals refused to sign a petition launched in his defence. On the right François Coppée agreed to sign but only 'as a member of the society for the protection of animals'. Alphonse Daudet was stunned that he could even have been asked to associate himself with such an initiative. 'As a family man,' he declared, 'I can only express my horror and indignation.' On the left, Jules Renard agreed to sign but only on condition that Wilde 'did the honourable thing and agreed not to write again'.[29] At the very same time, however, there were plenty of 'decadent' writers producing daring work and leading indulgent lives. Between the two world wars it was freely admitted that the 'artistic life' easily transgressed the limits imposed by the normal codes of social behaviour. Better than that, it was assumed that the artist had a duty to provoke. His mission was to challenge the morality that guided the steps of the great majority. Perversion made the artist. And to prove the point André Gide, in his Socratic discourse on homosexuality, has his spokesman Corydon remark: 'I would almost go as far as to say that those few periods or regions without uranism are also those periods or regions without art.'[30]

What exactly was the situation? There is no doubt that in France there were a significant number of intellectuals who indulged in licentious behaviour, sometimes turned it into a way of life and who did their best to defend it wherever possible. Homosexuality was always one of the great issues. From 1810 onwards in France it was no longer punishable as a crime and thus it became above all a moral issue, frequently dismissed by public opinion as a form of deviance to be condemned because it was either 'against nature' or as an absurd obsession. To defend or to recommend it did not therefore entail the same legal risks as in England. Nevertheless, there existed in France a level of moral pressure that was such as to ensure that during the first quarter of the century homosexual writers were only able to evoke their homosexuality by indirect routes. Proust, as is well known, was obliged in *A la recherche du temps perdu* to turn Albert into Albertine and to treat homosexuality as a form of deviance. Nevertheless, he had the audacity to bring to literature, in the same way that today they are brought to the screen, the most blatant homosexual scenes. The beginning of *Sodome et Gomorrhe*, for example, constitutes one of the most outrageous seduction scenes in French literature: 'deciding to grant M. de Charlus the favour that he had just asked of him, Jupien, after various remarks lacking in refinement such as 'What a big bum you have!' said to the Baron with an air at once smiling, impassioned, superior and grateful: 'All right, you big baby, come along!' '[31] Similarly, André Gide had finished writing the greater part of *Corydon* in 1908 but waited until 1924 before he published it and then not without hesitation and a considerable element of intellectual courage.

We would therefore be mistaken to see France as a country where the intellectual was entirely unrestrained. Decency imposed limits upon everyone and few were the intellectuals and artists who transgressed them before the Second World War or even before the 1960s. There were undoubtedly a few examples. In 1907, an intellectual as distinguished as Léon Blum, a former student at the *Ecole normale supérieure* but who had also frequented the anarchist-inspired literary circles of the end of the nineteenth century, published a treatise on marriage which was decidedly non-conformist in orientation. He here displayed an understanding of incestuous relationships between brother and sister, attacked marriage as it existed in contemporary society and recommended the sexual initiation of young people before marriage by partners older than themselves.[32] That Jean Jaurès, the political companion of Blum, should be shocked by such remarks is easy to explain. His puritanism was such as to prevent him displaying any sympathy for such propositions, despite his advanced opinions. More singular, however, was the reaction of Gide:

> I accept that it is clever but, for all that, it is also dangerous. The Jews are past masters in the art of destroying our most respected and venerable institutions, even those institutions which form the

basis and the strength of our western civilisation, and this to the advantage of I do not know what kind of licence and moral looseness. Fortunately our good sense and our latin instinct of sociability revolts at this.[33]

We do need, however, to understand the true extent of the moral liberalism to be found amongst intellectuals. In truth, there were many who were only too eager to defend the established ethical order. So, for example, if Gide was shocked by the writings of Blum, then by the same token the dramatist Paul Claudel never ceased to reproach Gide himself for his own moral non-conformity. Writing to Gide on 2 March 1914, he remarked: 'If you are not a pederast why this strange predilection for that kind of subject? And if you are, cure yourself.' The efforts of François Mauriac to repress his homosexual desires are also well-known. Between the two wars public opinion at best tolerated the homosexuality of intellectuals. Nevertheless, in 1931, the press gave a very bad reception to Roger Martin du Gard's play, *Un taciturne*, in which Louis Jouvet played the part of a man who finished up by committing suicide after realising the love he felt for his young male secretary. Roger Martin du Gard, Nobel prize winner in 1937, was also the author of the unfinished *Le lieutenant-colonel de Maumort*, a book where the underlying theme was homosexuality and which was published posthumously only as recently as 1987.

Equally, the idea of a 'homosexual plot' directed by intellectuals and artists, the agents of decadence and dissolution, has been a recurrent theme in anti-intellectual literature in the twentieth century. The surrealist poet André Breton, for example, vigourously attacked intellectuals in his review *La Révolution surréaliste*: 'I accuse the pederasts,' he wrote in March 1928, 'of propagating a doctrine which is morally and mentally defective and which threatens all the things that I respect'.[34] Even in our day this theme has not entirely disappeared. 'Whilst the authorities try as best they can to hide the frightening increase in AIDS,' Jean-Paul Pigasse wrote in 1987, 'there is a section of the western intelligentsia which seeks to gain acceptance for the idea that this disease can strike anyone, anywhere and at any time.'[35]

The climate does, however, seem to have changed since the 1950s: the level of tolerance accorded to intellectuals has undoubtedly increased. The post-war existentialist craze and the numerous 'scandals' that it gave rise to, for example, definitely made their mark. The model relationship personnified by Sartre and de Beauvoir and which was self-consciously opposed to that of the traditional family was reproduced throughout all levels of the intelligentsia. Moreover, in the 1970s intellectuals, disillusioned with politics, turned their attention to a whole series of moral issues. Jean-François Sirinelli, in a recent work devoted to the study of petitions and manifestoes,[36] has shown in particular how this occurred in the period after 1968 and here it is sufficient to cite the so-called petition of the '343' supporting abortion, that of 18 June 1976 demanding the de-criminalisation of cannabis and the petition launched in January 1977 in support of Bernard Dejager, Jean-Claude Gallien and Jean Burckardt, all of whom had been accused of sexual offences against minors. From this vantage point the 1950s seemed a long way away and few were the intellectuals who now felt compelled to hide their homosexuality. This was, however, the case with Barthes and Foucault and not surprisingly these intellectuals themselves became symbols. In New York on 26 June 1983, in a demonstration organised to raise public consciousness about AIDS, portraits of Gide, Cocteau and Barthes were carried aloft.[37] As the writer Jean-Louis Bory remarked – he himself consistently complained about the discrimation suffered by homosexuals and had no hesitation in proclaiming his own homosexuality – intellectuals have the privilege of being able to say what others must keep quiet. This itself tells us something about the peculiar place that the intellectual occupies in French society and the rights that it confers.

THE INTELLECTUAL: CLERIC OR ARISTOCRAT?

The Intellectual as Cleric?

It is very easy to establish a link between the intellectual and the cleric and so much so that the two terms are often seen as being interchangeable. The success of Julien Benda's book is itself proof of this and more recently Jacques Le Goff, one of the most eminent historians of the Middle Ages, has successfully imported the word 'intellectual' into the vocabulary of the medieval historian.[38] But is a medieval cleric such as Jean Gerson really the same as one of our contemporary intellectuals? Certainly when an intellectual accepts a doctrine, a philosophy or an ideology – all of which could easily pass as a faith – the required ingredients seem to be there and thus if the intellectual is not exactly a cleric then there is a metaphorical resemblance. But is this metaphor anything more than an attractive image and does it really help us understand the place and role of intellectuals in French society?

Let us recognise straight away that there are many arguments in support of this position. The cleric does undoubtedly *resemble* the intellectual. And this is true of both his attitudes and his behaviour. The cleric is a scholar, a man of learning and of reflection. He is also a man who through speech guides and instructs, a 'seller of words' as Jacques Le Goff describes him, and he is of necessity attached to the world of the city.[39] Nor is he without political influence or aspirations. In the name of morality and of intellectual honesty he is the adviser to princes. He is finally and without doubt a man of intellect. But is any of this to say that he is an intellectual fighting on the side of faith? What have we established by these parallels? Has the modern intellectual self-consciously imitated his earlier religious counterpart? It is, for example, highly unlikely that the model of the cleric had any impact upon the emergence of the Dreyfusard intellectual and it is this episode which remains the point of reference for the contemporary intellectual. Emerging out of an environment characterised by a profound hostility towards the Church, firmly attached to republican values – the intellectual is secular by definition – the modern 'cleric' has only the outward appearance of a cleric. What constitutes the originality of the intellectual is precisely that he does not owe his social authority to an institution. He is neither a man of the State nor of the Church. Yet as Jacques Le Goff remarks, with a clear debt to Gramsci, 'the intellectuals of the middle ages were above all 'organic' intellectuals, the faithful servants of both Church and State'.[40] Exceptions to this rule are limited to a few very unusual cases. Moreover, Benda himself implicitly accepts this point when he denies the status of intellectual to party intellectuals, especially those associated with the Communist Party. In short, the assimilation of the intellectual with the cleric too easily forgets the claim to autonomy which is central to a definition of his moral and political role.

The cleric, however, is not the only figure who bears a resemblance to the intellectual: the eighteenth century in particular provides, in the shape of the *philosophe* or the man of letters, a model which many historians have wanted to establish as both his precursor and predecessor.[41] Thus Christophe Charle in his last work felt able to elaborate a 'historical and social genealogy' of the intellectual based upon the assumption that from the eighteenth to the end of nineteenth century there existed an element of continuity and which, beginning with the *philosophe* – in this case Voltaire defending Calas – went on to trace the different stages dominated in turn by the man of letters, the poet, the artist and the *savant*.[42] But even the author himself admits that these comparisons need to be treated with care and that they in no way diminish the originality of the intellectual's status. 'In him,' writes Charle, 'is not only to be found the traces of earlier forms that he supersedes but also the impact of the peculiar circumstances of the 1890s.' In other words, even if one accepts that the roots of the intellectual are to be found in the distant past, it is only much later and at a specific moment that he fully appears. The rise of democracy, the age of the masses, the spread of public education are all related to the emergence of a new social type of which the socialist variant is one of the best examples.

Aristocratic Behaviour

We can perhaps push this analysis a little further by recognising that there is in fact another model which accords more accurately with our analysis of the function and the functioning of the intellectual. With very little difficulty it seems possible that from what has already been said it can be shown that there is an element of aristocratic behaviour in the conduct of the intellectual, despite the fact that in a very real sense he is the product of the Republic. For example, the anti-intellectual stances of both the right and the left have made much of this criticism. On the left, at the turn of the century, Georges Sorel, Edouard Berth and Charles Péguy repeatedly criticised the 'caste' mentality of the intellectuals and the aristocratic character of their behaviour. On the right the violent diatribes directed against the intellectuals by the likes of Maurice Barrès and Charles Maurras from the Dreyfus Affair onwards have their roots in an almost identical response. Looked at another way, the intellectuals were the aristocracy required by the Republic: in effect, the new régime needed an element of quality, of distinction, the support of intellectual élites; and it is in this context that republican élitism – which from Jaurès to Edouard Herriot and via the school system sought to unearth the best of each generation – is best understood. For the Republic the question was how to reconcile democracy with aristocracy.

Moreover, intellectuals themselves have practised patterns of sociability that have served to isolate them from other people and which are far more easily equated with those of the aristocrat than of the cleric. The existence of the *salon* – including those frequented by the left-wing intellectual – is a case in point. Many others testify to the desire of intellectuals to confine themselves to their own company, to inhabit an environment where discussion is possible and where the merits of the intellect are beyond question. A hierarchical conception of society is retained.

Many of the biographies recently devoted to contemporary intellectuals – as if the latter themselves had a right to treatment formerly reserved for kings and the great of the nation – disclose events and facts which confirm this analysis. For example, in the interviews that he conducted with Simone de Beauvoir in 1974, Sartre had great difficulty reconciling his own élitism with his desire to appear as just an ordinary person. As a young man, these conversations reveal, along with Paul Nizan he saw himself as a 'superman' and at the Sorbonne where each of them was obliged to take a couple of courses these two students of the prestigious *Ecole normale supérieure* had the unpleasant reputation of treating their 'simple' fellows with contempt. This, explained Sartre, was because 'the Sorbonne students represented beings who were not quite men'.[43] His refusal to accept either honours or prizes derived equally from an aristocratic gesture: 'the men who give the honour, whether it's the *légion d'honneur* or the Nobel prize, are not qualified to give it. I cannot see who has the right to give Kant or Descartes or Goethe a prize'.[44] How then can one be a democrat? Sartre, in effect, was unable to answer the question and was obliged to dodge the issue:

Sartre: I think that I might have a little more talent than another man, a slightly more developed intelligence. But these are only phenomena whose origin remains an intelligence equal to my neighbour's or a sensibility equal to my neighbours. I do not think that I have a superiority of any kind. My superiority is in books, insofar as they are good, but the next man also has his superiority – it may be the bag of hot chestnuts he sells at the café door in winter. Each man has his superiority. For my part, I have chosen this one.
De Beauvoir: You don't believe that entirely since you think there are some people who are fools and swine . . .
Sartre: But I don't think they were so to begin with. They have been made so.[45]

Thus by disinvesting man of personal responsibility Sartre was able to safeguard his intellectual élitism whilst leaving his democratic options open. But it should be clear that even amongst left-wing intellectuals an aristocratic attitude towards the world soured their relations with other social groups. Other examples can easily be found, as the two recent biographies of Barthes and Foucault prove. Barthes was only too happy to play the role of an aristocrat, even during his long stays in hospital. Attending his seminars at the *Ecole pratique des hautes études*, it is said, as akin to attending court. His attendance at some of the fashionable *salons* of Paris, his 'dandyism', his refusal to engage in any form of political activity, despite his radical views, only serve to confirm this impression. The same applies to certain aspects of Michel Foucault's behaviour, even during his period of political activism. Is there not something vaguely aristocratic about combining time spent on the barricades with hours spent stubbornly at the *Bibliothèque nationale* and in preparing for election to the *Collège de France*?

To conclude, therefore, it seems that, if one accepts that the analysis of the place and role of intellectuals in society is linked to that of cultural production, then it makes sense to try to understand how intellectuals actually behave. We need, as Lucien Febvre would have put it, to analyse the 'mental equipment' of the intellectual and one of its manifestations is precisely how he responds to the demands of daily life. This is not to say, however, that we must establish a direct and unequivocal connection between what the intellectual does and what he says and writes but if we can come to understand the complex nature of this link it will enable us better to understand their work. The intention then is not to construct a psychology of intellectuals but rather a history of their behaviour. Thus, for example, it seems clear that the attitude of intellectuals towards money has changed considerably according to the place that money has occupied in society as a whole. Equally we have seen that important modifications took place in the sexual behaviour and discourse of intellectuals. Even if the secular republicanism which France enjoyed allowed intellectuals an element of licence it is also clear that over a considerable period of time moral pressure greatly restricted their possibilities of expression. Nevertheless, intellectuals have always been tolerated in France and it is this no doubt which in part explains the privileged position that they have enjoyed. And, of course, this situation inevitably contributed to the development amongst intellectuals of a taste for abstraction, a passion for theory at the expense of technical or financial knowledge. What the hackneyed theme of the death of the intellectual really signifies is the reversal of these values. The model of the 'liberal intellectual' born at the end of the nineteeth century seems set to give way at the end of the twentieth century to that of the intellectual as engineer, banker or power broker. It remains to be seen to what extent this evolution represents a decisive turning-point.

Notes

1. See J-P. Honoré, 'Autour d'intellectuel', in G. Leroy (ed.), *Les écrivains et l'affaire Dreyfus* (Paris, 1983) pp. 149–57.
2. See J-F. Sirinelli, 'Les intellectuels', in R. Rémond (ed.), *Pour une histoire politique* (Paris, 1989) pp. 123–49.
3. P. Ory and J-F. Sirinelli, *Les Intellectuels en France, de l'Affaire Dreyfus à nos jours* (Paris, 1986).
4. See P. Ory (ed.), *Dernières questions aux intellectuels* (Paris, 1990).
5. P. Bourdieu, *Homo Academicus* (Paris, 1984). In English see the Polity Press 1988 edition under the same title.
6. C. Charle, *Les élites de la République, 1880–1900* (Paris, 1987).
7. For a discussion of this concept see P. Bourdieu, *Distinction* (Cambridge, Mass, 1984).
8. See pp. 53–6 above and P. Bourdieu, 'The Corporatism of the Universal: The Role of Intellectuals in the Modern World', *Telos*, 81, 1989, pp. 99–110.
9. See here, for example, C. Charle and E. Telkes, *Les professeurs du Collège de France, Dictionnaire biographique, 1901–1939* (Paris, 1988) and *Les professeurs de la Faculté des sciences de Paris, Dictionnaire biographique, 1901–1939* (Paris, 1989).
10. See the special issue devoted to 'Réception et contresens', *Revue de synthèse*, 1, 1989.
11. According to Foucault an *episteme* is 'the total set of relations that unite, at a given period, the discursive practices that give rise to epistemological figures, sciences and possibly formalised systems . . . The episteme is not a form of knowledge . . . or a type of rationality which, crossing the bounderies of the most varied sciences, manifests the soveriegn unity of a subject, a spirit, or a period: it is the totality of relations that can be discovered for a given period, between the sciences when one analyses them at the level of discursive regularities': see M. Foucault, *The Archaeology of Knowledge* (London, 1977) p. 191.
12. See in particular Z. Sternhell, *La Droite révolutionnaire: 1885–1914* (Paris, 1983) and *Ni droite ni gauche* (Paris, 1983). The latter appeared in English translation as *Neither Right nor Left*. For a selection of the literature on Sternhell's work see M. Winock, 'Fascisme à la française ou fascisme introuvable', *Le Débat*, 25 May 1983, pp. 35–44; S. Sand, 'L'idéologie fasciste en France', *L'Esprit*, 80–1, 1983, pp. 149–60 and J.

Julliard, 'Sur un fascisme imaginaire', in J. Julliard, *Autonomie ouvrière* (Paris, 1988) pp. 269–85.

13. See in particular P. Bourdieu, 'Champ du pouvoir, champ intellectuel et habitus de classe', *Scolies*, I, 1971, pp. 7–26. A *habitus*, according to Bourdieu, is a system of shared social dispositions and cognitive structures whilst the notion of a *field* is conceived as a space occupied by various dominant and dominated groups or fractions.
14. J-L. Calvet, *Roland Barthes* (Paris, 1990) pp. 14–15.
15. A. Thibaudet, *La République des professeurs* (Paris, 1927).
16. J. Benda, *La Trahison des clercs* (Paris, 1927).
17. Quoted in J. Verdès-Leroux, *Au service du Parti. Le Parti communiste, les intellectuels et la culture (1944–56)* (Paris, 1983) pp. 269–70. See also D. Caute, *Communism and the French Intellectuals* (London, 1964).
18. See especially B-H. Lévy, *Eloge des intellectuels* (Paris, 1987).
19. A. Finkelkraut, *La Défaite de la pensée* (Paris, 1987). This work has been translated as *The Undoing of Thought* (London, 1988).
20. See L. Mercier, *Les Universités populaires: 1880–1914* (Paris, 1986).
21. See E. Ritaine, *Les stratèges de la culture* (Paris, 1983).
22. G. Bernanos, *Les grands cimetières sous la lune* (Paris, 1938), p. 318.
23. The reference here, of course, is to Proust's *A la recherche du temps perdu*.
24. P. Soupault, *Mémoires de l'Oubli, 1897–1927* (Paris, 1927); reference is to Paris, 1986 edition, p. 15.
25. R. Barthes, 'Quelques paroles de M.Poujade', *Mythologies* (Paris, 1957) pp. 85–7.
26. H. Hamon and P. Rotman, *Les Intellocrates: Expédition en haute intelligentsia* (Paris, 1981).
27. S. de Beauvoir, *La cérémonie des adieux* (Paris, 1981) pp. 483–4: see S.de Beauvoir, *Adieux: A Farewell to Sartre* (Harmondsworth, 1984) p. 342.
28. See H.M. Hyde, *The Trial of Oscar Wilde* (London, 1948).
29. D. Fernandez, *Le rapt de Ganymède* (Paris, 1989) p. 81.
30. A. Gide, *Corydon* (Paris, 1924) p. 129.
31. M. Proust, *A la recherche du temps perdu* (Paris, 1954) II, p. 610: see *Remembrance of Things Past*, II (Harmondsworth, 1981) p. 632.
32. L. Blum, *Du mariage* (Paris, 1907).
33. A. Gide, *Corydon*, p. 115.
34. D. Fernandez, *Ganymède*, p. 100.
35. J.P. Pigasse, 'Bloc-Notes', *L'Express*, 17 April 1987.
36. J.F. Sirinelli, *Intellectuels et passions françaises: Pétitions et manifestes au XXe siècle* (Paris, 1990).
37. G. Vincent,'Une histoire du secret?', in P. Ariès and G. Duby(eds), *Histoire de la vie privée*, V (Paris, 1987) p. 374.
38. J. Le Goff, *Les intellectuels au Moyen Age* (Paris, 1957).
39. Ibid. (Paris, 1985) p. II.
40. Ibid. p. III.
41. See R. Darnton, *The Literary Underground of the Old Regime* (Cambridge, Mass. 1982) and 'A police Inspector Sorts His Files: The Anatomy of the Republic of Letters', *The Great Cat Massacre* (New York, 1984) pp. 145–90.

42. C. Charle, *Naissance des «Intellectuels»* (Paris, 1990) pp. 20–64.
43. S. de Beauvoir, *La cérémonie*, p. 351: *A Farewell*, p. 245.
44. *La cérémonie*, p. 354; *A Farewell*, p. 247.
45. *La cérémonie*, p. 233: *A Farewell*, pp. 161–2.

4 The Concept of an Intellectual Generation

Jean-François Sirinelli

The central question that needs to be addressed in this article is whether the notion of a generation has any explanatory value. More generally, can it be used by the historian and, if so, how can it be utilised in the study of intellectuals?[1]

A CONTESTED CONCEPT

The use of the concept of a generation has always posed problems. In the first place it is not exactly clear what the object is that is being discussed. Apart from the obvious difficulty of confusion with such related notions as youth or the young it is also not easy to distinguish between different types of generation, be they demographic, social or political. Secondly, for some considerable time the concept itself has been treated with both suspicion and reticence. Suspicion because, given that the existence of age groups is a phenomenon inherent to all societies, it is thought that there is the risk of producing analyses that are utterly banal. And reticence because the concept of a generation is itself associated with two other ideas that have frequently been rejected by what has been the dominant school in French historical research: restricted time span and concentration upon events. Generation, by definition, relates to periods covered at best by decades and this is all too brief when we are invited to consider subjects only in the context of the medium or the long term. Moreover, it is virtually impossible to dissociate the notion of a generation from that of events. Events are crucial, it has to be acknowledged, in determining the appearance of a generation and, conversely, certain events are very much a reflection of the emergence of a generation. However, and as the *Annales* school demonstrates, events are not part of the historian's concern!

But looked at more closely it is clear that there has not always been total opposition to the concept or notion of a generation. For example, if Lucien Febvre, in the very year that the journal *Annales* was established, was unequivocal in his judgement – 'best forget all about it', he commented – then in 1941 Marc Bloch was less categorical: 'it seems destined,' he wrote, 'to play an ever increasing role in our analysis of human affairs'.[2] Thus rather than being completely rejected it has been more the case that the idea of using the concept of a generation as an explanatory device has always been treated with caution and uncertainty. And it is this which explains why, if in 1953 Yves Renouard could publish an article in the *Revue historique* entitled 'La notion de génération en histoire', then over thirty years later Jacques Le Goff could still proclaim himself 'uneasy about the use in the study of history of the concept of a generation'.[3]

However, the return to the writing of political history that has been such a marked feature of developments in historiography from the 1970s onwards could not but remove some of these doubts and objections. It has, moreover, been particularly in the field of the history of intellectuals that the idea of the existence of generations has shown itself to be particularly useful. And this has been so for at least two reasons. Firstly, because in the world of the intellectual the manner in which ideas are passed on plays a crucial role. An intellectual defines himself in part via a relationship to a certain cultural inheritance and, whether there exists an element of continuity or a complete break with that past, nevertheless it remains a vitally important implicit or explicit point of reference. Secondly, an analysis of the impact of age and of generational phenomena – as we will define them below – upon the environment of the intellectual has more than mere descriptive value. Both exercise an active and sometimes determining influence upon the workings of intellectual society and thus a knowledge of the way they operate can help us understand that very society.

Thus the impact of age is particularly noticeable in the world of the review. In effect, a review can serve to facilitate the entry of a new group or stratum of intellectuals into the 'network' of the intelligentsia. A student of Pierre Bourdieu, Anna Boschetti, has shown, for example, that *Les Temps Modernes* worked as a sort of Trojan horse for Sartre and Merleau-Ponty, both then in their forties.[4] In other words, in the struggle between different age groups a review plays an important strategic role. On the one hand, it is part of a process of legitimation; on the other, thanks largely to its frequent and regular publication which 'enables it quickly to discuss important issues' as well as the 'homogeneity of its editorial policy' it is in many ways 'the instrument best suited to allow intervention into the areas of culture and ideology'.[5]

The review, then, can provide a route into the intellectual environment and as such for a particular age group it can exist almost as an ante-chamber inhabited immediately prior to gaining entry to the inner citadel. It can also be on occasion the location for the diffusion of ideas and of intellectual fashions which have a durable influence. Moreover, the review can equally operate as a 'compression chamber'[6] allowing movement from one area of the intellectual environment to another. This can occur in various different ways: for example, gradual advance within a review that already exists, with the younger members being responsible for certain columns whilst their elders remain in general control, the 'juniors'[7] essentially gaining experience; conversely, immediate and total control established through the actual creation of reviews, in each case in specific historical conditions that themselves merit examination. Between these two extremes there are undoubtedly a whole series of intermediary positions. The point is that this relationship between generations makes its mark upon the life of reviews. And if, therefore, one wants to focus upon 'a history of ideas which concentrates upon the creation and the influence of reviews'[8] there are, in effect, two types of phenomena that need to be examined, namely, the impact of broader cultural trends and the struggles between different age groups.

Thus the age structure of different generations can have both a significant and varied influence upon the intellectual environment. And again it needs to be emphasised that an analysis of such factors can have a genuine explanatory value. Indeed, one could cite numerous examples of the way this has improved our understanding of recent French history. For example, if the division between the left and the right is one way of comprehending how French intellectuals responded to the Algerian crisis, then it is also the case that age group needs to be taken into consideration, especially on the left where divisions over Algeria were far greater than has been previously realised.[9]

Such details indicate, therefore, that there is a need for closer study of the specific ways in which phenomena related to age and to generation have an impact. What, for example, are the mechanisms which serve to link different age groups? Are they self-contained or open to outside penetration? Who were their intellectual mentors or 'guides'? How does one generation replace another? Why, for example, is it so that in certain cases a group of young intellectuals attains a position of influence and power twenty years after they themselves were twenty whilst in other cases it occurs earlier or later? Sometimes it is simply the age structure of the population that provides an answer, as was the case for the so-called 'non-conformists of the 1930s' who, given that so many of their elders had been killed in the

First World War, faced little in the way of obstacles.[10] Equally, political circumstances can have a role, as the post-war purge that accompanied the liberation of France in 1944 demonstrates, although in this latter case, as tempting as it is to see events in terms of a conflict between generations,[11] it is probably more accurate to speak of a rupture within a generation: in effect, a second branch of the 'generation of 1905' came into the ascendant as a consequence of the discredit suffered by the first branch.[12] In other words, the factors operating could be structural – demographic, in particular – as well as historical – for example, the ideological context or the political situation – with each element having an influence upon the other.

GENERATIONAL PHENOMENA

The majority of the examples and the situations cited above and which for convenience sake have been described as generational phenomena can perhaps more properly be seen as the consequences of certain age patterns, patterns which have an undeniable impact and whose analysis can prove to be extremely fruitful. It is this, for example, that provides the context for Raoul Girardet's comment, made in 1972, stressing 'the importance of generational change as an element in the renewal of styles of thinking and feeling'.[13] But several years later the same historian, with some reason and without necessarily contradicting his earlier position, cast doubt upon the validity of a more general use of the notion of a generation.[14]

The truth of the matter is, of course, that the identification of generations, understood not merely in terms of age pattern but as autonomous layers or clusters possessing their own identity, is not at all easy to achieve.[15] It can, however, as Girardet himself noted, be done in areas where there is ample evidence and this, happily, is the case with the environment occupied by the intellectual. Nevertheless, even here the identification of intellectual generations, and from this the description of the way they have succeeded one another, is not without its problems. Several objections come readily to mind.

The first is that it is by no means obvious that the intellectual milieu develops in a uniform way, the latter being very much the result of various different political, 'ideological' and cultural influences. Certainly, if one can regard the political context as being virtually the same for everyone – although here also there necessarily enters an element of subjective perception – then the cultural and 'ideological' environment undoubtedly varies, depending upon which intellectual sub-groups are being studied.

Secondly, the event – be it political or intellectual – which is responsible for bringing a generation into existence must, in order for it to have acted as a catalyst, be of a considerable magnitude. By definition, therefore, it affects other age groups and thereby loses any claim to a specific relationship with one particular age group. We can, in other words, no more talk of a First World War generation than we can of an Algerian war generation, each war having an impact upon French history in general. Here, however, the contradiction is only apparent. An event can have an impact upon a whole society whilst at the same time bringing into existence a new generation. In short, it seems 'possible to accept that an event can be capable of forming a generation for those who have not been exposed to an earlier event that was itself responsible for forming a generation'.[16] As Jean Luchaire, writing in a 1933 issue of *Notre Temps* devoted to 'the generation gap and the crisis of democracy', emphasised:

> a generation is a collection of individuals marked by one big event or by a series of such events. A mind, with very few exceptions, is influenced fundamentally by an event only when it has not been influenced by other ones, when, that is, the *determining* event occurs at a moment when the mind is free from earlier elemental impressions.[17]

There is also a third, rather embarrassing, objection. If we move from the particular – for example, specific case studies – to the more general – is the notion of a generation a useful concept in a history of intellectuals? – do we not inevitably run up against the problems associated with actually defining or demarcating an intellectual generation? Here again, however, the obstacle is not insurmountable as the way to proceed is through empirical investigation. It is only by painstaking and detailed research that a generation can be situated within the fabric of history, as, for example, an analysis of the students preparing for and gaining entry to the *Ecole normale supérieure* during the 1920s and their subsequent careers reveals a 'generation of 1905'.[18] Naturally this approach will only produce results if it is replicated in further studies and research: if it is not it will be only one part of a generation that is disclosed and defined.

Such an empirical process – based, as it is, necessarily upon the analysis of selected material – does, however, run the risk of only confirming a previously formulated thesis or hypothesis. Hence the need also to analyse a generation from the inside, to see it in terms of the perceptions of its contemporaries and in the context of its own day. In this way an *a posteriori* reconstruction of a generation can be avoided and there can emerge a picture drawn from the collective self-perceptions of the time.

FURTHER APPROACHES

Given, then, that it is possible to position and to characterise an intellectual generation, there are several different strategies that can be utilised to further our inquiry into their existence.

An Historical Approach

In essence, this amounts to answering one central question: how are generations born? What are the circumstances, in other words, that produce the 'Big Bang'?[19] Here we will limit ourselves to emphasising that the crucial event could occur in the realm of ideas and that even though cases like this are less dramatic than those that arise out of national conflicts or crises their capacity to form a generation is no less effective. Events, it is true, are usually thought of in terms of a narrow time span, whilst the impact of ideas tends to be spread over a longer period, but their impact can be as great. Indeed, it could be argued that in the fields of cultural and political history there is a place for the concept of an 'ideological event'.

The question of the birth of a generation leads on to another essential fact: that each generation has a history. Once a generation has appeared it progresses through time according to the pace of its members. As Charles Péguy noted in 1912: 'A generation, an age group, is a human wave. As a mass it moves forward in the same direction, and as a mass it disintegrates like a wall of water crashing against the shore.'[20] Here, no doubt, it could be objected that the very diversity of the routes taken by the members of a generation brought into existence by a particular event would be sufficient to deprive it of all homogeneity and therefore of any existence, but such a conclusion would be ill-considered. Beyond this undeniable diversity – which, in any case, follows certain patterns and thus enables us to outline the anatomy of a generation – each generation from its birth carries what might be termed an element of genetic baggage as well as a common memory derived from its first years of existence, innately and externally marking it for life.

What, moreover, should be clear from this is that the historical study of intellectual generations operates on two dimensions: at one level it follows the journey through time of a particular generation; at another, it analyses the composition of the different layers of successive generations that make up the intellectual environment at any given moment.

A Structural Approach

If an intellectual generation is the product of history then it is also in part the consequence of a demographic sub-structure and is defined by its own organisation and composition.

Demography

The importance of the demographic make-up of a generation should be sufficiently obvious as to not need emphasising in a chapter of this length. Suffice it to say that this aspect of the study of a generation is indispensable regardless of the chosen line of inquiry. Demography determines not only the statistical basis of an intellectual generation but also its internal operation, especially with regard to the respective strength of successive generations. Demography, in short, has an impact upon the history of intellectuals, at certain moments serving to open up new routes to influence as the young and the vigorous come knocking at the door of their still powerful but increasingly numerically fragile elders. Conversely, population size is also itself the product of history, and again this has its effect. As has already been indicated, it was the imbalance in age structure that existed after the First World War that made possible the relative rapid ascent of the 'generation of 1905' towards positions of power.[21]

Composition

However, the demographic source from which an intellectual generation is drawn must not only be studied quantitatively. The evolution of French society has undoubtedly modified the cultural character and shape of each new age group and this evolution has naturally played its part in the constitution of succeeding intellectual generations. For example, the spread and then generalisation of primary school education obviously served to re-fashion their cultural inheritance. And who could doubt that such profound socio-cultural changes did not have reverberations upon the world of politics? The reading of daily newspapers and the general improvement in the level of education could not but have affected the relationship of the 'masses' to politics. In much the same way several decades later the 'explosion' of secondary education served again to improve the cultural level of the population. If it was Victor Hugo who had reigned supreme in the age of the primary school then it was to be Jean-Paul Sartre who inspired the generations produced by the secondary school . . . and the paperback book, which first appeared in 1953.

And, of course, this expansion of secondary school education led inevitably to new generations of university students. Here notably there is a probable connection between this unparalleled numerical increase and the appearance of such serious weekly journals as *France-Observateur* – later *Le Nouvel Observateur* – or *L'Express*. The years of Sartre's dominance gave way to a craze for the social sciences. And again all of this undoubtedly had an impact upon the way that these generations related to politics. Moreover, at the very moment when politicians in France are again talking about rapid expansion in higher education, this phenomenon continues: the socio-cultural baggage of recent generations – including that of what we might call the present 'generation of the image' – owes more to the world of the audio-visual media than it does to the university or to the world of the written word. The proof of this was perhaps to be seen when students took to the streets in November and December 1986 and the manner in which the slogans used and the patterns of behaviour differed markedly from those of their forebears in May 1968.

A Functional Approach

Having located a generation within a particular historical context and analysed its demographic basis, there remains the task of observing the mechanisms through which it operates. In this sense a generation is seen as a form of micro-organism. Crucial to this enterprise is the notion of sociability, where people meet and where they work, because it is this which allows us to see how an intellectual generation is structured, how it is sometimes kept together and how often it is divided within itself. Through it, moreover, can be brought to light those locations and environments which exert particular influence over the intellectual as well as the existence of intellectual micro-societies or sub-groups within the intellectual community.

This notion of sociability was first formulated by the historian Maurice Agulhon in his research on the region of the Var during the nineteenth century. In his usage the expression had a very precise meaning and was used to describe 'the earlier intensity and vitality of communal life in Provence',[22] but it seems to us that it can also be used in a much broader sense to characterise the 'networks' of sociability that structure the French intellectual environment. Thus understood, the word 'sociability' has a double sense, denoting at one and the same time these 'networks' as well as the 'micro-climates' that make up this environment.[23] Moreover, in order to study these two aspects of sociability, what is required is an attempt to recover their origins and this, in the specific case of intellectuals, means that we need to look at their university years, at the age when friendships are easily formed and where influences tend to have their maximum impact. In this way, by concentrating upon the sources of intellectual and political awakening, we can map out and trace those who acted as mentors and who inspired successive intellectual generations. And it is here that the study of the Latin Quarter[24] allows us to reconstruct the connections and networks – of friendship, of intellectual affinity, of education – that are sometimes to be found still in existence some twenty or thirty years later and which operate as a form of sociability amongst intellectuals who now occupy centre stage.[25]

As we have already seen, it is in this context that an analysis of reviews can prove extremely useful, especially given that by definition they are a form of inclusion as well as exclusion. Another possible perspective is the examination of those manifestoes and petitions signed by intellectuals in such abundance since the beginning of the twentieth century.[26]

An Ideological Approach

The central question raised here is how it is that young intellectuals come to think in a particular way. Clearly this is a very important question and one that lies at the heart of any reflection upon the political awakening of successive intellectual generations. At this point let us simply restrict ourselves to remarking upon the fact that at any given moment there exists an element of discontinuity between the form of this awakening and the political atmosphere experienced by the great majority of the population. And in truth this discontinuity has its source in the character of the particular environment under investigation, that of the intellectual. This environment is essentially one dominated by ideological struggles rather than by politics or by electoral contests in particular. And so this discontinuity – or gap – has an almost permanent existence.[27] It was certainly very visible, for example, during the 1920s. The victory of the *Cartel des Gauches* in May 1924 undoubtedly marked the apparent political triumph of radicalism but amongst the 'upper intelligentsia', where the tendency to ideological stagnation and to cultural inertia, although not negligible, was less present than in the rest of society, radicalism as a doctrine, nourished as it had been in the anti-clerical struggles of the end of the nineteenth century, had long since been dead. As is always the case in such situations it was precisely young intellectuals, free from any ideological past, who were the first to take this course and who did so with the greatest ease. For them, on the left at least, the slogan was more likely to have been 'rather Blum than Herriot'.[28] Certainly such young men were likely to have been more numerous than those attracted to the avant-garde of intellectual society – the surrealists, for example – and who, a further step forward, were already being drawn towards communism.

This in itself, however, poses the problem of the avant-garde. Without wishing to say that 'every avant-garde is prone to excess and to confusion'[29] it is nevertheless the case that an avant-garde is necessarily defined in terms of a rupture with the past and therefore tends to be essentially 'activist', thus often making it the most visible component of an intellectual age group. It is furthermore incontestable, as Annie Kriegel has argued, that the 'the selection of examples is not legitimised by numerical preponderance but rather derives from their capacity to highlight different identities'.[30] But to conclude from this that a generation is 'the impetuous avant-garde of an age group'[31] is a step which the historian ought not to take. If he does so he will find himself writing a history of avant-gardes and that would be nothing more than a mythical history of generations.

Notes

1. For a more general discussion of the methodological problems raised by this question, see my 'Le hasard ou la nécessité? Une histoire en chantier: l'histoire des intellectuels', *Vingtième siècle*, 9, 1986, pp. 97–108; 'Les intellectuels', in R. Rémond (ed.), *Pour une histoire politique* (Paris, 1988) pp. 199–231; *Génération intellectuelle: Khâgneux et Normaliens dans*

l'entre-deux-guerres (Paris, 1988) pp. 9–19; and *Intellectuels et passions françaises: Manifestes et pétitions au XXe siècle* (Paris, 1990) pp. 9–20. Specifically on the concept of a generation, see my 'Effets d'âge et phénomènes de génération dans le milieu intellectuel français', *Les Cahiers de l'IHTP*, 6, 1987, pp. 5–18 and 'Génération et histoire politique', in *Vingtième siècle*, 22, 1989, pp. 67–80. The present study draws heavily upon these two articles.

2. L. Febvre, 'Générations', supplement to *Revue de synthèse historique*, XXI, 1929, p. 43 and M. Bloch, *Apologie pour l'Histoire* (Paris, 1974 edition) p. 151.

3. Y. Renouard, 'La notion de génération en histoire', in P. Nora (ed.), *Essais d'Ego-histoire* (Paris, 1987) p. 238.

4. A. Boschetti, *Sartre et 'Les Temps Modernes': Une entreprise intellectuelle* (Paris, 1985). See also my 'Pas de clercs dans le siècle', *Vingtième siècle*, 13, 1987, pp. 127–34.

5. J-M. Domenach, 'Entre le prophétique et le clérical', *La revue des revues*, 1, 1986, pp. 21–30.

6. The use of this expression is taken from the analysis of the review, *Arguments*, by G. Delannoi and O. Corpet.

7. See A. Anglès, *André Gide et le premier groupe de 'La Nouvelle Revue Française': l'âge critique, 1911–1912* (Paris, 1986) p. 110.

8. M. Decaudin, 'Formes et fonctions de la revue littéraire au XXe siècle', in *Situation et avenir des revues littéraires* (Nice, 1976) p. 19.

9. See J-P. Rioux and J-F. Sirinelli (eds), *La Guerre d'Algérie et les intellectuels français* (Brussels, 1991).

10. See J-L. Loubet del Bayle, *Les non-conformistes des années 30* (Paris, 1969).

11. See A. Cohen-Solal, *Sartre: a life* (London, 1985) pp. 218–9 and P. Assouline, *L'épuration des intellectuels* (Brussels, 1985) p. 140.

12. See J-F. Sirinelli, *Génération intellectuelle*.

13. R. Girardet, *L'Idée coloniale en France* (Paris, 1972) p. X.

14. R. Girardet, 'Du concept de génération à la notion de contemporanéité', *Revue d'histoire moderne et contemporaine*, XXX, 1983, p. 261.

15. Apart from my already cited *Génération intellectuelle* and its discussion of the 'generation of 1905', see my 'Les intellectuels et Pierre Mendès France', in F. Bédarida and J-P. Rioux (eds), *Pierre Mendès France et le mendésisme* (Paris, 1986) pp. 87–100, and 'Les normaliens de la rue d'Ulm après 1945: une génération communiste?', *Revue d'histoire moderne et contemporaine*, 4, 1986, pp. 569–88. For an outline of generations this century, see P. Ory and J-F. Siriuelli, *Les Intellectuels en France, de l'Affaire Dreyfus à nos jours* (Paris, 1986) and M.Winock, 'Les Générations intellectuelles', *Vingtième siècle*, 22, 1989, pp. 17–38.

16. P. Favre, 'Génération: un concept pour les sciences sociales?', unpublished paper, 1981, p. 13. See also J. Crête and P. Favre, *Générations et la politique* (Laval, 1990).

17. J. Luchaire, 'Querelle des générations et crise des démocraties', *Notre Temps*, 201–2, 1933, column 606.

18. See J-F. Sirinelli, *Génération intellectuelle*.

19. See P. Balmand, 'Les jeunes intellectuels de l'"esprit des années trente': un phénomène de génération?', in *Les Cahiers de l'IHTP*, 1987, p. 57.
20. C. Péguy, *Le Mystère des Saints Innocents* (1912) in *Oeuvres poétiques complètes* (Paris, 1941) p. 455.
21. See B. Parain, *Retour à la France* (Paris, 1936) p. 203. and P. Ory and J-F. Sirinelli, *Les Intellectuels en France, de l'Affaire Dreyfus à nos jours*, pp. 61–76.
22. M. Agulhon, *La République au village* (Paris, 1979) p. II.
23. See J-F. Sirinelli, 'Le hasard ou la nécessité', pp. 103–4.
24. See *Génération intellectuelle*, pp. 219–56.
25. For specific case studies see the second and third parts of J-F. Sirinelli, *Génération intellectuelle*, pp. 219–644. On the *khâgne* as the cradle of these networks, in addition to the above see my contribution to P. Nora (ed.), *Lieux de mémoire: La Nation III* (Paris, 1986) pp. 590–624.
26. See, in particular, J-F. Sirinelli, *Intellectuels et passions françaises*.
27. An exception to this would possibly be the era of the Popular Front: the electoral victories of the Socialist Party in 1981 would, however, be a good example of such a gap: see J-F. Sirinelli, *Intellectuels et passions françaises*, pp. 293–318.
28. See J-F. Sirinelli, 'Serres ou laboratoires de la tradition politique? les khâgnes des années 1920', *Pouvoirs*, 42, 1987, pp. 93–103.
29. M. Crouzet, 'La bataille des intellectuels français', *La Nef*, 1962–3, p. 63.
30. A. Kriegel,'Le concept politique de génération: apogée et déclin', *Commentaire*, 2, 1979, p. 395.
31. G. Liebert, *Contrepoint*, 1, 1970, p. 11.

5 Academics or Intellectuals? The Professors of the University of Paris and Political Debate in France from the Dreyfus Affair to the Algerian War

Christophe Charle

Of all the great European universities, the University of Paris is the most paradoxical. Established in 1253, it ceased to exist as a single institution with the Revolution of 1789 and found itself divided into autonomous faculties and colleges. The latter remained divided throughout the greater part of the nineteenth century, only to be brought together again at the end of the century under the title of the University of Paris. However, the habits acquired as a result of this separation of disciplines were such as to ensure that this formally unified administrative body was in reality an entirely empty shell. An *esprit de corps* existed only at the level of such smaller units as the faculty of law, and the faculties of medicine, letters and sciences. Moreover, this fragmentation of the professorial body was sharper than in other French or foreign universities because of the sheer size of the University of Paris. In terms of student numbers each faculty was more important than every other university in the country.

To this first paradox of a body lacking internal cohesion is to be added another arising from its position in the capital city of France. At the beginning of the twentieth century, Paris was one of the world's two or three biggest cities. It was, more importantly, not just the political and administrative capital of France but also its economic and cultural capital as well. This disequilibrium – which is so characteristic of France and which is also probably unique in the world – was such as to bestow a quite exceptional status upon the city's academics. In short, they came to consider themselves to be the élite of their profession. For example, given the status of the municipality of Paris after the fall of the Commune in 1871 as a city administered from above and therefore lacking any real autonomy in its relationship with central government, they had contacts not with the local élite but directly with the national élite.

It is these facts which provide the context and explain the choice of approach behind this study. The intention of this chapter is to describe an historical cycle; that of the emergence, prominence and progressive decline of 'intellectuals'. As is well known, 'intellectuals' first came fully into view at the time of the Dreyfus Affair and it is this moment that constitutes the point of departure for our study. In their ranks academics, and especially Parisian professors, played a crucial if not exclusive role. We will return later to the reasons for their appearance as a political grouping at the end of the nineteenth century. The point of arrival is, however, a little more arbitrary. The Algerian war has often been compared to a new Dreyfus Affair because of the intellectual debate that it engendered and which, broadly speaking, gravitated around the issues of the use of torture and respect for the rights of man.[1] Given the gap of sixty years it allows us to see the changes and the continuities in the political role played by Parisian academics as 'intellectuals'. But, above all, the Algerian war stands at the moment when the new University of Paris inaugurated by the Third Republic began to break down under the pressure of demographic factors and changes within academic disciplines. After the Algerian war the conditions of university and intellectual life were so changed that the internal problems of the University took precedence over external ones, or at least these external problems were totally re-interpreted through the perspectives of a university community which had lost all unity and even the minimum level of cohesion.

Our aim, therefore, is to answer two questions: Why did a significant minority, and upon some occasions a majority, of Parisian academics assume the role of intellectual in the important national debates which shook French political life? Secondly, given that political debate entails rifts and differences, how did these rifts arise and upon what did these differences between the various groups of academics rest? It is clear that for academics there were other possible roles than that of the intellectual, roles which themselves reflected opposing conceptions both of the university profession and of the relationship between the university élite and other élites. Indirectly this will tell us something about the substance and the limits of the notion of the intellectual in French society in the twentieth century.

Thus, after a broad survey of both the academics and of the University of Paris throughout this period designed to explain the general factors underlying the intervention of academics in the life of the State, we will analyse their role at the time of the Dreyfus Affair. Then, via a more cursory examination of later political crises and episodes in intellectual life, we will be able to assess to what extent this model of behaviour continued to exist, which issues gave rise to the greatest activity and involvement, and which groups were the most and the least liable to participate. This will enable us finally to answer our two initial questions and also to gauge the degree of autonomy and heteronomy enjoyed by Parisian academics.

THE PLACE AND ROLE OF THE ACADEMICS OF THE UNIVERSITY OF PARIS IN UNIVERSITY AND POLITICAL LIFE

The Prominence of the University of Paris

The prominence of the University of Paris in French university life is very considerable and can be measured both quantitively and qualitatively. In terms of numbers, at the time of the Dreyfus Affair the teaching staff in Paris made up roughly one-fifth of the total number of academics in French higher education (here we are counting only university faculties and are excluding such separate institutions as the *Collège de France* and the *Ecole Pratique des Hautes Etudes* which would further reinforce the domination of Paris). This percentage was maintained up to the beginning of the 1960s, indeed in certain faculties even slightly increased to reach almost one-third. The continuation of this heavy centralisation of the teaching profession in Paris – despite the efforts made during the Third Republic to strengthen provincial universities – can be explained by the even greater concentration of students in the capital. In 1897–8, for example, 39.2 per cent of French law students pursued their studies in Paris. This was also the case, respectively, of 51.2 per cent and of 37.1 per cent of arts and science students whereas in medicine the faculty of medicine was in the majority with 53.4 per cent of the total number of students. In the

1930s and 1950s these figures hardly changed, indeed if anything they got worse. For the academic year 1934–5 in law and in the arts the total share of students in Paris increased (respectively to 58.6 per cent and to 59 per cent) whilst it declined slightly or remained at the same high level in medicine and the sciences (42.1 per cent for both faculties).[2]

At the time of the Algerian war a slight decrease occurred (in all faculties the proportion of Paris students declined) but everywhere the figure remained above 30 per cent (44.1 per cent for law, 41.9 per cent for medicine, 32.2 per cent for the sciences, and 30.7 per cent for the arts).[3] This persistent imbalance in favour of the University of Paris, despite the creation of new universities in the provinces, can be explained by the existence in Paris of specialist research institutes, the prestigious *grandes écoles*, and so on, and by the strong attraction exercised by the university over foreign students, an attraction based upon the assumption that the most senior and the most well-known academics were gathered in the faculties of Paris. This quick numerical sketch provides us with another conclusion. In Paris, the university community, its teachers and its students, constituted a self-contained city within a city. In 1901, for example, the full professors of the four principal faculties plus the School of Pharmacy made up a theoretical Senate of 130 members and with the other categories of staff (assistant professors, senior lecturers, lecturers and so on) one reaches the numbers of a small parliament.

As for the students of Paris, at the time of the Dreyfus Affair had they been put together, they would have formed a population equal to that of a small town (more than 12 000). In the 1930s there were more than twice as many academics as in the period of the Belle Epoque before the First World War, whilst by the end of the 1950s there were more than four times as many. Assembled together they would have been almost as numerous as the members of the National Assembly. The student body of the 1930s was equal to the size of a sub-prefecture, with more than 36 000 young men and women, and of a medium-sized prefecture by the end of the 1950s (more than 66 000 people). What is more a knowledge of these figures enables us to deduce certain important consequences for the behaviour of Parisian academics. From the end of the nineteenth century onwards they benefited from a set of favourable circumstances which allowed them to assert their presence upon the national political stage: the prestige of forming an élite small in number but nevertheless sufficiently diverse and extensive such that in Paris alone its collective strength was equivalent to that of a significant minority of the total number of academics. In addition, Parisian professors had a very sizeable student audience the mobilisation of which increased their influence. Equally, the process could be the other way around. Upon certain occasions, it was the political commitment of the students which prompted the capital's academics to show their support for a cause or on the contrary publicly to distance themselves from and to criticise the positions adopted by their students.

The Conditions Determining the Politicisation of Academics

These general details, on the other hand, are not sufficient on their own to explain the specific political role played by the academics, or the students, of the University of Paris from the end of the nineteenth century onwards. First of all, from the beginning of the last century there occurred student 'agitation' in defence of academics persecuted for the political positions they had taken. Amongst the most well-known could be cited, during the Restoration, Guizot, Cousin and Villemain and Michelet, Quinet and Mickiewicz towards the end of the July Monarchy. The university community, even before it had reached its size of the twentieth century, had very quickly become aware of its potential symbolic strength and of its concentration in a specific part of Paris, the Latin Quarter, where it reigned supreme.[4] Nevertheless, this tradition, which goes back to the Middle Ages, of a city within a city changed at the moment where our study commences, and this because of three new factors.

Firstly, a new equilibrium came into existence between the Sorbonne (the faculty of arts and sciences) and the law and medical schools. Throughout the nineteenth century professorial power and prestige was heavily concentrated in the latter two faculties. Alone, they possessed a large number of students, their subjects were of uncontested social utility and their teaching body was more easily able to gain entry into the governing élite. At the end of the century, helped by the reforms of the 1880s, the spread of the German university model coupled with the support for science on the part of republican politicians, the Sorbonne became an important element in university reform. Vis-à-vis university teachers in law and medicine those in the arts and sciences also found themselves from now on before a body of full-time students constituted by those in receipt of a grant for studies at degree and doctoral levels or in order to obtain the State teaching qualification (the *agrégation*). Previously they had faced either amateurs or society people (in the case of the arts) or auditoria full of poorly motivated students pursuing compulsory courses (as was the case in the sciences with first year medical students). It was out of this new environment which saw itself as the intellectual avant-garde of the nation that emerged both the innovatory concept of the Dreyfusard 'intellectual' and the revisionist cause's best supporters.[5]

Secondly, a community life – so important in German universities at this time – began to appear in the Latin Quarter and in the provincial universities. It took various forms. Amongst the students it was primarily in the shape of non-political associations (strongly encouraged by the Republic and by such reforming professors as Ernest Lavisse and Gabriel Monod) that the signs of maturation of a younger generation breaking with the turbulent traditions of the Latin Quarter were to be seen. In Paris the *Association générale des étudiants* suffered from the intellectual and geographical separation of the different faculties and the sheer number of students made the creation of a sense of belonging at the level of the University even more difficult to attain, but nonetheless this organisation offered the possibility of less formal meetings between students and academic staff and helped the students to free themselves from the apathy, interspersed with brief, violent explosions, that had characterised their behaviour in the past. What is more, in parallel to this there also appeared at this time a series of more political student organisations which were to play the role of active minorities in the mobilisation of students and academics at the time of the Dreyfus Affair (be they socialist or anarchist, Catholic or conservative students).[6]

Finally, the academics in their turn, at least at the level of the faculties and sometimes over more general issues at the level of the University, began to learn about a more collective form of life. The autonomy acquired by the universities and the lesser interference by the State in the internal life of the faculties transformed the various academic councils, at the level of the faculty, the University, the Academy of Paris and the Education Ministry into places of university power and discussion, thus strengthening the sentiment of an *esprit de corps*, encouraging much wider debate, and, in brief, turning the professor from an isolated individual secure in the possession of his chair into a more or less active citizen of a city of scholars who were obliged to voice their opinion upon its future. This new situation, which followed from the reforms of the two previous decades, had a greater impact in Paris simply because of the greater size of the faculties, the means at its disposal and, above all, the dominance of

Parisian academics within the decision-making machinery of the university system . To this should be added the more frequent lines of personal contact that many academics had established with higher civil servants and members of the political class.

Thus took form a new function for Parisian academics, that of councillors to the Prince and of experts in the service of the government administration. This role, which continued to expand throughout the twentieth century, was not however the only professional model available to academics. The new prestige conferred upon the universities by the reforms combined with the pro-science ideology encouraged by the Republic and the centralisation of cultural life in Paris opened up other routes for the academics of the University of Paris to exert influence upon both informed and broader public opinion: the writing of works of synthesis, the editing of prestigious collections for publishers, the editing of influential reviews and regular collaboration with them, plus writing for daily newspapers (then at the height of their power and influence). In short, at the end of the century and at the moment when the Dreyfus crisis got under way and as the ideal of the 'intellectual' came into view all the requisite conditions existed to ensure that Parisian academics would consider themselves to have the right to play a decisive political role.

The 'Intellectual' Versus the 'Notable'

We must be beware, however, of over-simplification. The analysis of the positions taken by Parisian academics at the time of the Dreyfus Affair shows that not all of them necessarily accepted this newly-emerging ideal of the 'intellectual'. Firstly, by definition the holding of an academic post in Paris was a form of consecration. Many academics still belonged to an older generation formed by a more traditional and more strictly academic university system. Under this system the academic was at one with the established order and was bound to it by numerous ties: frequent membership or desired membership of the academies that made up the *Institut de France*, where they came into contact with members of the other élites; recognition of their worth by the State through the award of honorary decorations; the multiplication of posts and therefore of salaries, which in certain cases was such as to produce a notable amongst notables. Finally, but less frequently, admission into the governing élite was achieved through the possession of an electoral mandate at a local or even national level.[7] Thus in the 1890s several members of the Parisian faculties were either parliamentary deputies, senators or, if only for a brief period, even government ministers. These were, however, increasingly to be special cases.[8] The liberal democratic régime in effect brought about a professionalisation of political life which was itself increasingly incompatible with the greater specialisation demanded of a university career. An academic career in Paris, for example, demanded a very considerable commitment to research, international contacts and active participation in the life of the discipline through such things as the editing of scholarly journals and the chairing of learned societies. Moreover, it became more and more difficult for academics to develop the local ties necessary to win the votes of their fellow citizens. In this context it is significant that the two greatest representatives of science in the 1870s, Ernest Renan and Louis Pasteur, should have suffered electoral defeat, whilst under the July monarchy both Joseph-Louis Gay-Lussac and Jean-Baptiste Dumas, not to mention Guizot, were virtually impossible to remove from parliament. Paradoxically, it was provincial academics who were prepared to forgo their highest intellectual ambitions who found it easiest to secure votes in the towns where they worked, the most famous cases being Jean Jaurès, a local councillor in Toulouse, and much later Edouard Herriot in Lyons.

PARISIAN ACADEMICS AND THE DREYFUSARD REVOLUTION

The Dreyfus Affair has sometimes been described as a revolution. This is even more true for the world of intellectuals and especially of Parisian academics than it is for the rest of the actors in French politics. And this is so because this crisis had three very important consequences.

In the first place it made academics adopt a new form of political conduct that differed markedly from previously established patterns of behaviour. Academics, and especially those in Paris, committed themselves both publicly and collectively through the means of petitions published in newspapers to one or other of the two rival camps. In this way they departed from the normal channels of political life which stipulated that political problems should be left to the elected representatives of the people. Moreover, in this crisis, as opposed to those of earlier decades in the nineteenth century, it was not only well-known personalities acting as the spokesmen of their peers or as representatives of public opinion who intervened but intellectuals, whatever their personal reputation.

In addition this novel form of agitation, which for this group of intellectuals at least was a new type of activity, had a profound and durable impact because it was accompanied by a clear-cut internal division between the two camps, thus shattering the traditional sense of solidarity that had existed amongst teachers in higher education. There were those who tried to find a third route, a middle way between the excesses of the anti-Dreyfusard nationalists and the anarchist or anti-militarist tendencies of some Dreyfusards,[9] but it was only the supporters and the opponents of a review of the trial of Dreyfus who succeeded in collecting a large number of signatures and this behind two incompatible systems of values: the defence of the Army and of order on one side and that of Truth and Justice on the other. Such was the force and extent of this division that upon the occasion of other political crises later in the twentieth century it re-surfaced in an identical form and served to re-mobilise academics in an analogous way.

After this summary of the conditions that made possible this form of activity we must now attempt to determine why this specific combination of circumstances led to such an unexpected result, in brief we need to understand how Parisian academics defined their own political role.

The Emergence of the New Model of the 'Intellectuel'

Like all revolutions the Dreyfusard revolution occurred by surprise and its magnitude could only be measured after the event. In the same way that those aristocrats who had hastened the crisis of the Ancien Régime had not desired the collapse of the old order so too the first Dreyfusards, who were themselves often people well placed in society, could not have imagined that their obstinate pursuit of a revision of the trial of Dreyfus would have set in motion a political crisis whose two outstanding results were the entry of the first socialist minister into a bourgeois government and an abortive attempt at a *coup d'état*. But in order to break the wall of silence they were obliged to resort to indirect methods (for example, a press campaign after the publication of Zola's open letter 'J'accuse'), calls for support designed to influence public opinion ('J'accuse' and the so-called manifesto of the intellectuals in 1898), the organisation of public meetings and the creation of associations which to an extent competed with those conventional vehicles of parliamentary democracy that remained closed to them. At the outset it was chance alone that was responsible for the fact that it was well-known academics who were among the first to find themselves won over to the cause of Dreyfus and who therefore in their turn set out to convince the members of their own professional world. And, as is always the case in politics, the successful mobilisation of support rested upon something of a misunderstanding. The first Parisian academics who signed the so-called manifesto of the intellectuals did so believing that they were thereby respecting the values of Justice and Truth which, as Durkheim later pointed out in their defence, they regarded as an integral part of their 'professional practices'.[10] The mission of the teacher, and especially of the university academic, was it not to seek truth and to award university qualifications to pupils solely on the grounds of justice? As servants of truth and of justice were not the members of the teaching profession obliged to defend these values everywhere, be it in the lecture room or in public life? Thus, in order to demonstrate that it was this concern which alone motivated them and which also gave them the right to act, they ensured that in the petitions they signed their academic or university title appeared after their name! From this point of view Parisian academics were even purer 'intellectuals' than those writers and journalists who supported the first Dreyfusards. In the literary and political polemics in which they participated the latter did not always defend just causes and they were in general more involved in the events of their day than were academics. Moreover, the intervention into the political arena of academics was even more striking because it occurred in this way for the first time and on such a scale. Finally, the symbolic capital possessed by a writer was more individual than that attached to a university qualification, which was by definition both impersonal and universal.

This theoretical justification of the right of university academics to involve themselves in matters which did not directly concern them and to challenge decisions made by the State when they were themselves employees of that State (a reproach voiced on many occasions by the anti-Dreyfusards) was not, however, always so obvious to everyone. If one takes as an example the first petition, the so-called manifesto of the intellectuals which brought together 1200 signatures, in terms of numerical importance those in secondary and higher education constituted the second largest group (22 per cent), behind journalists and writers and before students, but they still represented only a small minority of the total number of university academics (no more than 260 out of several thousand) although measured as a proportion of the actual size of the group their level of participation was the highest of any intellectual profession. For all their abstraction these figures show that the pattern of commitment amongst intellectuals operated slightly better in the University than elsewhere and in part this is explicable in terms of the existence of networks of personal acquaintance, the confined geographical space of Paris and the presence amongst academics of a much stronger community of values than existed amongst writers and journalists who were often divided by fratricidal struggles and whose movements were less free because of their dependence upon the press, then overwhelmingly anti-Dreyfusard. The successful emergence of the model of the intellectual within university circles was, however, only relative. In terms of absolute numbers even within higher education in Paris the Dreyfusards were in the minority. The fact that they were able to attract several big names to their cause was deceptive: the greater proportion of those teaching at the Sorbonne did not support them, whilst most of their recruits came from such research institutions as the *Ecole Pratique des Hautes Etudes* and the *Ecole des Chartes* or from places where the teaching staff were young, such as the *Ecole normale supérieure*.

As a form of agitation the signing of petitions by Parisian academics really bagan in the autumn of 1898 with petitions supporting Major Picquart, that is, after such dramatic events as the suicide of Colonel Henry had begun to swing informed opinion behind calls for a re-trial of Dreyfus. The quantitive success of this tactic within the university faculties, however, was such as to convince the anti-Dreyfusards that they in their turn needed to use the same means if only, amongst other things, to show that not everyone had sided with the opposing camp. For the intellectual right the channels used to gather support were more traditional. Members of the *Académie française* and more generally of the *Institut de France*, formed an association, the *Ligue de la patrie française*, and then under the cover of defending the army, the homeland and tradition, sought to bring university academics and writers together, indeed to assemble those who, they believed, made up France's moral, spiritual and social authorities. As such this league was an attempt to fuse the traditional model of the notable with that of the intellectual and in so doing to challenge the pretension of the Dreyfusards to represent the entire intellectual élite.[11] Judging from the list of its supporters it did indeed fulfil this aim, since if many of its members taught in higher education they did not enjoy the relative preponderance that had characterised the so-called manifesto of the intellectuals.

The Strength and the Role of Parisian Academics within Both Camps

This general survey has already revealed a dissimilarity of functions played by academics inside the two factions. In one they had a directing and leading role, whilst in the other they represented one element of support within a much larger coalition. However, how one assesses the level of participation and role of Parisian academics depends upon the perspective adopted. In terms of levels of participation amongst both Dreyfusards and anti-Dreyfusards the already existing disequilibrium between Paris and the provinces was further accentuated. According to my own figures Dreyfusard and anti-Dreyfusard academics working in Paris made up 45 per cent of the total number of academics who signed the principal petitions. Amongst the Dreyfusards, the creators of this new role for the intellectual, the disequilibrium was even more marked: the Parisians being in the majority, with 91 signatures against 82. Conversely the anti-Dreyfusards, who rejected this notion of the intellectual, had a strong provincial base: 101 provincial academics joined the *Ligue de la patrie française*, compared to 59 from Paris. This difference in the geographical breakdown of the two groups is indicative of the continued attachment of provincial academics to both the established order and the earlier conception of the academic role of teachers in higher education that has already been outlined. In the provincial towns of France academics saw themselves as notables closely allied to the other élites and with whom they had extensive contacts. By contrast, in the capital the size of the national élite, the much greater differences of status and in material and cultural levels within its ranks, combined with the internal diversification of the academic community, were such as to accentuate the distance between the world of the university and other élites. This made possible an element of autonomy and, for the most advanced members of the profession and those least integrated into the establishment, gave rise to the call for an independent political role of which the emergence of the idea of the intellectual was itself proof.

This contrasting geographical base of the two camps must not let us forget, however, that with regard to this new type of political activity there was a third party, more numerous than the first two, that of the abstentionists. Even in Paris 55 per cent of academics refused to sign one or other of the petitions, whilst in the provinces the proportion was a little less than 80 per cent. However, these figures themselves hide significant variations in levels of commitment according to institution. At the head of the list is the *Ecole des Chartes* and then in descending order come the fourth and fifth sections of the *Ecole Pratique des Hautes Etudes*,[12] the *Ecole normale supérieure*, the Faculty of Arts in Paris, the *Collège de France* and the faculty of sciences. The dominated pole of the university field was more disposed to this new mode of action because, more than their rivals, they were excluded from other forms of power.[13]

Even more clear-cut than these differing levels of involvement in the struggle is the breakdown of the two camps according to faculty. All of the faculties (with the exception of one, that of law) were divided, but in each case the majority leant in a different direction according to the side of the Rue Saint-Jacques on which they were situated (the Rue Saint-Jacques being the principal geographical dividing line within the Latin Quarter). To the right (or the east) of this road if one looks towards the north the anti-Dreyfusards were in the majority: for example at the *Collège de France* 62 per cent of the academics were anti-Dreyfusard, at the *Muséum d'histoire naturelle*[14] the figure was 83.3 per cent whilst at the faculty of law it was 100 per cent. To the left or to the west it was the opposite with the Dreyfusards in the majority: at the *Ecole des Chartes* support stood at 83.3 per cent, the fourth and fifth sections of the *Ecole Pratique des Hautes Etudes* at 80 per cent, the arts and science faculties of Sorbonne at 64 per cent and 70 per cent respectively, whilst at the faculty of medicine it stood at 59 per cent thanks largely to the backing of non-professorial staff. What these very simple figures show is that the greater the size of an institution's teaching staff the less uniform were the views of its professors (except, that is, for the case of law, where very few professors took a position). By contrast, in the confined world of the research institution the determined minority were able more easily to acquire a position of hegemony whereas the more traditional academic was subject to numerous external influences and to power-ful social interests that restricted the possibility of non-conformism. Thus for Parisian academics the Dreyfus Affair had the appearance of a quarrel between the ancients and the moderns (the new Sorbonne against the old Sorbonne, research institutions on the German model against the great institutions inherited from the ancien régime, scholarly faculties against vocational faculties) and also of being a quarrel between generations: it was the younger generation of academics and those least promoted within their institution who most easily adopted the posture of the intellectual, and then usually on the side of the Dreyfusards.

In this respect there existed an undeniable interaction between students and their lecturers. To the extent that it can be known, the breakdown of Dreyfusard and anti-Dreyfusard students according to faculty parallels exactly that of their teachers.[15] The Dreyfusards were in the majority in the arts and science faculties of the Sorbonne, as were the academics of these two faculties, just as they were marginally in medicine, where again the same comparison applies. They were in the minority in law and in the oldest of the *grandes écoles*. It was as if the academics found it easier to commit themselves when they sensed broad support amongst their students: either because the students undertook to lend their support to petitions at the side of those academics to whom they felt the closest or, conversely, because the example of commitment given by their masters inspired them, as disciples, to do the same thing. There is, however, one exception to this general pattern. At the *Ecole des Chartes* the open endorsement of the Dreyfusard cause by the academic staff incited on the contrary a large number of their students to adopt the opposite position in order to express their disapproval. This perhaps reflects a social division: those academics most professionaly committed to their discipline turned it into an instrument in the quarrel between experts that characterised the Dreyfus Affair; their students, who for the most part attended the *Ecole des Chartes* without any thought of their career and in the amateurish style typical of the future notable, were shocked by this intellectual pretension which stood as the antithesis of the traditionalist image that they themselves had of their college.[16]

This brief and schematic analysis of the positions adopted by Parisian academics at the time of the Dreyfus Affair has already in part answered the two questions posed in the introduction. The acceptance by Parisian academics of the new model of political behaviour associated with the intellectual was undoubtedly aided by the organisational conditions of the French university system which put Parisian academics directly into contact with national political problems. However, the break with the traditional university *habitus*[17] varied according to the social contacts that existed between academics and other élites, the extent of the changes introduced into the composition of teaching body by the university reforms, as well as according to discipline and academic status. In order to complete our investigation it remains now to show that the structure put in place at the beginning of the century came into operation again on various other occasions between the 1920s and the end of the 1950s and in roughly similar ways.

DREYFUS AFFAIRS? FROM THE RIF WAR TO THE ALGERIAN WAR

Methods and Sources

Despite the unique character of the circumstances surrounding the Dreyfus Affair it was the case that the methods used to intervene in political debate inaugurated by intellectuals in 1898–9 were re-used at regular intervals in the course of the twentieth century. What was at issue, however, was sometimes very different. How then can we explain the later reappearance of the intellectual's petition: a reappearance, moreover, that from some quarters was to be criticised for its over-ritualistic character? Three principal reasons can be cited.

A proportion of the intellectuals who experienced their political baptism of fire at the time of the Dreyfus Affair continued to act and to express themselves politically during this period and certainly did so up to the Second World War. When circumstances demanded their leaders could fall back upon reflexes created in 1898–9. Given their status as civil servants and the length of their careers it was, from this point of view, academics who were the most consistent in their pattern of behaviour. Secondly, the success achieved by this method during the Dreyfus Affair was sufficient to preserve a belief in its effectiveness. Finally, this mode of action had the advantage that it did not challenge the deep-seated individualism of the academic and saved him from any long-term organisational commitment. As we shall see, the petitions that were the most successful were those that appeared the least partisan and the most overtly intellectual.

However, the course of history has worked against the petition. In the twentieth century the mobilisation of public opinion has increasingly been achieved by such permanent, and more or less official, instruments as the trade union, the political party and other similar associations. To the extent also that the number of academics increased and became more dispersed, then the artisanal and spontaneous procedure of organising a petition became less and less successful in assembling an impressive list of signatures. In effect a return has had to be made to the élitist petition, signed by only a few well-known – and very often the same – celebrities.

Despite these reservations these documents remain very good indicators of the level of involvement of Parisian academics in national political life, because they alone at regular intervals provide a cross-section picture of opinion within the university community. Other forms of analysis, for example the utilisation of individual monographs, are inadequate, for two reasons. Only a very small minority of academics were politically committed and publicly displayed their position in a continuous manner: thus to confine oneself to these exceptions would be completely to falsify the picture. For the remainder the only means of defining their position is precisely through the study of these petitions, especially given that indirect testimony of non-published political opinions must always be subject to caution and to differences of interpretation. The great advantage of the petition in terms of a quantifiable study is their relative homogeneity, their public character which therefore presupposes a minimum level of support for the cause endorsed and their continued existence over a long period of time.

For our analysis we have concentrated upon several different types of petition: (1) those with near unanimous support that were relatively free from political influence but which reflect an issue of general social concern, such as the manifesto of intellectuals and academics (published in the *Revue des études coopératives* in October 1921) calling for co-operation in industry and the petition against the anti-semitic measures taken by Hitler (published in *Le Temps* in April 1933); (2) nationalist or patriotic right-wing petitions such as that supporting the Rif war (*Le Figaro*, 7 July 1925), that protesting against the sanctions imposed on Italy during the Ethiopian war (*Le Figaro* and *L'Echo de Paris*, October 1935) or supporting Spanish nationalist intellectuals (*L'Occident*, January–February 1938) and, finally, that in favour of the cause of French Algeria (*Le Monde*, 7 October 1960); (3) left-wing petitions, such as that supporting the imprisoned trade unionist Durand (*L'Humanité*, January–February 1911) and those founding the *Comité de vigilance des intellectuels antifascistes* (*Europe*, 15 April 1934), supporting republican Spain (*Commune*, December 1936) and calling for peace in Algeria (*Le Monde*, 6 October 1960). In terms of period-isation the breakdown is reasonably even, with the obvious exception of times of war and the 1950s. The latter saw the publication of an important petition signed by university academics, the subject of which was the European Defence Community, but the newspapers of the day reported it without giving a detailed list of its signatories, thus making it unusable in an inquiry of this kind.[18]

Unequal Levels of Mobilisation

The level of commitment of Parisian academics, judged by comparing the number of signatories with the total number of university teachers at the time, was always higher than that of other academics, a conclusion already established with regard to the Dreyfus Affair. However this rate only exceeded the level attained at the time of the Affair for those petitions which were the least partisan and the least controversial and which only raised issues of general principle. Here we could cite the manifesto of October 1921 (signed by almost 80 per cent of the academics in the faculty of arts) and the petitions protesting against the anti-semitic measures in Germany (signed by almost 60 per cent of the faculty of arts, almost 40 per cent of the faculty of science, 44.6 per cent in law and 26.5 per cent in medicine). In this case the university élite fell in behind traditionally liberal and humanitarian values. By contrast, the members of the various faculties felt themselves much less concerned when the cause being championed had overt political connotations. If they wished to play the role of the intellectual then, with the exception of the most militant, they took care not to be equated with vulgar party intellectuals. Thus, for example, the petition supporting the army at the time of the Rif war which, in many respects, was identical to that of the *Ligue de la Patrie française* in 1899 (it arose from an initiative on the part of members of the *Institut de France* and was opposed to a manifesto published in *L'Humanité*, itself signed by members of the literary avant-garde and judged to be scandalous in government circles) succeeded in mobilising, beyond the confines of the conventional right, academics who saw it as an expression of patriotism (the names of several former Dreyfusards figure there, for instance).[19] Equally, the numerous petitions of the 1930s, heavily influenced by either the left or the right, only aroused support from the most politicised academics. The scenario of the Dreyfus Affair, the game of petitions and counter-petitions, was therefore re-used in order to seduce the maximum number of intellectuals, but academics in the strict sense of the word were visibly reticent about enrolling behind causes that were more and more international in their implications and concerns (for example, Ethiopia or Spain) or which had been 'exploited' by the various political parties that confronted each other so bitterly at the time.

The Algerian war marks the culmination of this tendency towards a decline in the model of the intellectual established by the Dreyfus Affair. Academics in general had great difficulty in fully comprehending a war where the conflict of values was so complex and where conventional schemas did not easily apply, and it was out of this that there arose some surprising affiliations.[20] Even if we add together the number of signatories on the two most important petitions published in 1960, one supporting French Algeria and the other (sponsored by the *Fédération de l'Education nationale*) peace in Algeria, one discovers that, with the exception of the faculty of arts, they succeeded in mobilising only a few isolated individuals: 16 for French Algeria in the four principal faculties out of a total of more than 400 tenured staff (3.8 per cent) and 25 for peace in Algeria (5.9 per cent). What this statistical evidence indicates is that we are now arriving at the end of a historical cycle we set out to describe. The model of the intellectual will remain alive (as an image if not a reality) for a further fifteen years at least but, in contrast with its period of emergence, the Parisian academic will figure less and less as a point of reference, and this for several reasons: the ageing of the teaching profession, growing specialisation and a decline in internal sociability, to the advantage of wider forms of association.

The Persistence of Divisions

If, however, we abandon this perspective, with its pessimistic conclusions, for a more structural analysis of relative continuities of behaviour, then the persistence of the divisions first brought to light during the Dreyfus Affair seem obvious. So, for example, the teachers of medicine, who at the time of the Dreyfus Affair had leaned slightly to the left, had definitely gone over to the conservative camp by the time of the 1920s. Thus the opposition between the vocational faculties and the scholarly faculties, analysed by Pierre Bourdieu in *Homo Academicus*[21] and which Kant referred to as the right and left of the parliament of knowledge, offers the most satisfactory key to an interpretation of those petitions under consideration. When the cause championed was patriotic, nationalist or conservative, it was professors of law and of medicine who committed themselves; when it was pacifist, left-wing or in defence of the oppressed, it was the academics in the faculty of arts and, to a lesser extent, in the faculty of science and the *Collège de France* who were the most numerous.

Thus 31.8 per cent of academics teaching medicine and 21.2 per cent of those teaching law endorsed the manifesto supporting the Rif war; by contrast respectively only 14.2 per cent and 12.2 per cent of academics in the faculties of science and of arts did so. Similarly, in one way or another between 13.3 per cent and 36.3 per cent of those teaching medicine stood up for the policy of Mussolini in Ethiopia in the name of defending the West, something which not a single academic at the Sorbonne did. Conversely, republican Spain was supported by only one medicine professor and by not one single teacher of law. On the other hand, nine academics at the Sorbonne and three at the *Collège de France* signed a petition in its favour. Two years later six academics teaching law and two teaching medicine explicitly showed solidarity with Franco's Spain.

Twenty-four years later the same pattern was reproduced over Algeria. Out of the fifteen academics of the University of Paris who declared their support for French Algeria eight belonged to the faculties of medicine and of law. The arts and science sections of the Sorbonne provided at least twenty-one of the twenty-five Parisian signatures calling for peace in Algeria (compared with two jurists and one physician). This left/right polarisation, even when it had been attenuated by the decline in the model of the intellectual, proves therefore that upon each occasion that they were brought into play the systems of values operating reflected different conceptions of the university profession: worldly and attached to the established order and the nation in the case of law and medicine; more autonomous and attached to non-temporal values in the case of the sciences and, especially, the arts. However, this principle of professional and political classification is not sufficient to account for the logic that lay behind the taking of positions, because each faculty was to an extent split by this division. Even the faculty that was most consistently on the left and which remained most faithful to the Dreyfusard model, that of the arts, was not homogeneous. The expansion in university staff, coupled with the appearance of new disciplines, in effect introduced new grounds for conflict which reflected different conceptions of the relationship of the university to society: in science, between the applied and pure sciences; in the arts, between the classical disciplines and the social sciences; in medicine, between clinicians and researchers; in law between traditional jurists and the defenders of social and political science and so on.

If from this perspective one analyses the two petitions on Algeria one finds a more subtle difference between disciplines. Here we have extended the basis of our analysis to include provincial academics so as to ensure that the numbers involved are not too small. As at the time of the Dreyfus Affair the disciplines most represented, that is to say where the academics were most willing to commit themselves, were philosophy, psychology, history and geography: these four alone accounted for twenty of the sixty-one signatures scrutinised. Mathematicians and representatives of the experimental sciences (physics, astronomy, biology) only gave their signatures to the petition organised by the *Fédération de l'Education nationale.* The same applies for the social sciences: anthropology, sociology and political science. Conversely, the medical sciences and the traditional law disciplines (civil law, the history of law, and so on) are only to be found amongst the defenders of French Algeria. Of those academics specialising in classical literature and in archaeology, who as a result of their training were strongly attached to the Mediterranean world and to the presence of France overseas (some had previously taught in Algiers), all sided with French Algeria. Those teaching French, comparative or foreign literature signed up behind peace in Algeria. The historians and geographers were both more numerous and more divided, with six on the left and four on the right. The demarcation line between ancients and moderns, liberals and conservatives, decolonisers and nationalists split them into two. On the left one finds, not surprisingly, Charles-André Jullien and Ernest Labrousse, both long-time socialists, the Marxist geographers, Jean Dresch and Pierre George, the historian of Germany and of socialism, Jacques Droz, and Robert Mandrou, disciple of Lucien Febvre and director of studies at the *Ecole Pratique des Hautes Etudes*; on the right, the monarchist and historian of pre-revolutionary France, Roland Mousnier, and the geographer of traditional France, Roger Dion, and the modernists, François Bluche and F. Baure, both disciples of Mounsier.

CONCLUSION

The historical cycle that we have attempted to describe, that of the role of Parisian academics as intellectuals, can only be properly understood when placed in the context of university and, more generally, political life during this period of sixty years. It began before modern political parties had been formed and when the prestige associated with academic life was at its height. It came to an end as the university system entered a long crisis of adaptation and when political parties dominated political life. The room for intervention available to academics was therefore either reduced or turned towards other objectives, for example the reform and increasingly complex management of the universities. Those Parisian academics who, in the Fifth Republic, wished to play a role in national political life did not need to be local notables, as had been the case at the time of the Dreyfus Affair and between the wars. They could penetrate as far as the ante-chambers of power by becoming ministerial advisers or via any one of the numerous commissions and enquiries set up by government, sometimes going as far as to arrive at the very top. The career of Raymond Barre, a former professor of economics at the Paris law faculty who subsequently became prime minister, is the classic example of this.

The unequal propensity of the different categories of academic to adopt the role of the intellectual has already referred us to the unequal possibilities available to academics to perform alternative functions in society. The non-commitment of law professors, a constant throughout the entire period, was not merely an expression of the traditionalism of this self-recruiting body and of its professional respect for the established order, but of the greater frequency of political careers within its ranks. In 1928, for example, four full professors out of forty-seven had either been or were parliamentary deputies. In the same way the less prominent position of Sorbonne scientists in comparison with those in the arts disciplines is explicable in part by their concern, beyond partisan divisions, to further the broader interests of the scientific community in order that it might obtain from government (whatever its colour) or from other sources (individual patrons or private enterprise) the resources and funding increasingly demanded by modern science.

The decline in this form of public intervention by academics is finally related to the expansion of this social group itself. The symbolic power of academic titles appended to petitions designed to support a particular cause is not the same when they are held by several hundred, if not several thousand, individuals and not a few dozen. After the democracy of the intellectuals brought into existence by the Dreyfus Affair we have had to return, it could be said, in the age of the mass university to the restricted suffrage of celebrities who hold centre stage through their utilisation of the mass media.

But in history, and especially in intellectual and political history, the memory of outstanding moments can still have a political impact long after the social conditions which produced them have disappeared. Thus, at a recent conference on intellectuals and the Algerian war, an American historian showed how some of the methods and the tactics used by American academics against the war in Vietnam had been inspired by the struggle of French academics against the Algerian war.[22] But if they, like the great 'media' intellectuals who continue to want to exercise this magisterial role, threw themselves or throw themselves again into the battle it is because at the beginning of the century obscure academics set the example.

Notes

1. See J-P. Rioux and J-F. Sirinelli (eds), *La Guerre d'Algérie et les intellectuels français* (Paris, 1991).
2. See *Statistiques de l'enseignement supérieur (1889–1898)* (Paris, 1899); *Minerva* (Paris, 1936).
3. See *The World of Learning* (London, 1960–1).
4. See J-C. Caron, *Générations romantiques: Les étudiants de Paris et le Quartier latin (1814–1851)* (Paris, 1991).
5. See my doctoral thesis, *Intellectuels et élites en France (1880–1900)* (University of Paris I, 1986) and my *Naissance des «intellectuels»* (Paris, 1990).
6. G. Weisz, 'Associations et manifestations, les étudiants français de la Belle Epoque', *Le Mouvement social*, 1982, pp. 31–44.
7. See N. and J. Dhombres, *Naissance d'un nouveau pouvoir: sciences et savants en France, 1793–1824* (Paris, 1989) and J.Verger (ed.), *Histoire des Universités en France* (Toulouse, 1986). See also R. Fox and G. Weisz (eds), *The Organisation of Science and Technology (1808–1914)* (Cambridge, 1980); T. Shinn, 'The French Science Faculty System, 1808–1914: Institutional Change and Research Potential in Mathematics and the Physical Sciences', *Historical Studies in the Physical Sciences*, 10, 1979, pp. 271–332; R. Fox, 'Science, the University and the State in Nineteenth-Century France', in G. Geison (ed.), *Professions and the French State* (Philadelphia, 1984) pp. 66–145. Also to be recommended are the excellent biography written by M. Crosland, *Gay-Lussac, Scientist and Bourgeois* (Cambridge, 1978) and J.M. Burney, *Toulouse et son université, Facultés et étudiants dans la France du 19e siècle* (Paris, 1989). Finally see also my biographical dictionary: *Les professeurs de la Faculté des lettres de Paris (1809–1908)*, I (Paris, 1985).
8. See my *Les élites de la République (1880–1900)* (Paris, 1987) pp. 407–54.
9. See here the *Appel à l'Union* which appeared in *Le Temps*, February 1899.
10. E. Durkheim, 'L'individualisme et les intellectuels', *La Revue bleue*, 2, 1898, pp. 7–13.
11. See J-P. Rioux, *Nationalisme et conservatisme, La Ligue de la Patrie française* (Paris, 1977).
12. The *Ecole Pratique des Hautes Etudes*, founded in 1868, was split into five sections: mathematics, physics and chemistry, the natural sciences, history and philosophy, religious sciences.
13. For a discussion of the concept of a field of power see P. Bourdieu, *Distinction* (Cambridge, Mass, 1984).
14. The *Muséum d'histoire naturelle*, apart from its connections with the *Jardin des Plantes*, has attached to it various professorial chairs, all of them in the natural sciences.
15. C. Charle, 'Les étudiants et l'affaire Dreyfus', *Cahiers Georges Sorel*, 4, 1986, pp. 61–78.
16. The *Ecole nationale des Chartes*, established in 1821, was concerned principally to train archivists, librarians and specialists in palaeography.
17. On the concept of *habitus* see P. Bourdieu, *Outline of a Theory of Practice* (Cambridge, 1978).

18. See here the testimony of Ernest Labrousse, the man behind this petition, in 'Entretiens avec Ernest Labrousse' in C. Charle, *Actes de la recherche en sciences sociales*, 32–3, 1980, p. 120.
19. For example, Paul Appell who had been a fervent Dreyfusard in 1898.
20. See J-F. Sirinelli, 'Guerre d'Algérie, guerre des pétitions?', *Revue historique*, 565, 1988, pp. 73–100 and *Intellectuels et passions françaises* (Paris, 1991).
21. See P. Bourdieu, *Homo Academicus* (Oxford, 1988) pp. 62–3.
22. D. Schalk, 'Algérie et Vietnam', in J-P. Rioux and J-F. Sirinelli, *La Guerre d'Algérie et les intellectuels français* (Brussels, 1991) pp. 365–76.

6 Intellectuals, Pacifism and Communism: The Mandarins and the Struggle for Peace (1914–53)

Yves Santamaria

A matter of months before having to face up to the crisis engendered by the abortive August 1991 coup in the Soviet Union, the French Communist Party (PCF) believed itself capable of restoring at least part of its declining support by participating in the anti-war movement associated with the conflict in the Gulf. Despite the favourable signs created by opinion polls which indicated the existence of a strong pacifist sentiment, this initiative came to nothing, and this for the simple reason that, as with the previous campaign against the Euromissiles in the 1980s, it succeeded in evoking a wave of anti-Munich sentiment amongst what was probably a majority of France's intellectuals.[1] Not only did this episode illustrate both the importance and the limits of the autonomy enjoyed by the world of the intellectual in times of national crisis but it was also added proof of the divorce that had taken place between France's intelligentsia and communism.

This further setback for the PCF does, however, have a broader context in what since 1917 it has seen and described as *the struggle for peace*.[2] This campaign has taken a variety of different forms, but from the Treaty of Brest-Litovsk in 1918 through to the Korean war via support for the propositions put forward by Hitler in 1939 and later participation in the fight against imperialism, it has been, as Stéphane Courtois has shown, one of the principal means used to define the global relationship between the communist and non-communist worlds. Indeed, understanding this aspect of PCF strategy amounts to grasping the place it allots to war – either real or imagined – in the attainment of its overall revolutionary goal.

It is, moreover, within this perspective that the intellectual, placed alongside the working class, figures as a crucial element in what is perceived as an anti-war alliance. To the extent that he intervenes in public life the intellectual constitutes an element that has to be won over to the cause or, at worse, neutralised.[3] Thus, despite its heterogeneity and the inherent difficulties demonstrated by each successive attempt at mass organisation, the aim, if possible, has been to influence and control the environment inhabited by the intellectual. Just as significantly, it was from out of this universe that came the *compagnon de route* or fellow-traveller. Originally coined by Trotsky in October 1922 and used extensively in his *Literature and Revolution*, published in 1923, this term has since taken on a wider usage and meaning but in general it has been employed to describe those members of the intellectual community who, under the guidance of the Communist Party, were prepared to locate and interpret Marxism–Leninism as part of the tradition of European humanism and progressive thought.

On its own a horror of war, despite forming an important part of this vision, was clearly not sufficient to explain the endorsement by intellectuals of communism: in addition to a refusal to countenance the destruction of civilisation or the desire to be rid of the old world, other, more positive factors clearly played a part in engendering this fascination with Marxist doctrine. Nevertheless, beyond the fact that the struggle for peace has had a place at the heart of communist strategy, the approach adopted here to survey the links that have existed between the intelligentsia and the PCF has the added attraction that it can serve to clarify the relationship – beyond the narrow world of the intellectual – of French society as a whole with a conception of revolutionary violence that, as Jean-Paul Sartre remarked, like Achilles' spear is capable of healing the wounds that it makes.[4] The issue raised, in short, is that of the relationship of means – in this case violence – to ends.

THE RESPONSE TO 'IMPERIALIST CARNAGE' (1914–31)

What evidence, if any, is there to suggest that immediately prior to 1914, as with war in the Gulf, intellectuals in France were more ready to entertain the idea of war than were the public at large? Whilst conclusive proof is lacking it was nevertheless the case that alongside the gains made by the Socialist Party in the elections of April 1914 there was also a definite increase in patriotic sentiment evident not merely amongst the student population but also in a whole series of literary texts. Here, following historian Michel Winock, it is perhaps sufficient to cite Roger Martin du Gard's novel *Jean Barois*.[5] The hero, a former Dreyfusard, has his past conduct criticised by an emblematic representative of the new generation in these terms: 'This mandarin's existence, which leads to total inaction, is now repugnant to the new France, to the France threatened by Germany, to the France of the Agadir crisis.' The mandarins who were the targets of this invective quickly draped themselves in the folds of a Republic endangered by Prussian feudalism. In this respect the response of the *Ligue des Droits de l'Homme* (LDH) was typical. Led by Victor Basch, behind the awful reality of war it identified a holy war fought to secure the triumph of the ideas for which it had been formed in 1898. Similarly, on the eve of the Brest-Litovsk treaty it warned the Bolsheviks of the consequences of their actions. 'In siding with the Allies,' the LDH argued, 'you will bring forward the hour of democratic peace ... By consenting to a separate peace you will dishonour yourselves for ever.' Not surprisingly, the Bolsheviks regarded membership of the LDH as being incompatible with allegiance to the Comintern. Lenin for one found its moralising tone to be intolerable.

The Leninist reply to the arguments of President Wilson was brought together under the title of *Letter to American Workers*.[6] Extensively distributed by the PCF in the inter-war period it utilised the logic of capitalism and concentrated upon a cold-hearted calcula- tion of the likely costs and benefits of war. International imperialism, Lenin argued, had slaughtered millions of victims. 'If,' he went on, '*our war* ... results in half a million or a million casualities in all countries, the bourgeoisie will say that the former casualities are justified, while the latter are criminal. The proletariat will have something entirely different to say.' The Bolshevik leadership frequently used this argument in their attempts to win over those who, after the European cataclysm, were in search of radical solutions.

But was it the case that the vision of the cruiser *Aurore* bombarding the Winter Palace in the course of the Bolshevik Revolution was just as influential in determining the choices made by individuals as the memory of mass carnage? Certainly, for many of the early leaders of the PCF who came from intellectual backgrounds – for example, Boris Souvarine and the schoolteacher Albert Treint – their involvement in the conflict, as they themselves testified, constituted a vital landmark in their political evolution. And here, from Raymond Lefebvre to Paul Vaillant-Couturier, even a superficial glance at Jean Maitron's *Dictionnaire du Mouvement ouvrier français* reveals numerous other similar cases. However, whilst we cannot ignore the importance of this communism born at the Front we have to agree with Nicole Racine that the theme of violence, stressed by communists at the outset to characterise the means of revolutionary action, 'was the issue that evoked the greatest opposition'. Concluding a recent article entitled 'Pacifisme, socialisme et communisme naissant'[7] she asserts that 'pacifism provided both a route of access into communism as well as a barrier to its influence'. As we have already seen, the attitude of the Bolsheviks was met by incomprehension on the part of the LDH and this, as Victor Serge recalled in his memoirs,[8] was even more the case amongst the French working class.

The 3rd Congress of the Communist (Third) International, held in December 1921, recognised that this was the case. In France reaction against the war developed more slowly than it did in other countries. And so, for example, the sense and joy of victory was such as to produce a pacifism built around a defence of the status quo that was both objectively anti-Bolshevik and paradoxically in harmony with the positions endorsed by Romain Rolland. Even if at the time a young intellectual such as Jean de Saint-Prix could place the author of *Jean-Christophe*, with its sympathetic portrayal of German culture, on a par with Trotsky,[9] it is quite clear that the former did not share the same vision of the world as the chief of the Red Army. An advocate of franco-german reconciliation, Rolland had also been heavily influenced by the example of Gandhi and he could not therefore but distance himself from the Leninist position. Moreover, his stance was such as in late 1921 to invite a personal attack – to which he replied the following year in *L'Art Libre* – penned by Henri Barbusse in the pages of *Clarté*.

An army volunteer at the age of forty one the pacifist Barbusse made his name with the publication in 1916 of *Le Feu, journal d'une escouade*. The result of eleven months spent at the Front, this controversial work enjoyed an enormous success. However, after joining Raymond Lefebvre and Paul Vaillant-Couturier in establishing the *Association Républicaine des Anciens Combattants* (ARAC) in 1917, Barbusse progressively moved from a support of President Wilson's peace proposals to Bolshevism. When in 1921 the *Clarté* movement, created in 1919 as an international organisation of anti-war intellectuals, set up its own periodical he had already joined the new Communist Party formed the previous year at the Congress of Tours.

Likewise the review owed much to the influence of Raymond Lefevbre, whose mysterious disappearance at sea on his return from the 2nd Congress of Communist International the previous year had generated considerable debate and controversy. His death occurred shortly after his remarkable speech at the Strasbourg Congress of the Socialist Party in February 1920. There this brilliant former student of the *Ecole libre des Sciences politiques*, who in the past had been influenced by the monarchist *Action française* and by Tolstoy, spoke out – as a survivor of the war – in the name of the 'massacred generation' before some of the very people who had defended the *Union sacrée*.

His former fellow pupil at the prestigious *Lycée Janson-de-Sailly*, Paul Vaillant-Couturier, had also like him (and like so many others) seen death at close quarters. Although he himself did not devote the greater part of his efforts to the review – he was to be heavily involved as the PCF's spokesman on intellectual affairs – his participation was such as to contribute to a general tone that was closer to humanist indignation and outrage than it was to orthodox Marxist analyses of recent events in terms of the final stage of capitalism.[10] Whilst references to Marxism cannot be ignored completely, read today the overriding impression created by the articles published in *Clarté* is one of bitterness suffered in isolation but mixed with a sense of fraternity. Such sentiments are evident in the numerous passages where, for example, it is regretted that the combattants 'had not taken the opportunity to march 50 kilometres in order to hang the government, shooting a few generals on the way'. At the same time, however, the contributors to the pages of *Clarté* also recognised that they represented at best a 'much-despised handful of survivors' whose 'crime' was still to feel strongly about the slaughter that had occurred.

This sense of distance from public opinion was to an extent diminished by the support given to the review by Anatole France, then at the height of his fame. Coming after the espousal of an ardently patriotic position in the first years of the war, France then played an important role in the campaigns against military intervention in Russia and against the Treaty of Versailles. The latter had been especially evident in his speech accepting the award of the Nobel Prize for literature in 1921. Above all he was to be the man who coined the phrase – endlessly repeated by communist propaganda and published first in *L'Humanité* on 18 July 1922 – to the effect that: 'we thought that we were dying for the homeland; we were dying for the industrialists'. Four years earlier he had defended André Marty, condemned after his part in the mutiny of the French Black Sea Fleet sent to aid the counter-revolutionaries in Russia, and even after he had distanced himself from the communist movement in 1923 he remained true to his pacifist ideals. Nevertheless, with his death in 1924, *Clarté* did not hesitate to criticise France. Under the title 'Contre Anatole France, Cahier de l'Anti-France' Jean Bernier, Edouard Berth, Marcel Fourrier and Georges Michael denounced in France an author whose prestige was such as to constitute the grounds for the formation of a new *'Union sacrée'*, praise being heaped upon him from the recently formed centrist and socialist *Bloc des gauches* as well as from *Action française.*[11]

Following on shortly after *Clarté's* protest at the unanimity of emotion that had accompanied the death of nationalist writer Maurice Barrès in 1923 this denunciation of Anatole France – described in a telegram sent by *Pravda* to *L'Humanité* as 'the outstanding representative of capitalist art' – stood as the high-water mark of their assault upon bourgeois culture, and was clearly intended to embrace even its supposedly 'left-wing' form. Moreover, if it lacked the tact displayed by such figures as Barbusse and communist Marcel Cachin towards France, it was in line with the stance of 'class independence' adopted by the Communist Party at the time of the 1924 elections and which had seen the PCF's *Bloc Ouvrier et Paysan* pitted against what it saw as the two sections of the bourgeoisie, the *Bloc national* and the *Bloc des gauches*. What explained this hatred towards what the members of the *Clarté* group regarded as the various 'hotbeds of humanism' was not just the experience of war but their conviction that these events had exposed the decadence of the West. In this they shared the sentiments of Romain Rolland. Just as significantly, it also announced a rejection of the figure of the *artist*, henceforth discredited by his chauvinism and his outdated aestheticism, and the emergence of a *new type of intellectual*.

But did this mean that in someone like Barbusse one could find the lineaments of a pre-Gramscian theory of the 'collective' intellectual as Jean Relinger has recently argued?[12] Here the position is more complex than it might appear because beyond the calls to the 'manual and intellectual workers', typical of his anti-war activities, one also finds in Barbusse a constant mistrust and suspicion of those he frequently characterised as the ignorant multitude. In addition this ambiguous, if not contradictory, response to the literary transcription of the Leninist model of the relationship between the masses and the avant-garde was also evident in his attitude towards the leaders of the various anti-war campaigns. By the side of the intellectual–worker stood the sage, the guide, the enlightened, with Anatole France himself cast in the role of 'the most admired and revered figure of French letters'.

Such veneration for France did not, however, find support amongst the writers who made up the newly-formed surrealist group. In October 1924 six of its members – Louis Aragon, André Breton, Joseph Deltail, Pierre Drieu La Rochelle, Paul Eluard and Philippe Soupault – published a pamphlet entitled *Un Cadavre* in which, to great controversy, they decreed the second death of the former Dreyfusard. At the same time, however, Aragon made it plain that he did not expect much of the Russian Revolution, speaking in the same breath of a 'senile Moscow' and the 'swinelike Maurras'. In July 1925, the same group, all members of the First World War generation, sent a letter to dramatist and diplomat Paul Claudel expressing the desire that 'revolutions, wars and colonial uprisings will annihilate this Western civilisation whose vermin you are protecting in the East'. But for them the turning-point and the step to commitment came that summer.

In Morocco the Rif war, pitting the French Republic against rebel leader Abd-el-Krim, allowed Henri Barbusse to launch a series of calls for united action, in the process asking France's 'intellectual workers': 'yes or no, do you condemn the war?' The response came on 2 July 1925, in the pages of *L'Humanité* and in the shape of a petition placing them 'by the side of the proletariat against the war in Morocco'. Along with the names of the editorial board of *Clarté* were also to be found those of the surrealists as well as those of various personnalities associated with the pacifist intellectual left, such as Henri Jeanson, Victor Margueritte and Marcel Martinet. Without wishing to underestimate its importance, it should be said that this episode did, however, serve to demonstrate the limited extent of the support that existed for the ideas of pacifist communism. Barbusse's initiative not only produced a counter-petition, published in *Le Figaro* and bringing together many of the leading figures of the scientific and literary Establishment, but it also failed to gather the requested support of such as the LDH's Victor Basch.[13]

The relative lack of success of this undertaking did not, though, generate the scorn of the Communist International. In 1922, Lenin had lectured his People's Commissar for Foreign Affairs, Chicherin, to the effect that: 'You and I have fought against pacifism as a part of the programme of a proletarian revolutionary party. That's clear enough. But has anyone ever denied that our party can use pacifists as a means of breaking up the bourgeoisie?' The same year Karl Radek, if he warned against the temptation of forming an alliance with 'a fraction of the liberal bourgeoisie suffering from the malady of pacifism', also recognised that in terms of potential tactical support it was necessary to distinguish between those 'pacifists who represented elements of the bourgeoisie truly disgusted by war' and those who represented 'intellectuals tired by war'. Nevertheless it was only after the diplomatic crises of 1926–7 that the Communist International began a systematic policy designed to gather support from these quarters.

As Moscow abandoned its line of the struggle for peace in order to replace it with a new campaign against imperialist war,[14] so the number of initiatives or front organisations directed at intellectuals multiplied. Behind them often stood the remarkable figure of the German Willi Münzenberg. After the formation of the *Ligue contre l'Impérialisme et l'oppression coloniale*, whose first conference was held in Brussels in February 1927, there came in December of that year the *Amis de l'URSS*. Whilst intellectuals were not specifically designated as the target, the latter was placed under the direction of Barbusse, Panaït Istrati and architect Francis Jourdain. It was soon to enjoy the support of Romain Rolland. Moscow's obsession with the threat of imminent war and the insistent call to defend the USSR was matched by Rolland's recognition, in the pages of the fellow-travelling *Libération*, that Russia was in danger. He was not subsequently to waiver from this position. The same year Barbusse launched his new journal, *Monde*, intended as a forum for intellectual debate.

Thus Moscow's tactics did have a limited success. But it was only limited. In the discussions about French security that took place at the time of the Geneva conference of the League of Nations in 1926, Soviet declarations in favour of total disarmament were received with little enthusiasm, if not scepticism. Likewise the signing of the Briand–Kellogg Pact in 1928 by the Soviet Union and its simultaneous condemnation by the Communist International engendered incomprehension. Certainly, then, up to 1930 the various initiatives directed by the communist movement towards the pacifist intelligentsia largely ended in failure.

THE FIGHT AGAINST FASCISM (1932–45)

If henceforth, in the eyes of Stalin, it was to be Paris that was regarded as the capital of the warmongers it was from Japan, an ally of France, that in 1931 came the real threat. Thus it was the invasion of Manchuria and then, in February 1932, the creation of the nominally independent state of Manchukuo that lay behind the first really serious attempt to defend the USSR, the Amsterdam Congress against imperialist war, attended by between 2000 and 3000 delegates, of whom over 500 were from France. Presented subsequently by communist historiography as the first sign of the Popular Front it was in reality, and as the private notebooks of communist leader Marcel Cachin make crystal-clear, an attempt to rally opinion against the League of Nations and against the Socialists. Preparations for the Congress were accompanied in France by the setting up in March 1932 of the *Association des Ecrivains et Artistes Révolutionnaires* (AEAR). Again the tone was set by the passing of a resolution, inspired by Vaillant-Couturier, condemning war and fascism, whose impeccable orthodoxy was such as not to recommend it to a wider audience of sympathisers. 'We,' it declared, 'who today hold a pen and who tomorrow will carry a rifle. . . . we will fight with the proletariat through the most self-conscious and well-organised defeatism to transform imperialist war into civil war.'

The tactics of the communists, in short, were characterised by the desire to make use of the potential afforded by intellectuals. And this was something that was clearly articulated. Guy Jerram, for example, informed the Party's Central Committee, on 4 June 1932, that the task was 'to bring into existence, through the cover provided by intellectuals, organisations based in the war and transport industries and in the ports'. The time, in other words, seemed right for the implementation of the programme sketched out by Barbusse before the Soviet Commissar for Public Instruction, Lunacharsky: 'the practical and logically organised association of the intellectual and artistic worlds with the policies pursued by the International'.

But even in those sections of the PCF with specific responsibility for intellectual affairs the tactic of subordination engendered an element of misunderstanding and confusion that was especially evident with regard to the Amsterdam Congress and the attitude to be adopted towards the journal, *Monde*. For the intelligentsia Barbusse's review was the principal vehicle of the pro-Amsterdam campaign but it was the object of considerable suspicion and criticism from a party press (for example, the *Cahiers du Bolchévisme*) that was largely ignorant of Barbusse's real standing. The latter's untouchability and independence, in effect, derived from his contacts with those at the very summit of the communist movement. Marcel Cachin's notebooks, for example, indicate that in January 1933 Stalin informed Barbusse that the three principal axes of his 'intellectual labour' should be: '1) do not be a communist 2) remain within the law 3) speak about other things than the USSR'. Moreover, Barbusse's talents as a political manoeuvrer were such as to attract veiled hostility from other sources. This was especially the case with Romain Rolland, with whom Barbusse worked very closely in preparing the Amsterdam Congress. Writing to his sister he commented: 'You must understand that with a reptilian creature such as B[arbusse] one must always use the same fork if one wants to stop the beast from escaping'.

Whatever judgement one might make of Barbusse's character, however, it has to be admitted that the achievements of this opening towards intellectuals were much more impressive than earlier such attempts. Circumstances undoubtedly played a part and here the atmosphere of pessimism, evident in the personal accounts of the period that are now available and above all in Louis-Ferdinand Céline's emblematic and influential novel, *Voyage au bout de la nuit*, was crucial. The sense of concern and impending catastrophe, visible at the Geneva Disarmament Conference and heightened by the situation in Germany, was such as to encourage expressions of support, most notably from writers André Gide and Jean-Richard Bloch. The latter case was all the more significant, given that in the past he had always rejected Barbusse's numerous advances.

The impact of the Amsterdam Congress upon intellectual opinion was also discernible in the reaction of the *Ligue des Droits de l'Homme*, a body, as we know, broadly representative of a wide section of France's intellectuals. Whilst its leadership, in the person of Salomon Grumbach, continued to be insulted by the communist press, the membership of the *Ligue* proved responsive to the calls for a conference signed by Rolland and Barbusse. Faced with this situation the LDH decided to send a representative to Amsterdam before finally authorising individual membership of the movement it gave rise to, the *Comité contre la Guerre et le Fascisme*. Advocates of participation in the organisation were able to group themselves around a committed pacifist core led by Félicien Challaye (then a close friend of Rolland's) and Armand Charpentier and were also to receive support from a crypto-communist element associated with the Secretary of the French section of the Women's International League for Peace and Freedom, Gabrielle Duchêne.

If at the time of the right-wing riots of February 1934 the Amsterdam–Pleyal movement (so-called because its second congress was held at the Salle Pleyal in Paris) gave ample proof of its ineffectiveness it nevertheless continued, under the concealed guidance of the PCF, in its efforts to bring together all those forces hostile to the extra parliamentary Leagues – the *Jeunesses Patriotes*, the *Croix de Feu* and so on – taken to support both Hitler and French imperialism. In this crisis the Communist Party, under instruction from Moscow, abandoned its strategy of 'class against class' but refused to give priority in its policies to intellectuals, preferring rather to build a United Front at the level of the workers through its own communist-controlled trade union organisation, the CGTU.

It was, however, from amongst intellectuals that came the principal anti-fascist organisation, the *Comité de Vigilance des Intellectuels Antifascistes* (CVIA), so named despite the efforts of Paul Langevin (vice-president of the LDH and increasingly a PCF sympathiser) to have the word 'intellectual' omitted from its title. Initially the PCF attempted to direct anti-fascist activity around its own mass organisation – Amsterdam-Pleyel – but given the lack of success it was obliged to counternance entry into a movement – through the infiltration of its elected governing committee, for example – that, under the patronage of pacifist philosopher Alain, sought 'to save France from an oppressive régime and the misery of war'.

From the outset, then, for the CVIA the struggles for peace and against fascism were intimately connected and this was understood to mean that it was to be the fight against the internal enemy that took precedence, with French imperialism being seen in the same light as German expansionism. This placing of Paris and Berlin on an equal footing was clearly not a position that the PCF could accept for long, especially as it was about to begin a process of revising its policy of national defence that would lead in December 1936 to a vote approving France's military budget. The unity of the CVIA was first shattered in May 1935, following Stalin's breathtaking announcement of support for France's security requirements, thus opening up the way for another *Union sacrée*. After this, despite the facade of unity, the PCF attempted to set up a *Centre international de liaison et de défense des intellectuels* designed to offset the pacifism of the CVIA but this, like the equivalent *Centre de Documentation antiguerrière*, had little impact. Rather opportunely the invasion of Ethiopia re-forged agreement amongst the ranks of the anti-fascists as the threat of war with Italy forced them into a battle of petitions, their own, in the name of '*écrivains et artistes français*' and headed by novelist and playwright Jules Romains, responding to that of Mussolini's supporters describing themselves as '*Intellectuels français pour la paix en Europe et la défense de l'Occident*'.

Discord, however, re-surfaced with Hitler's re-militarisation of the Rhinelend in March 1936. No one, given the proximity of parliamentary elections, was in favour of the use of armed intervention but discussion centred upon the merits or otherwise of a policy of collective security (and, to a broader extent, on whether war was inevitable) and this necessarily raised the issue of the Franco-Soviet military alliance. Finding themselves in a minority and conscious that they could not reverse its anti-war stand, in June the communists resigned from the CVIA's governing committee.

At this time, however, the communist movement nourished greater ambitions of forging unity through the International Peace Campaign, yet another fellow-travelling body produced by the fertile imagination of Willi Münzenberg. Corresponding to a new line of policy applied equally to Germany and Italy as to the remaining democracies, the emphasis fell upon defending what was broadly defined as a culture under threat from the impending cataclysm. Within this vast projected international front opponents of appeasement such as Churchill and Paul Reynaud were deemed to be far more important than the leadership of a movement of intellectuals paralysed by the mortal contradiction between pacifism and anti-fascism. In Paris the pro-communist daily *Ce Soir* was launched, as the communist historian Danielle Tartakowsky has remarked, in order to undertake 'the conquest of a public opinion blinded by pacifism'.[15] 'The petit-bourgeois,' Maurice Thorez explained before the Communist International in September 1936, 'fear Hitler because they still remember the great victory and they do not want to see this victory compromised. They could be capable of nationalism but this sentiment clashes with the desire to preserve the peace.'

The middle classes were not, however, alone in being contaminated by the 'pacifist depression'. Intellectuals, on this view, shared what Thorez described as their 'timorous nature' and this, in the PCF's eyes, was confirmed when in 1937 the leading elements of the CVIA began to forge an alliance with the anti-communist wing of the *Confédération Générale du Travail* gravitating around René Belin and his *Syndicats* group. Nevertheless, despite this general mood and the reticence to contemplate going to war amongst the intelligentsia, there remained in certain quarters a very real admiration for what from a distance were seen as heroic courses of action. Beyond the obvious example of republican Spain, the LDH displayed an undeniable fascination for what it clearly took to be a Soviet version of Jacobinism and this at the time of the Moscow show trials. Indeed, in October 1936, a report commissioned by the *Ligue* and written by Raymond Rosenberk concluded that the accused were guilty! Thus the split that occurred in 1937 within the LDH brought two kinds of blindness to light. As Christian Jelen as shown,[16] whilst a horror of Hitlerism led the majority of the members of the LDH to fail to recognise the reality of the Bolshevik system, the ultra-pacifism of men such as Léon Emery and Michel Alexandre, if it did at least give them a clear picture of Stalin, led them to turn a blind eye towards the Nazi regime.

After this the positions taken remained fixed until the outbreak of war. The German invasion of Austria saw *Ce Soir* publish an appeal to national unity, probably inspired by the PCF, and signed by, amongst others, Georges Bernanos, Henry de Montherlant, François Mauriac, André Malraux and Jules Romains. To this the pacifist current responded with a counter-appeal under the title of *Refus de penser en choeur*, signed by Alain, André Breton, Jean Giono and others keen to deny the threat of imminent invasion.[17] The final organisational phase of the Communist International's attempts to consolidate support around the struggle for peace followed on from the Munich Agreement. Without renouncing earlier initiatives such as the *Comité contre la Guerre et le Fascisme*, a new structure, the *Union des intellectuels français pour la justice, la liberté et la paix* (UDIF), was created. On 30 August 1939, a week after the signing of the Nazi–Soviet pact, the UDIF erupted, its most eminent members (including Frédéric and Irène Joliot-Curie and Paul Langevin) expressing their 'stupefaction before the *volte-face* which has reconciled the leaders of the USSR with the Nazi leaders'.

Not without some justification, David Caute has argued that the atmosphere of war led to far more defections from the Communist Party amongst intellectuals in France than it did amongst British and American fellow travellers.[18] The PCF's most notable loss was the resignation of Paul Nizan. Certainly, to the extent that it could be heard from its new position of illegality, the campaign of the French section of the Third International in support of the struggle for peace whilst the pact was in operation met with little comprehension amongst the intelligentsia. Here the letter sent to Prime Minister Edouard Herriot immediately after the crushing of Poland requesting a discussion of the Soviet–German peace proposals did little to help the situation. Despite an increase in communist support amongst the student population, evident in the autumn of 1940, it was only in the summer of 1941, and with the German attack upon the Soviet Union, that this trend was reversed. But could one then really speak of the struggle for peace?

'PEACE' OR 'LIBERTY'? (1945–53)

'Drunk with glory and with sorrow', to cite Jeannine Verdès-Leroux, post-1945 the PCF benefited greatly from the 'Stalingrad effect' and from the respect accorded to its 'martyrs' in the Resistance. Without doubt the sudden appearance of American modernity was not an insignificant attraction and even in the pro-communist press – for example, in the journal *Action*, where an article entitled 'J'aime les Américains' was published by Claude Roy[19] – it was in evidence. American military presence on French soil was not without its opponents but the first graffiti demanding 'US go home' found little immediate support in the writings of the time. However, for the intellectual generation born out of the Resistance and for that about to reach adulthood, the attractions of Hollywood, of Chet Baker and of Lucky Strike could not rival the general atmosphere of pro-Soviet sentiment. As proof of the strength of this climate it is perhaps sufficient to cite Simone de Beauvoir's *La Force des choses* and the description she there provides of the attitude she shared with Sartre. 'There were,' she writes, 'no reservations in our friendship for the USSR; the sacrifices of the Russian people had proved that its leaders embodied its true wishes. It was therefore easy, on every level, to cooperate with the Communist Party.'

In September 1947, in response to the Marshall Plan and the Truman Doctrine, Stalin created the Cominform, the Communist Information Bureau. The analysis of the international situation provided by its organiser, André Zhdanov, clearly found a resonance in the preoccupations of an important section of France's intelligentsia, especially those either disappointed by the post-Liberation period or eager to follow in the steps of the Resistance. The resolution presented at the Cominform's inaugural meeting defined its role as that of organising the struggle against American plans to enslave Europe and, to that end, the various communist parties were allotted the task of 'bringing together the friends of peace and all democratic and antifascist forces in the fight against the new plans for war and aggression'.

It seems evident that this Cold War vision informed the motives of Charles Tillon, a member of the PCF's political bureau, when in November 1947 he made contact with some of the leading personalities of the Resistance, including the writer Vercors and Emmanuel d'Astier de la Vigerie. Three months later, in February 1948, the *Combattants de la liberté* put out a call to all those united against the occupier. In the name of national independence they rejected American proposals for the economic and military re-building of Germany. Moreover – and as with the 1930s – concern about the re-activation of fascism abroad was matched by the desire internally to support the republican régime and the intention 'to prevent the return of fascism and of dictatorship'.[20] Given the similarity between the objectives of the *Combattants* and those of the Cominform, as well as the presence amongst its ranks of such dependable fellow-travellers as novelist Roger Vailland and the Abbé Boulier, it is not surprising that the PCF progressively gained control of the movement. The stages of this process were, in fact, easily discernible in the successive changes of its title, the *Combattants de la liberté et de la paix* eventually being superseded by the *Combattants de la paix*.

An even more important stage in the establishment of communist hegemony was achieved when the World Congress for Peace met at Wroclaw in Poland in August 1948. With this was successfully realised the project that had always met with failure in the inter-war years of bringing together different national groups at an international level and in a situation where the communists could exercise maximum influence. Led by Laurent Casanova, the member of the PCF's political bureau responsible for intellectuals, the composition of the French delegation could not but have pleased the party's leadership. Out of twenty-seven members, sixteen were communists and amongst these was biologist Marcel Prenant, the renowned former leader of the *Francs Tireurs et Partisans* (for which he suffered at the hands of the Gestapo), who personally constituted a point of intersection between the PCF's Central Committee, the Resistance and the world of the University. Whilst there they all had the pleasure of witnessing the bravura performance of the president of the Soviet delegation, Alexander Fadayev. 'If,' Fadayev proclaimed, 'jackals could learn to type and if hyenas knew how to write what they would produce would undoubtedly resemble the books of Miller, Eliot, Malraux and of Sartre.'

The integration of the French *Combattants* into the international movement occurred at the second world congress, held in Paris in

April 1949. The withdrawal of both Jean-Paul Sartre and David Rousset, co-founder of the *Rassemblement démocratique révolutionnaire*, was in part eclipsed by the support received from Charlie Chaplin and singer Paul Robeson but above all – in a brilliant publicity coup on the part of Laurent Casanova – it was Pablo Picasso's white dove, conceived as the rally's symbol and first distributed through the pages of *Les Lettres françaises* on 24 March, that gave a mark of distinction to the congress and which seemed to indicate that it would have a durable impact.

A further success for Casanova was the acceptance by Nobel Chemistry prize winner, Frédéric Joliot-Curie, of the presidency of the movement.[21] This distinction was all the more appreciated by the communists given that Soviet approval of Lysenko's genetic theories was running the risk of creating a breach with the scientific community. High Commissioner of the Commissariat for Atomic Energy, Joliot-Curie further developed the thesis already popularised by Maurice Thorez in response to the question: 'what would you do if the Red Army were to occupy Paris?' Before the XIIth Congress of the PCF, Joliot-Curie proclaimed: 'never will progressive scientists, never will communist scientists, give any of their science for war to be made against the Soviet Union'. Less than a month later, in April 1950, to great controversy, he was dismissed from his post by the government. Beyond the personal misfortune involved, however, the significance of Joliot-Curie's action – he was later to take part in the creation of the anti-war Pugwash movement in 1955 – was to draw attention to the direction taken by the communist-controlled peace movement in France: henceforth, even in its title, it abandoned any reference to liberty.

'A beautiful girl easily seduced': such in effect was the conception of liberty held by Marxist philosopher and party spokesman Roger Garaudy, a witness in the case brought by Victor Kravchenko against the communist weekly *Les Lettres françaises* and which opened in January 1949 in Paris.[22] The success of Soviet defector Kravchenko's *J'ai choisi la Liberté* (approximately 500 000 copies were sold in France alone) was itself testimony to the resurgence of liberal values at the very time that the author of *J'écris ton nom, Liberté*, the poet Paul Eluard, joined the Greek partisans on Mount Grammos in their defence of 'world peace'. The opposing camp happily took up the theme forsaken by the apologists of the new Popular Democracies in Eastern Europe. The gaullist *Rassemblement du Peuple Français* launched its monthly journal, *Liberté de l'esprit* (with the participation of Claude Mauriac, Raymond Aron, Jules Monnerot, André Malraux and Roger Caillois) as the trial was in full swing, whilst in Berlin the review *Preuves* – with American financial help – organised a *Congrès pour la Liberté de la Culture* supported by Benedetto Croce, John Dewey, Karl Jaspers and Bertrand Russell. These iniatives directed towards intellectuals found their popular counterpart in the anti-communist movement, *Paix et Liberté*, set up in September 1950 and which used the exact name of one of the journals set up by Amsterdam–Pleyel in the 1930s.

The battle enjoined by the PCF against Kravchenko was fought therefore under the banner of the struggle against the warmongers, a strategy which saw appear in court the former founder of the *Rassemblement Universel pour la Paix*, Pierre Cot, as well as Joliot-Curie, future winner of the Stalin peace prize. In order to entertain those accused by Kravchenko a dinner was organised at *La Coupole*, one of the great meeting places of intellectuals, where, in the presence of Soviet General Rudenko, 197 guests followed Aragon, Eluard, Vercors and Elsa Triolet in swearing not to fight against the USSR.

Amongst Parisian *clercs* the trial and the reply it evoked from the communists engendered a typically ambiguous response. If Sartre, in *Les Temps modernes*, was soon to acknowledge the existence of the Soviet labour camp system he also let it be known that he had no desire to allot himself a rôle in the 'campaign of preparation for war'. By the same token, whilst Camus published the anti-Marxist *L'Homme révolté* in 1951, Sartre was not prepared to allow himself to be thrown into confusion by what he regarded as the 'imbecilic duel of two abject worlds'.

However, signs of disenchantment flourished all the more easily, given that the recent Soviet condemnation of the 'belligerent acts and war propaganda of the Tito government' had induced several defections from the ranks of the fellow travellers. In January 1950 novelist Jean Cassou resigned from the *Combattants de la paix*, soon to be followed by Jean-Marie Domenach. This episode, as revealing as it is about the absence of autonomy in the peace movement, is, though, of only limited significance when placed beside the most remarkable communist initiative for peace, the Stockholm Appeal.

The text was first made public on 16 March 1950. Quickly distributed throughout the world, it demanded 'the complete banning of atomic weapons' and affirmed the necessity of 'rigorous international control'. Describing their potential utiliser as a 'war criminal' it further invited 'all men of good will' to sign the appeal. Given that the

USSR at the time had already acquired the incriminating weapon, as well as its general defiance on the question of control, it is hard to discern the motives behind this strategy – perhaps they related to short-term necessities (it was the eve of the Korean crisis) or to Stalin's thesis on the substitution of inter-imperialist conflicts for the East–West clash – but the fact remains that it aroused considerable enthusiasm. To limit ourselves to the French case, the figure of approximately ten million signatures represented a remarkable achievement. In the university world the breakthrough was particularly noticeable in sectors that had been untouched by the Cominform's earlier campaigns. Finally, after the International Committee of the Red Cross, it was the turn of France's cardinals and archbishops who, on 20 June 1950, declared that 'in this nightmarish atmosphere the Stockholm Appeal has attracted very many well-intentioned people'.

The crossing, on 25 June, of the 38th parallel by North Korean troops, if it increased the anxieties of Catholic consciences, again unleashed the energies of activists. Moreover, in its campaign for a victorious peace the PCF was not totally isolated. Whilst completely accepting the reality of North Korean aggression, *L'Observateur*, a journal broadly representative of the progressive intellectual left, on 29 June drew attention to the ineluctability of the Korean 'revolution', given both the international environment and the 'shameful police dictatorship of Syngman Rhee'.[23] Neutralism amongst intellectuals was further, and paradoxically, reinforced by the fear – expressed notably by André Fontaine of *Le Monde* – that a massive American military commitment in what was thought to be a peripheral theatre of operations would be accompanied by a reduction on the principal front, Europe. The concern at being abandoned was itself an important element of the general climate. Whereas, for example, *Samedi soir* responded in a positive frame of mind to its headline asking 'Should we be frightened?', Maurice Duverger on 14 July spoke in *Le Monde* of a 'Europe in distress' and Simone de Beauvoir was later to recall in her memoirs, *La Force des choses*, that 'in Paris it was total panic'. The same work, however, also bears witness to the coexistence – widespread amongst French opinion – of both the fear of being isolated and of anti-Americanism. Talking to Albert Camus of the American GIs she had recently seen de Beauvoir recounts the following exchange: 'I really felt,' she remarked, 'that I was back in the Occupation.' To which, in astonishment, Camus replied: 'Wait a little while. You'll see a real Occupation soon – a different sort altogether'.

Certainly the impact of neutralist and pacifist sentiments amongst intellectuals must not be over-exaggerated. As Raymond Aron makes plain in his own *Mémoires*, 'with the exception of the communists American intervention was not severely criticised . . . at least at the time'. However, the Korean war gave rise to another issue of controversy. As a guarantee of American commitment to the Old World, NATO decided to set up its headquarters in Europe under General Eisenhower and this implied French acceptance of German participation in the defence of the West. Immediately afterwards, in January 1951, the *Combattants de la paix* attempted to exploit their success of the previous year by launching another campaign. This, not surprisingly, received the support of the PCF's political bureau which announced that 'at the present time the fundamental task in the fight to defend peace is the collection of millions of signatures protesting against German rearmament'. Only eleven days later, on 17 February, an interview with Stalin that appeared in *Pravda* brought everything to a sudden halt. No, Stalin declared, war was not inevitable; yes, a peace agreement was possible between the five great powers. Opening the way to 'peaceful co-existence' the words of the 'Great Leader' dealt a significant blow to the energies of the French movement. The *Combattants de la paix*, for example, saw itself obliged to re-direct its efforts behind a campaign for a superpower pact which to many seemed far removed from their immediate concerns, most notably the war in Indo-China.

In the absence of party leader Maurice Thorez (undergoing hospital treatment in Moscow) Communist Party activists did, however, indulge themselves in a hatred of the biological warfare supposedly initiated in Korea by the forces of American imperialism. Jacques Duclos' notebooks, confiscated after his arrest in May 1952, talk of 'the difficulties being experienced by Casanova in getting the peace movement to accept the necessity of action against this now-notorious bacteriological warfare': but after a moment's hesitation, especially on the part of those in the medical profession sympathetic to the cause, the offensive launched by the New China news agency was taken up with enthusiasm. Both Joliot-Curie and Marcel Prenant, the party's two leading scientists, stood up bravely to the scepticism expressed by the *Institut Pasteur* and many intellectuals – for example, left-wing Catholic Jean-Marie Domenach who voiced his disquiet in the August 1952 issue of *Esprit* – lent their support.

The ending of the PCF's initial isolation was considerably aided by the demonstration organised on 28 May 1952 against the arrival of

General Ridgway ('*Ridgway-la-peste*' in André Stil's famous formulation). Co-ordinated by the *Mouvement de la paix* it represented one of the final expressions of proletarian violence on the streets of Paris. Moreover, following the ensuing police repression that took place, it showed that the capital of sympathy enjoyed by both the party and its mouthpiece amongst intellectuals remained considerable. The most spectacular expression of support came from Jean-Paul Sartre, whose writings were still viewed with disapproval by the PCF!

In *Les communistes et la Paix*, a text of over 300 pages published in *Les Temps modernes* from July 1952 onwards, Sartre commented: 'I have looked hard but in the course of the last three decades I cannot find any evidence of the desire for aggression on the part of the Russians. I see rather a distrustful and hunted nation.' Rediscovering the fears that had already been perceptible at the time of Western intervention in Korea, he unambiguously disclosed one of the most powerful sources of neutralism: 'You are so frightened of the communist régime that you do everything possible to provoke it into action. Today there is peace, the Americans are here and the Russians are in Russia. But tomorrow, if there is war, the Americans will be in America and it is the Russians who will be here.'

The backing of Sartre coincided with Stalin's confirmation in October of that year of what was taken to be the inevitability of war between capitalist countries and it was therefore in the context of the demands for East–West negotiations that the *Combattants de la paix* were henceforth obliged to orientate their activities. Internally this meant a united campaign for 'national independence', symbolised in the French delegation to the Vienna World Peace Congress where Sartre found himself side by side with non-communist writers Maurice Druon, Michel Leiris and Hervé Bazin.

The death of Stalin and the reduction of tension immediately visible on the Korean front was soon to change the terms of debate. If, beginning in the autumn of 1953, the polemics surrounding the proposal for a European Defence Community proved particularly intense in France's universities, then soon the interest of her intellectuals turned towards other areas of confrontation. The repercussions within France and between her people of the Cold War gave way to the deep divisions that accompanied events in North Africa. Inevitably the support given to the champions of independence was clothed in the slogan of 'peace in Algeria', but this very particular struggle for peace belongs to another study.

The end of the French Empire, if it brought about a shift in the content of intellectual pacifism, was – as Jean-François Sirinelli has shown[24] – a period marked, in terms of the number of petitions that were drawn up, both by intense activity and a lessening of the specific impact of intellectuals upon the formation of public opinion. But this decline in the influence of intellectuals upon society should not lead us to idealise a golden age. And this consideration applies particularly to an area – the perception of the outside world – where the French intellectual has attempted to reconcile his propensity to think in universal terms with his eagerness to protect his homeland.[25] Evident after the Second World War and ever-present at the beginning of the 1980s in the debate on the relationship between Europe and the USA, this twin dimension of the intellectual's vision ran through and nourished the debates of the inter-war years.

Certainly this atavistic mentality, with which – with varying degrees of success – the communist movement had to deal, is a reflection of what Tony Judt has described as 'the holistic strain in French styles of thought'.[26] It was favourable to pacifism to the extent that the difficulty in recommending what was imperfect and contingent was accompanied by a distaste for intellectual doubt which itself could be transformed into self-hatred and which, in the last analysis, encouraged political commitment.

However, if the effects of this form of intervention by France's *clercs* is at present being re-assessed for the period after 1945 it seems only legitimate to push this 'revisionism' further into the past. Beyond its relevance to the sphere of the intellectual such an investigation would also allow us to gauge more accurately the impact upon French opinion of the modifications that took place in both the discourse and actions of communists directed towards the struggle for peace. Even given that the French people have short memories, one could then inquire about the repercussions of adherence to communism upon a complex of values – and here patriotism joins pacifism – the rejection of which appears to have been constitutive of the original ideology formulated by the PCF at its inception.

In terms of 1940 we would be inclined, for our part, to regard these effects as being secondary. If, for example, we rely upon the autopsy of the French defeat recently carried out by Jean-Louis Crémieux-Brilhac,[27] then the picture certainly has to be re-focused. Given the overwhelming evidence of the lack of military preparation and of quasi-biological exhaustion, combined with the fear of Germany, what could have been the weight of Barbusse's writings? A hundred years after the birth of the author of *Le Feu*, Jean Lacouture asked a similar question: 'Because,' Lacouture writes, 'he died in 1935 we cannot altogether attribute to him the tragic errors of a pacifism which, faced by a murderous nazism, was content to bare its soul and to chatter endlessly. Who can say what was the exact rôle of Amsterdam–Pleyal and what sentiments it inspired in Berlin: annoyance or secret jubilation?' To lean, as we are inclined to do, towards the second alternative does not imply an over-estimation of the place of the struggle for peace in the defeat suffered during the battle of May–June 1940. Such, however, was not perhaps the view of the German censor who waited until July 1942 before banning a collection of articles by Romain Rolland that had escaped the first proscribed list of September 1940. Published by the (Communist Party's) *Editions Sociales Internationales*, it carried the title, *Par la Révolution, la Paix*.

Notes

1. See here the special issue of *Pouvoirs*, 58, January–March 1991, devoted to *La France dans la guerre* as well as M. Winock, 'Le pacifisme à la française (1789–1991)', *L'Histoire*, 144, 1991, pp. 34–55.
2. S. Courtois, 'Le système communiste international et la lutte pour la paix, 1917–1939', *Relations internationales*, 53, 1988, pp. 5–22.
3. J. Verdès-Leroux, *Au service du Parti: Le parti communiste, les intellectuels et la culture (1944–1956)* (Paris, 1983) p. 21.
4. Quoted in A. Glucksman, *Europe 2004* (Paris, 1979) p. 472.
5. M. Winock, 'Au nom de la Patrie', *L'Histoire*, 107, 1988, p. 18.
6. V. I. Lenin, *Collected Works*, 28 (Moscow, 1965) pp. 62–75.
7. N. Racine, 'Pacifisme, socialisme et communisme naissant: Quelques documents concernant les intellectuels 1914–1920', *Communisme*, 18–19, 1988, pp. 34–49.
8. V. Serge, *Memoirs of a Revolutionary 1901–1941* (Oxford, 1975) p. 61.
9. D. Caute, *Communism and the French Intellectuals* (London, 1964) p. 65.
10. J-J. Becker, 'La revue *Clarté*', in O. Barrot and P. Ory (eds), *Entre deux guerres* (Paris, 1990) pp. 59–76.
11. N. Racine, 'Une revue d'intellectuels communistes dans les années vingt: *Clarté* (1921–1928)', *Revue Française des Sciences Politiques*, 1967, pp. 484–519.
12. J. Relinger, 'Henri Barbusse dans les années vingt: pour une nouvelle conception de l'intellectuel?', in D. Bonnaud-Lamotte and J-L. Rispail (eds), *Intellectuels des années trente* (Paris, 1989) pp. 83–8.

13. J-F. Sirinelli, *Intellectuels et passions françaises: manifestes et pétitions au XXe siècle* (Paris, 1990) pp. 62–3.

14. S. Cannone, 'De la 'lutte pour la paix' à la 'defense de l'URSS': le débat sur le danger de guerre dans le Komintern 1926–1927', *Communisme*, 18–19, 1988, pp. 50–70.

15. D. Tartakowsky, review of C. Serrano, *L'enjeu espagnol: PCF et guerre d'Espagne, Cahiers d'Histoire de l'Institut de Recherches Marxistes*, 29, 1987, p. 161.

16. C. Jelen, *Histoire ou Staline, le prix de la paix* (Paris, 1988), pp. 172–83.

17. N. Racine, 'Bataille autour d'intellectuel(s) dans les manifestes et contre-manifestes de 1918 à 1939', in D. Bonnaud-Lamotte and J-L. Rispail (eds), *Intellectuels des années trente*, pp. 234.

18. D. Caute, *The Fellow-Travellers* (London, 1973) pp. 185–99.

19. M. Winock, 'L'âge d'or des intellectuels', *L'Histoire*, 83, 1985, p. 28.

20. O. Lecour-Grandmaison, 'Le Mouvement de la paix pendant la guerre froide: le cas français, 1948–1952', *Communisme*, 18–19, 1988, pp. 120–38.

21. A. Kriegel, *Ce que j'ai cru comprendre* (Paris, 1991) p. 503.

22. G. Malaurie and E. Terrée, *L'affaire Kravchenko: Le Goulag en correctionnelle* (Paris, 1982).

23. P. Rigoulet, *La guerre de Corée: images et implications politiques en France* (D.E.A., Ecole des Hautes Etudes, 1990).

24. J-F. Sirinelli, *Intellectuels et passions français*, pp. 206–24.

25. P. Grémion, 'Le rouge et le gris: les intellectuels français et le monde soviétique', *Commentaire*, 24, 1983–4, pp. 767–80.

26. T. Judt, *Marxism and the French Left* (Oxford, 1986) p. 174.

27. J-L. Crémieux-Brilhac, *Les Français de l'an 40* (Paris, 1990) 2 vols.

7 French Intellectuals and a German Europe: An Aspect of Collaboration

Daniel Lindenberg

During the four years of his presence on French soil the Nazi occupier benefited from the active support of a not inconsiderable number of writers, *savants*, artists, journalists and university academics as well as other members of the intelligentsia. In a country such as France, where the role of the intellectual is traditionally taken to be of decisive importance, such collective behaviour has posed a problem for the national conscience and so much so that a resort to selective memory has seemed the most appropriate response. Those who paid with their life or who were obliged to accept the punishment demanded of them (Robert Brasillach and Drieu la Rochelle, for example) remain, at the end of the day, the only ones to be identified unanimously as 'collaborators', a term which is equated with 'treason' but which itself is also not without its own conceptual problems. All the others are still up for discussion even when, for the impartial historian at least, the case is as clear-cut as that of someone like Céline. Nevertheless, there exist relatively straightforward criteria for defining a collaborator or, as they themselves preferred to be called, a 'collaborationist'. A collaborationist was an individual who believed that the alliance of France and Germany represented the solution to a crisis of civilisation that had had two successive world wars as its primary symptom. A collaborationist, therefore, was to be distinguished from a fascist, a pacifist, a socialist or an old-style Jacobin republican precisely because he believed that, thanks to franco-german collaboration, he had transcended the contradictions and weaknesses inherent to those ideologies whose impotence and harmfulness had been demonstrated by the defeat of 1940. But why Germany? Why was the 'hereditary enemy' given a messianic role?

The 'German mirage', analysed first by Jean-Marie Carré,[1] has a long history in France. Indeed, what has been described as the German crisis of French thought is something that has been re-lived by every intellectual generation since 1810, with love so mixed up with

140

hatred that in the relationship between the two peoples, and especially their élites, it is difficult to separate the real from the imaginary in what are the competing myths of hereditary enemy and ally. It is, however, now clear that during the twentieth century pro-German sentiments have been far more prevalent amongst the French intelligentsia than official historiography would have us believe. During the supposed general patriotic mobilisation of intellectuals that occurred between 1914 and 1918 (a mobilisation that in 1926 Julien Benda was to condemn as 'treason' on their part) it was not only to be Romain Rolland and the international revolutionaries who stood 'above the fray'. The assassination of Jean Jaurès did not in reality put an end to the dream of mutual cross-fertilisation between a Jacobin and Saint-Simonian France and a Protestant and Marxist Germany: for the vast majority of its enthusiasts at the Sorbonne and amongst the advocates of 'university socialism' the project was only temporarily shelved. Less conspicuously there were also the Wagner and Nietzsche sects, the descendants of the symbolist movement of the 1890s, who continued obstinately to cultivate the ideal of an aesthetic community liberated from Judeo-Christian prejudices and drawing sustenance from the light of Bayreuth and the 'Aryan' sources of European heroism. The democratic, mercantile and egalitarian spirit was clearly alien to this world.

This, broadly speaking, was the position of Romain Rolland, of his friend Alphonse de Châteaubriant, and of Edouard Dujardin, standard-bearer of the symbolist tradition and friend of the prophet of political Wagnerianism, Houston Stewart Chamberlain. It was also to an extent the position of André Gide during part of the war. And this list is by no means exhaustive. There were, for example, many who, if not entirely indifferent to the quasi-religious attractions of Wagner and Nietzsche, were rather inspired by the virtues of German socialism considered, following the studies of Jaurès and Charles Andler,[2] as the heir to the Reformation and to Prussian rationalism. Seen in this light it is easier to understand why, via Spengler and Sombart, first in Germany during the 1920s and then in France during the 1930s, a whole section of the intelligentsia was able to see in national socialism the at last discovered form of 'European' socialism.

For Drieu la Rochelle, for example, fascism was 'a form of reformist socialism which . . . has more guts than the old traditional political parties'. Always the obsession was with energy, and this itself disclosed another more direct question: that of virility. At the time no school of thought was immune from this line of interrogation. Sartre, for example, explored this theme in 1939 in his short story, *L'enfance d'un chef*. Here we see a young member of the bourgeoisie, Lucien Fleurier, become a fascist in order to overcome a personal crisis of identity arising from a homosexual experience. Several years earlier, Soviet writer Ilya Ehrenbourg, passing through Paris for an anti-fascist conference, received a slap in the face from André Breton for having imprudently defined surrealism as a 'pederastic activity'. And we know that in the polemic directed by the Resistance against the collaborators the suggestion that latent homosexuality was involved was a common line of attack. This view itself was nourished by the abundant use of sexual metaphors in the writings of men such as Drieu la Rochelle, Lucien Rebatat and, of course, Brasillach ('we have all', the latter wrote, 'to an extent slept with Germany'), not to mention the far less ambiguous attitude adopted by such well-known homosexuals as Jean Cocteau, Abel Bonnard, Jean Genet, Marcel Jouhandeau and Henry de Montherlant. The same fear, expressed of course in nobler terms, of the stigma of impotence and of homosexuality (in all of this there was undoubtedly a strong smell of misogyny) was also felt strongly by Catholic élites amongst whom the question 'Has Christianity made man effeminate?' was repeatedly posed. To escape they recommended a 'virile Christianity' – the emergence of *Chrétiens de choc* in the phrase of Jesuit Pierre Beirnaert[3] – and resorted to a reading of Saint-Exupéry and the pursuit of mountaineering. An impotent body, it was suggested, resembled a female body in the sense that it was a weak body, a body which had more 'stomach' than it had 'heart' (one can easily imagine the cruder expressions employed by Céline to get across the same idea). This weakened body therefore needed to be toughened up, infused with a soul forged by the harshness and misery of the world. But the great difficulty faced by a political Catholicism of this kind as it attempted to evangelise the modern barbarians – the word in this context has no pejorative connotation – was clearly that it risked, as was recognised by the writers associated with the Jesuit seminary of Fourvière (for example Henri de Lubac and Gaston Fessard), 'losing its own soul', being won over by the new gospel, the gospel of force so prophetically denounced by Robert d'Harcourt in 1936.[4]

As early as 1932 the essayist and novelist Jean Prévost (later killed fighting for the Resistance) foresaw that the place left vacant by religious faith could only be filled by aesthetics.[5] In 1937 Henri Pollès, in what remains a little-known text,[6] saw in fascism a form of political opera. Today perhaps we would be more inclined to speak of a 'society of spectacle', the idea expressing the key to a form of seduction that both liberal and Marxist theories failed totally to explain. Equally, the writers associated with the so-called *Collège de Sociologie* (Georges Bataille, Roger Caillois and Pierre Klossovski) provided an interpretation of fascism as a phenomenon which emphasised what they themselves described as a 'sacred sociology' where prime importance was attached to rituals, liturgy and other similar forms of theatricalisation. All of this is linked in a more profound manner to what I have characterised in my own study, *Les Années souterraines*,[7] as the desire 'to put back enchantment into the world', as an attempted return to primordial tradition. As a witness to this intellectual mood, Jacques Laurent has commented that

> many writers were seduced by fascism as they would have been by a lyrical movement in which song and will were mingled together. For Drieu, obsessed as he was like all the followers of Barrès by the reign of decadence, fascism was the force that he had first expected to come from Moscow . . . For Brasillach fascism was not a political movement but rather a vast collection of symbols produced by a secret culture that was more true than anything to be found in books. He transformed fascism into a national poetry and Mussolini into a druid who, having re-awakened immortal Rome, launched new galleons upon *mare nostrum*. There were other magical poets: Hitler for example, who celebrated Walpurgis night and May day and who appeared to Brasillach in a garland of songs, dances and forget-me-nots.[8]

Was it not after all the Duce himself who said: 'I want to transform my life into a piece of theatre, into a work of art'? And thus it is with reason that Morris Eksteins in his recent work, *Rites of Spring*, comments: 'Nazism was grand spectacle, from beginning to end . . . When the legislature, elected on March 5, 1933, had to find a new meeting place . . . the choice fell on the Kroll Opera House. This was no accident and certainly not a question merely of convenience, space and seating. Politics was now to become 'genuine' theatre, as opposed to the pompous posturing of the democratic era'.[9] Let us just note in passing that the Vichy régime was born in the town's Grand Casino. As Jean-Pierre Maxence sensed in his *Histoire des Dix Ans*, published in 1937, the passionate yearning for a 'synthesis, after so many analyses' could not but make desirable a conception of politics as total art. More prosaically, it also appealed to the French enthusiasm for holistic thinking.

In December 1942, the former anti-fascist Armand Petitjean, writing in the review *Idées*, responded in the following way to the question of who were the friends of Vichy's National Revolution.[10] They were, he argued, those who had participated in the pre-war political battle against the old parties of both the left and the right and were to be found amongst 'the intellectual avant-gardes associated with *Je suis partout, Combat, L'insurgé, L'ordre nouveau, La Flèche, Critique sociale* and even *Esprit, Avant-postes*, and *La Révolution prolétarienne*. And that is by no means all'. What is particularly striking about this list is that it draws inspiration from the project associated with the 'renovators' and 'non-conformists' of the 1930s and their fight against the 'old parties' and the Establishment in general. Critics of all ideological persuasions, in other words, were welcome in Petitjean's personal pantheon and this went so far as to include left-wing opponents of Stalinism (*La Révolution prolétarienne*) as well as Catholic personalists (*Esprit*) even when it was clear that by the end of 1942 the latter were not (or were no longer) on the side of the National Revolution. Petitjean, like his friend Drieu la Rochelle, was pursuing a war of the new against the old and this with a fascination that he was never able to overcome for Marxism and its works. And the same applied for what he clearly took to be the French roots of the modern idea of revolution. Whom did he cite by the side of the German prophets of conservative revolution, by the side of Von Salomon and Ernst Jünger, spiritual brothers-in-arms and 'fellow combattants in the corrupt war of 1939-40'? Carnot and the Jacobins, the 'mystique of volunteer in struggle' merging with that of the soldiers of Year II.

If subsequently he made every effort to ensure that it was forgotten – and so much so that people were fearful of not describing him as the embodiment of liberalism – the writer and journalist Alfred Fabre-Luce was undoubtedly one of the ideologues of collaboration. More than this, he was in fact its encyclopaedist! It was from him that, in 1942, came the idea of 'making a useful contribution to the history of the spiritual origins of the new Europe' in the shape of a collection entitled *L'Anthologie de la nouvelle Europe*. The document itself provides a fascinating insight into the mind of collaboration and certainly shows the extent to which the cultural project which underpinned it could be systematic ... as well as seductive for those intellectuals who had lost their bearings. The selection made by Fabre-Luce skilfully mixes contemporaries, not all of them fascists or admirers of Germany (far from it, in fact) with the giants of

European culture, going as far back as the Renaissance! It is not perhaps therefore entirely surprising that in the Preface we learn that 'Proudhon, Michelet, Quinet, sons of '89 and active participants in '48 had already treated national-socialist themes: respect for force, a counter-religion, the cult of the family and of the homeland'. Far from simply exalting a reactionary political culture, in other words, the anthologist puts before us the classics of the Republic, sure in the knowledge that it was they who were preparing the true revolution of the future, a revolution that Fabre-Luce himself calls that of an anti-democratic Europe. Once again there is the appeal to a new religion, a 'Jewish influenced' Christianity being adjudged to have had its day. The Europe of the twentieth century, on this view, had religious yearnings that the traditional faiths could no longer satisfy and which could not be assuaged by international materialism. Nevertheless the impact of Marxism had left its mark. What is shown by this little-known text, written by one of the most intelligent intellectuals to have been momentarily led astray by this ideological phantasy, is that collaborationism wanted to reactivate the old dream previously articulated by Edgar Quinet, Eugène Pelletan . . . and Jean Jaurès of a 'religious revolution' inspired by the memory of the Great French Revolution of 1789.[11]

What also needs to be taken into account when assessing the consequences of the collapse of 1940 is the profound apocalyptic and eschatological mentality to be found amongst those disappointed by the Republic, by radicalism, by socialism and by syndicalism. The belief was that the wholesale removal of the past presented another opportunity for the supporters of the 'true' Republic, for those imbued with the authentic socialism of Jaurès, Louis Blanc, Proudhon and pre-First World War revolutionary syndicalism. Such hopes were originally placed in Vichy's National Revolution, but from around the beginning of 1942 they found a voice in a wider context and one in which Vichy's 'reactionary' mentality did not play a part. The new head of government, Pierre Laval, appeared not to present an obstacle to this project, especially as he never tired of repeating his attachment to the Republic – admittedly a Republic disencumbered of its parliament and that he wanted to see 'toughened up' – and to the socialism of his youth that he was never to renounce. The words of a cynical politician? It is not certain and this because there is ample evidence to suggest that Laval was personally convinced that he had 'liberated' his country from the grip of the British government and that in the partnership with Germany he saw a new opening for a

France exhausted by the quarrels between her political parties. But a
Laval surrounded by former politicians of the Third Republic and by
freemasons was hardly a 'revolutionary' as the term was understood
by those for whom it was a question not merely of borrowing from
national socialism the banal propaganda theme of the fusion of the
national with the social but also of accepting the obligation of forming
a Single Party, *le parti unique.* Here the most consistent advocate was
Marcel Déat, founder of the *Rassemblement National Populaire*
(RNP).

'The Jacobin State,' Déat announced, is 'a State similar to that
which the Germans describe as a *Kulturstaat.* It possesses a doctrine,
proclaims it and sets out to form citizens . . . it organises popular
celebrations which carry a message and which, in their way, are akin to
religious events.' Moreover, the leader of the RNP went on, 'the
German State is neither atheist nor even areligious. The Führer seems
to hold a philosophical position that is not far removed from that of
Robespierre. This could be the source of profitable reflection'.[12]
Certainly – and given that analagous views were expressed by other
ideologues from Drieu la Rochelle through to René Château, disciple
of Alain and one of the most ardent supporters of the secular ideal to
be found amongst the collaborators of Paris – it invites the following
question: how was it possible for religious believers to work together
with people who did not hide their conviction that it was they who
were soon to succeed the Church of Christ? Certainly the theme of an
anti-Bolshevik 'crusade' cannot explain everything if only because for
the same people the swastika represented the aggressive symbol of 'a
new paganism'.

As René Rémond and Michel Winock have remarked on many
occasions we should not underestimate the importance of 'hard-line
Catholicism' in the formation of the collaborationist mentality.
Faithful to the doctrine of counter-revolution formulated at the end
of the eighteenth century this body of ideas rested upon the belief that
the Revolution and the modern world to which it subsequently gave
birth were quite literally the product of a diabolic plot perpetrated by
freemasons, Protestants and 'men of letters'. To this list was soon to be
added Jews, who quickly took pride of place amongst the supposed
culprits. Having, with mixed fortunes, outstayed the nineteenth
century, the theory was then systematised and rejuvenated by Charles
Maurras and his friends. Clearly, it was from amongst the ranks of
counter-revolutionary Catholicism that *Action française* always nourished its support. The common problem faced by both of them was

this: how could the monstrous and unnatural society born of the Revolution be uprooted and replaced by a hierarchical and decentralised State on Maurras's model of 'Dictator and King'? In effect, the wheel of history was to be reversed and thus, despite the numerous crises of the Third Republic, the promised transfiguration was never realised. It was in this context of impatience and disappointment that a new star rose amongst those nostalgic for an idealised *ancien régime*: fascism.

For those who find this surprising it is sufficient to take a look at the penetrating analysis provided by Catholic historian and wartime anti-Nazi, Joseph Hours. Hours shows clearly that the patriotism of the disciples of Albert de Mun and La Tour du Pin, both legitimists and supporters of Social Catholicism, was of recent invention, that it arose primarily from tactical considerations (the need to place the republicans in the difficult position of being seen as 'bad Frenchmen') and that this superficial 'nationalism' could not hide a long-established 'ultramontanism' which, as everyone knew, implied a loyalty to the Pope both as a temporal sovereign and as head of the Church and which, less obviously, entailed the desire to reconstitute a Holy Empire around the values of tradition. The point is that the ultramontanes (the very people who, according to Clemenceau, took their orders from a foreign power) were mentally predisposed to expect salvation from a form of external intervention, in much the same way as their distant ancestors had sought it from Spain (at the time of the wars of religion), the anti-revolutionary and anti-Napoleonic Coalitions and the Holy Alliance. Maurrasian doctrine and its 'integral nationalism', in other words, owed more to an implacable hatred of democracy than it did to an unquestioning patriotism. Maurras, it is true, always remained a sincere Germanophobe and, like Pétain, believed that he truly defended the interests of France,[13] but, ultimately, the logic of his argument led those of his followers who were more logical than he was – this, for example, was exactly the position of Lucien Rebatet and Henry Charbonneau – into the ranks of Vichy's *Milice* and the SS and this in the name of the struggle against 'Judeo-bolshevism'.

Maurras, however, was not the only person to have found himself in this difficult position, even though in the case of the others their responsibility for events cannot be compared to his. There is, for example, another Provençal writer who merits our attention: Jean Giono (1895–1970), a man whose career is illustrative of a particular form of political responsibility often associated with intellectuals. Clearly, it is not a question here of re-opening a legal investigation nor, in this particular case, of trying to assess if the author of the pacifist *Le Grand Troupeau*, published in 1931, was deep-down a collaborator or whether he 'simply' allowed himself to be used and manipulated by the Nazis. Given that Giono, like so many Vichyite intellectuals who came close to expressing support for Hitler, never adequately explained his behaviour, we shall never know. We do know, on the other hand, that Giono's profoundly anti-modernist discourse had a direct influence upon the decision of a number of his young followers to collaborate.

This point has been made by several historians, most notably Jean Mabire[14] and Bertram M. Gordon.[15] Working on the impact of the movement associated with the community established by Giono at Contadour and on that of the youth hostel movement, the *Auberges de Jeunesse*, what they have brought to light are the obvious continuities that exist between the pastoral visions of the pre-war period and later much harsher stances. As their researches have shown, there is ample first-hand testimony to prove that this was the case. A good number of the former visitors to Contadour or to the *Centre Laïc des Auberges de Jeunesse* (CLAJ), sometimes both, were again to meet up in 1941 in the youth movement of the occupied zone, *Les jeunes du Maréchal*. Under the leadership of Jean Balestre, the organisation moved progressively towards collaboration. Its most prominent personality, however, was Philippe Merlin. A Breton, doctor in law and participant at Contadour he repeatedly paid hommage to Giono for having been the interpreter of 'youth' and for his idyllic vision of the world replete with its cult of nature and artisanal labour, his scorn of progress and of politics. Later Merlin was to join the Waffen SS. The same theme is found with Marc Augier, the former secretary of the CLAJ, who, under the pseudonym of Saint-Loup, was to become the eloquent propagandist of France's Anti-bolshevik legion, the *Légion des volontaires français contre le bolchevisme*. The problem is not, as his biohagiographers have pretended to believe, that Giono should have dined with Lieutenant Heller of the Propaganda Staffel or that his photograph was displayed at the German bookshop, *Rive gauche*, but rather that he did not utter a single word in denunciation of the use to which his ideas were being put. That he should have protected members of the Resistance and of the Jewish community and that he was persecuted by the communists is an altogether different issue and raises questions which by no means only apply to Giono himself.

In early 1942, Jean Giono, whose *Le Triomphe de la Vie* had been warmly received by the collaborationist press, was engaged in a lengthy public correspondence with Alphonse de Châteaubriant. The latter, one of the leading lights of intellectual collaboration, did, however, have one specific peculiarity: his collaboration began not in 1940 but in . . . 1937, with the publication of his bestseller, *La Gerbe des forces*, a veritable hymn to Hitlerian Germany. One of Romain Rolland's closest friends, Châteaubriant had flirted with the left before the First World War but he was in essence a traditionalist imbued with a nostagia for an idealised and romanticised vision of the Middle Ages and it was from this that was derived his infatuation for a Germany hostile to modernity and so much so that in intellectual terms he refused to go to war in 1914. The ambiguities of pacifism – which, it needs to be emphasised, did not date from 1933 – were such that in 1923 (although not without an element of hesitation) he was involved with the left-wing review *Europe* and then, in 1926, alongside Maxim Gorky, Henri Barbusse, Georges Duhamel and Henry de Montherlant, he paid hommage to Rolland on the occasion of his eightieth birthday. Nevertheless, as early as 1922, he teamed up with *La Revue universelle*, edited by monarchist Jacques Bainville, knowing full well that he would incur the wrath of his friend Rolland. It was, however, after his visit to Germany in 1936, first with his hugely succesful 1937 volume and then with the journal that he founded in 1940 and edited, *La Gerbe*, that Châteaubriant moved towards wholehearted collaboration. One phrase summarises his position: 'Germany,' he wrote, 'knows what France wants and sometimes she knows it better than France herself.' This, it must be remembered, was a man who admired the work of Giono (the esteem was mutual), who corresponded with him, and who was asked by his old friend Romain Rolland to intercede on his behalf in order to ensure that the latter's works were not taken off the school syllabus. Nothing was simple in the world of collaboration.

One thing, it is true, does, however, separate Giono from the great majority of collaborators: as a worshipper of Pan he was not fascinated by death but by life. This is in marked contrast to the champions of the 'New Europe' where one finds a literature characterised by a loss of hope (for example, Philippe Merlin indulged in a veritable rhetoric of despair and was ultimately to commit suicide in 1945), 'the appeal of nothingness' (for example, in the case of Saint-Paulien, alias Maurice-Yvan Sicard of Doriot's *Parti populaire français*), or quite simply (in relation to the fighting that followed the Normandy landings in 1944) a sense of futility. For these people nihilism was not a philosophical idea but rather a reality that they had lived through and in this sense Marcel Déat was right to say, as he did in his *Mémoires politiques*, that existentialism and the vogue for the Absurd, normally associated with the post-war period, actually began with them. However, not everyone was content to indulge in the morbid pleasure of resignation described by Montherlant in his novel *Service inutile*.[16] Decadence had to be struggled against, even if at bottom we knew it to be inescapable.

Here reference could be made to the ideas of Nietzsche, and especially to his distinction between 'passive nihilism' and 'active nihilism'. For many of the writers operating in France at the time at issue was the attempt to transcend the death of God through the creation of new élites. These, as Montherlant argued in *Je suis partout* on 29 November 1943, would further the triumph of 'the great adventurers of the new European civilisation over European mediocrity', of the creators over those who were nothing more than creatures, of harmony over chaos. Close to Montherlant stood Jacques Benoist-Méchin, the writer, but also the man of action who in the spring of 1941 sought to change the course of history through the so-called 'Protocoles de Paris', thereby committing France to a military alliance with Germany against England.

Benoist-Méchin's life reads like something out of a novel, especially as it perfectly embodies the phenomenon of the 'second life' typical of so many former Vichy sympathisers and Franco-Nazis. In this case, however, it is not surrounded by the usual halo of defeat and unfulfilment that one is used to and it has to be said that it has been Benoist-Méchin's contemporaries and some of his present-day admirers – of which there are a good few – who have done everything possible to throw a veil over a political commitment that for his part the author of *Soixante jours qui ébranlèrent l'Occident* never sought to hide. While we await the forthcoming publication of a biography[17] which will shed full light upon what was an extraordinary career we can rely for information upon what is nonetheless a remarkable document: the interview given by Benoist-Méchin to André Harris and Alain de Sédouy in 1977.[18]

What we there see straight away is that Benoist-Méchin, in revolt against the tedium he associated with his aristocratic family background, was inducted into germanophilia and into political action by the flower of France's left-wing intelligentsia: Romain Rolland, Ferdinand Buisson (President of the *Ligue des Droits de l'Homme*) and Lucien Herr, the man who first introduced him to Germany and which was then to become the great enthusiasm of this English-educated young man from Paris's fashionable seventeenth *arrondissement*. It was, however, Aristide Briand's goal of accommodation with Germany that led him, via his own *Histoire de l'Armée allemande* – the first part of which appeared in 1936 and which, despite its title, was in fact a history of the German nation in the twentieth century seen through its 'unifying myth' – to the dream of a France regenerated by a full-scale alliance, not to say fusion, with Germany. It was a matter of going far beyond the cautious position of the Vichy government, a régime for which Benoist-Méchin had only contempt, as his remark to the effect that 'going from Berchesgaden to Vichy was like passing from [Wagner's] *Tetralogy* to [Planquette's comic opera] *Les Cloches de Corneville*' amply illustrates. What was required, he believed, was the wholesale repudiation of the 'politics of the slave' and its unashamed replacement by the 'politics of the soldier' and this because Benoist-Méchin as well was obsessed by the possibility of the end of the civilised world, only in this case it was understood to mean that of the dominant white race.

In *De la Défaite au désastre*,[19] a manuscript written in 1944 but only published forty years later, he echoed the arguments of a book which he was amongst the first to recommend to a French audience: *Mein Kampf*. Benoist-Méchin argued,

> Let us hope that the final victor will not be chaos . . . because applied to a weakened Europe already drained of most of its strength these moves towards disintegration can only benefit the forces of disorder. Europe risks descending into complete political upheaval and then on the day, still far off, when it begins to climb out of the abyss or when some new order – communist or whatever – comes into existence the last vestiges of the aryan race will have disappeared. All that will remain would be a magma of crossbred and bastardised peoples, an appalling mixture of races, a mishmash of Whites, Blacks and Yellows. This would represent the triumph of a 'grey race' shorn of all creative reflexes, incapable of uniting and of organising itself, delivered over wholesale to the anarchy that lay in its blood, and in which the original flame had been extinguished.

In France that flame had already been extinguished: witness the pathetic farce of the Vichy régime! Much later, when a best selling writer and an author of a series of books exploring the 'broken dream' of pan-Arabism (including a biography of Lawrence of Arabia),[20] Benoist-Méchin turned for inspiration towards Islam. But he had not entirely forgotten Germany: in 1977 to Harris and Sédouy he announced his admiration for the Baader-Meinhof gang.

The writer Céline – in real life Dr Louis-Ferdinand Destouches – likewise had little faith in the capacity of the country's traditional élites to save France. 'Rapprochement with the bourgeoisie,' he wrote in July 1943 in the pages of *Je suis partout*, 'was still possible in 1914 but in 1943 it no longer is: the bourgeoisie is finished, sapped of energy, cowardly, has no national (or international) role to play. Once and for all it discredited itself in the war and gave ample proof of its death.' Put bluntly: it had been subject to Jewish influence. In 1939, even before the Occupation, he had written to Lucien Combelle, former secretary to André Gide and later editor of *La Révolution nationale*, complaining: 'You say nothing about Jews – nothing about alcohol – nothing about the vile flattery of the people and of our famous 'élites' by the press. What an opiate! Never in my opinion, not even under the Pharaohs, have the masses been subject to a form of treatment that is so debasing and so full of rubbish'.[21] Obsessed, like so many doctors of his generation, by the fear of the biological decline of the race, Céline was therefore hardly a 'populist' and, if anything, the course of action he recommended can be compared to that of Alexis Carrel, a Nobel prize winner in the field of medical research, advocate of the 'reconstruction of man' and another supporter of collaboration. As with the concept of totalitarian propaganda developed by Paul Marion,[22] Vichy Minister of Information between 1941 and 1943, questions relating to population – a central concern for Céline – were to be dealt with by a core body of specialists placed in positions of authority and without the involvement of the 'masses'.

Here we probably touch directly upon one of the major differences between the German national socialists and their French sympathisers. Amongst the latter one does not find a mystical faith in the *Volk*, in the idea of a pure ethnic group, as the source and guarantor of a future recovery. And how could it have been otherwise when in France there was a continuous debate – with roots deep in the national conscience – dividing northerners from southerners, supporters of the nation's celtic identity from the champions of latin civilisation? For want of knowing therefore who or what exactly was constituted by the 'French people' prudence dictated that resort be confined to these new élites. Paradoxically the style of argument was deeply influenced by Bolshevism, a movement which many collaborators (and especially those intellectuals amongst them) regarded as both an object of detestation and as an unavowed model.

But was it not vaguely absurd to make constant appeal to the need for 'iron will', 'risk' and 'adventure' – thus paraphrasing for the umpteenth time Sorel's *Réflexions sur la violence* – when direct action syndicalism was only a glorious memory? And what sense did it make to cite Sorel (or a Sorelianised Nietzsche, for that matter) to endorse the concept of a Church Party or of a Party of the Army? With his habitual lucidity, it was Drieu la Rochelle who saw clearly the formidable contradictions facing his friends. Writing, for example, of the young technocratic 'team' associated with the *Banque Worms* then exercising influence at Vichy, he commented in his *Fragments de mémoires*[23]:

they are incapable of making a real break with anything but they claim to be refashioning everything. It is this desire to break decisively with the past that is missing amongst the great majority of the French, be they on the right or the left and no matter to what class they belong. The only exceptions to this general incapacity are to be found amongst a handful of communists and a few fascists.

Drieu la Rochelle, like Marcel Déat, believed in the struggle to achieve the impossible[24] but the eternal 'moderation of France' was such that it always invited the same diagnosis: France suffered from too much intellectualising. A counter-model was required.

From 1937 onwards that model was to be Jacques Doriot, leader of the *Parti Populaire Français*. Full of enthusiasm, the normally melancholic Drieu was to write of Doriot as 'the great athlete', standing before France not like a big fat intellectual who watches 'his sick mother whilst smoking his pipe. He is an athlete who takes hold of the weakened body and breathes into it the spirit of which he is full'. We know, moreover, that the reading of Nietzsche – in which Drieu himself was not lacking[25] – was such as to legitimise for many thinkers of the day, and not merely for those who found themselves amongst the collaborators, the search for a new élite that would come out of the depths of the nation's soul. In their *La Fin du nihilisme*,[26] Raymond Soulès and André Mahé, the two leading ideologists of the *Mouvement Social Révolutionnaire* set up in September 1940, spoke of 'the three essential forces who together have determined the historical evolution of the French nation': a leader, powerful to a greater or lesser extent; an aristocracy, in turns loyal and secessionist, sometimes operating as an élite open to the people, sometimes as a closed caste; and finally the people, in turns enslaved and emancipated. Then, after the (inevitable) invocation of the Druids and the popular aristocracy of educators, wisemen and jurists, who, it is argued, reconstituted themselves more by a process of co-optation than by heredity and are associated with Clovis, the medieval knightly orders and 1789 – the authors justify the latter by reference to the bankruptcy of the landed aristocracy – comes the proposition to create 'a new Knighthood' drawn from the new popular élite. This allows them to brush aside the dream of the restoration of the monarchy still cherished by many at Vichy and then, drawing upon Alfred Rosenberg and his concept of a hierarchical State, the *Deutsche Ordenstaat*, to affirm in a peremptory fashion that 'there is no point struggling for an abstract form of monarchy or republic'. This itself serves to disclose the true meaning of republicanism for many post-nihilist 'revolutionaries': it was simply a matter, divorced totally from democracy, of countering the supporters of monarchical restoration. As such it was incoherent, if not contradictory, but then dreams are never coherent.

Nothing is more absurd or more ridiculous Raymond Aron wrote in 1945,[27]

> than the revolutionary phraseology of the collaborators who in turn or simultaneously deploy two contradictory themes: the acceptance of the German yoke in the name of historical reason and a moral revolution inspired by Nietzsche. The two themes cancel each other out. It can be wise, but not heroic, to accept necessity. If it is not always wise it is always heroic to fight against triumphant force. But where is the risk, the adventure, the audacity, in a totalitarian régime installed by the invader?

But were those involved aware of this contradiction? The question is worth posing. Following on from the work of Robert Paxton, French historians have come to accept the distinction between State collaboration and collaborationism as an essential means of understanding the Vichy régime. State collaboration was a policy which followed logically from the signing of the armistice and which meant that the government of Marshal Pétain, convinced that Germany had won the war, would seek to obtain from the Germans: (a) in the short term, the best possible conditions for a defeated France; (b) in the long term, a privileged place for France in the German Europe of the future. It needs to be emphasised therefore that State collaboration was compatible with nationalist sentiment and could be put into practice – in the name of *realpolitik* – by men who were sincerely anti-German, of whom some (including perhaps even Pétain himself) were convinced that they were 'duping *les boches*'. Similarly, the internal project that inspired State collaboration was a 'national revolution' that was closer to what was being attempted in Portugal and Spain than it was to national socialism. In particular, we need to take note of the influence of political Catholicism in Vichy as well as what Stanley Hoffman has already described as an anti-democratic liberalism reminiscent of Guizot in the July Monarchy.

With collaborationism we are inhabiting an altogether different universe. We are in Paris (in the occupied zone) rather than in Vichy (the effective capital up to November 1942). We are in the company of ideological visionaries rather than realist politicians. With men such as Déat, Doriot, Drieu la Rochelle, Céline, Benoist-Méchin, and the other 'collaborationnists', we are in a mental world characterised by 'an ethic of conviction', committed pro-Nazism, a world far from the compromises and trickery that they all condemned at 'Vichy'. For them France had died in June 1940, so the hope was for a new Europe whilst Germany – just like the Soviet Union for communist intellectuals – was of interest to the extent that it was the avant-garde of the Revolution. Collaborationism is therefore a different name for what is in truth a form of utopia: a Europe which has defeated nihilism, decadence and those responsible for decadence, beginning with 'Jewish-freemasonry' and all forms of 'materialism'. It is this point that Zeev Sternhell in his recent books on the subject has correctly perceived: a rejection of all forms of hedonism and materialism was the direct line that led many intellectuals towards 'the temptation of fascism'.

Notes

1. J-M. Carré, *Les Ecrivains français et le mirage allemand* (Paris, 1947).
2. J. Jaurès, *Les Origines du socialisme allemand* (Paris, 1959); C. Andler, *Les Origines du socialisme d'Etat en Allemagne* (Paris, 1897).
3. P. Beirnaert, *Chrétiens de choc* (Paris, 1942).
4. R. d'Harcourt, *L'Evangile de la force: le visage de la jeunesse du IIIe Reich* (Paris, 1936). In his preface, d'Harcourt comments that the youth of Germany have been given a 'false God'.
5. J. Prévost, *Histoire de France depuis la guerre* (Paris, 1932).
6. H. Pollès, *L'Opera politique* (Paris, 1937).

7. D. Lindenberg, *Les Années souterraines 1937–1947* (Paris, 1991).
8. J. Laurent, *Histoire égoïste* (Paris, 1976).
9. M. Eksteins, *Rites of Spring: The Great War and the Birth of the Modern Age* (Boston, 1989) p. 312.
10. A. Petitjean, 'Les Amis de la Révolution nationale', *Idées*, 14 December 1942, pp. 1–12.
11. A. Fabre-Luce, *Anthologie de la nouvelle Europe* (Paris, 1942) pp. I–XLV.
12. M. Déat, *Pensée française et pensée allemande* (Paris, 1944).
13. C. Maurras, *La seule France* (Paris, 1941).
14. J. Mabire, *Les SS français* (Paris, 1973–5).
15. B. M. Gordon, *Collaborationism in France during the Second World War* (Cornell, 1980).
16. H. de Montherlant, *Service inutile* (Paris, 1934).
17. E. Roussel, *Jacques Benoist-Méchin* (forthcoming 1992).
18. A. Harris and A. de Sédouy, *Qui n'est pas de droite?* (Paris, 1978) pp. 24–51.
19. J. Benoist-Méchin, *De la Défaite au désastre* (Paris, 1984–5) 2 vols.
20. J. Benoist-Méchin, *Lawrence d'Arabie ou le rêve fracassé* (Lausanne, 1961).
21. L. Combelle, *Péché d'orgueil* (Paris, 1978).
22. Paul Marion (1899–1954) was a former communist who, during the 1930s, became a neo-socialist and a member of Doriot's PPF. He left the latter in 1938 only later to become Vichy Minister of Information. Here he developed the idea of totalitarian propaganda originally sketched out by him in his book *Leur Combat*, published in 1939. After the war he was condemned to ten years in prison. He was released in 1951.
23. P. Drieu la Rochelle, *Fragments de mémoires* (Paris, 1982) p. 81.
24. The second part of Déat's memoirs, dealing with the period May 1940–April 1945, is entitled *Combat pour l'impossible*: see M. Déat, *Mémoires politiques* (Paris, 1989) pp. 513–946.
25. The second chapter of Drieu's *Socialisme fasciste* (Paris, 1934) pp. 63–9, is entitled *Nietzsche contre Marx*.
26. A. Mahé and G. Soulès, *La Fin du nihilisme* (Paris, 1943) pp. 201–14.
27. R. Aron, *La France libre*, November 1945.

8   Anti-intellectualism in French Political Culture
Pascal Balmand

1981: in his *Manuel de savoir-vivre à l'usage des rustres et des malpolis* the humorist Pierre Desproges deploys his biting wit to lampoon the world of the French intellectual:

> Like the Richter scale or the Centigrade thermometer, the intelligence of man can be located on a sliding scale. At the highest point is found the intellectual, who is clearly an exceptional being. The word 'intellectual' is derived from the latin 'intel' which means 'everybody' and from 'ectualus' which means 'I am not'. It follows that 'intellectual' literally means 'I am not like everybody else'. In fact, the intellectual is an exceptional being who spends his time thinking and meditating for other people. But how can we recognise an intellectual? In terms of external appearance the intellectual wears overalls and braces when he goes to eat a crab salad at *La Coupole*. At first sight we might be inclined to think that the intellectual dresses in this way in order to make fun of the working class. This is incorrect because in general he has never been close enough to a worker to know what he wears . . . Whilst he has rarely set eyes on a worker (there are very few of them at *La Coupole*) the intellectual writes things that are full of generous sentiments and incomprehensible words on the condition of the working class, typically he then solves the crisis in San Salvador in an article written for a professional magazine, then he examines the role of the West in the Third World food crisis, then he has a second crab salad, then for the seventh time he goes to see the English language version of Lubitsch's *The Merry Widow* because the work of the second assistant set designer seems to him to be better researched than that in the French version and where, in any case, Maurice Chevalier speaks in French, a very vulgar language (for an intellectual a vulgar language is a language that people understand.[1]

Almost a century before, at the time of the Dreyfus Affair, the anti-Dreyfusard Ferdinand Brunetière for his part attacked those who 'could only speak with authority about things they did not understand'[2] and went on to assert that he could not see 'by what right a professor of Tibetan could claim to direct his fellow citizens'.[3] Faced with what are in terms of tone and length two very different indictments we can, even if we accept that two quotations are not sufficient on their own to prove the point, easily imagine the extent to which in France the figure of the intellectual has been the object of a tradition of criticism at least as significant as the very special place he has occupied in the nation's political culture.

Is this anti-intellectual tradition, however, susceptible to an unequivocal and conclusive definition, especially given that it has been visible both in certain parts of the world of politics and amongst elements of the intelligentsia itself? Clearly, the answer is that it is no more so than, for example, anti-semitism, a phenomenon with which, moreover, it is often associated. All too frequently, what we are dealing with is a question of degree and subtle variation and obviously the methodological approach initially taken will have an impact upon how we approach the subject: should we, for example, establish a strict distinction between 'moderate' anti-intellectualism (satire devoid of malice, for example) and 'radical' anti-intellectualism (the obsessive denunciation of intellectuals as the bearers of all ills) or should we on the contrary accept that it is only a short step from the first to the second? Given these questions, would it not be unduly premature if at the outset we were to fix upon a rigid definition? A definition, if there is to be one, should after all result from observation, rather than precede it. However, we all know that something can be observed only if it has been subject to preliminary delimitation and it is after this that one can progressively fill out the picture. In line with this, therefore, we propose to designate under the term 'anti-intellectualism' any discourse or ideological position which in an overt way displays a general hostility towards intellectuals when regarded specifically as actors in political life.

THE ROOTS OF THE ANTI-INTELLECTUAL TRADITION

Like the dark side of the moon, anti-intellectualism is in a way integral to the existence of the world of the intellectual itself. Here it is sufficient to recall, for example, that the term 'intellectual' was first deployed as part of an argument that was specifically anti-intellectual in content: in response to the various Dreyfusard petitions it was Maurice Barrès, the leading spokesman of anti-Dreyfusard nationalism, who in the 1 February 1898 issue of *Le Journal* published a scathing attack entitled 'La protestation des intellectuels' and in so doing 'invented' a noun bearing explicitly negative connotations. The title was, however, immediately adopted as a rallying call by those concerned.

Anti-intellectualism, in other words, appeared precisely at the very moment when intellectuals first emerged as a specific socio-cultural category in France and did so in such a way as immediately to clarify its place and role in the nation's political culture. It took root, moreover, primarily in two very different environments: those of the anti-Dreyfusard and nationalist right and of revolutionary syndicalism. Despite their obvious differences and opposition to each other, what these two stances had in common was their separation from the dominant political culture that had been built around the republican consensus. On both the extreme left and the extreme right there existed bitter opposition towards what was seen as the Republic of the middle classes and towards the ideology of the Radical Party. To the extent therefore that, in a democratic France that was becoming ever more secular, intellectuals were increasingly seen to be performing the social functions previously assigned to the clergy it was not surprising to see the principal opponents of the republican system remorselessly attacking those features that were taken to be symbolic of the whole edifice.[4] Certainly even at this stage anti-intellectualism was multifaceted and it is clear that the version associated with working-class protest cannot be superimposed totally upon that of the extreme right, but it was nevertheless undoubtedly the case that both to an extent used the same images and similar points of criticism.

More particularly, as it developed from the Dreyfus Affair onwards, anti-intellectualist discourse sought to deny any legitimacy to intellectuals and to criticise their propensity, either real or imagined, to think and to speak on behalf of other people. As is well known, the end of the nineteenth century saw a series of attempts within both the trade unions and the socialist movement to bring the world of the working class and that of intellectuals closer together. Despite their limitations the effect was to bring about an element of integration at two levels: the socialist movement began to participate in conventional political debate whilst, on the other hand, republican culture started to find its way into socialist thinking.[5] There were, however, whole sections of opinion which, in the name of the necessary autonomy of the revolutionary movement, remained fundamentally hostile to any attempted fusion of working-class activists and intellectuals. It was through this that there came into existence a virulent form of left-wing anti-intellectualism that considered intellectuals not only as the representatives of the bourgeoisie but also as an obstacle to the activities and complete emancipation of the working class.

Such a stance was especially characteristic of the advocates of revolutionary syndicalism grouped around Georges Sorel and his principal disciples, Hubert Lagardelle and Edouard Berth, all of whom never ceased to denounce the arrogance of those well-bred young men adjudged and accused of having 'gone to the people' out of a sense of guilt and only in order to further their own interests.[6] For example, Lagardelle, the man who had set up *Le Mouvement socialiste* in 1899, repeatedly denounced the illusions of what he saw as an unnatural alliance between members of the proletariat and intellectuals, the latter being bourgeois by definition. 'It is a matter of fact,' he wrote, that 'the majority of intellectuals virtually despise manual workers, and believe themselves unquestionably to be the best equipped to understand everything, the most capable of governing everything, the most worthy of directing everything.'[7] Berth for his part devoted several articles to the subject in *Le Mouvement socialiste* before bringing them together on the eve of the First World War in what was a veritable manifesto of pro-working class anti-intellectualism, *Les Méfaits des intellectuels*.[8] Drawing as much upon Proudhon and Nietzsche as upon Marx and Bergson, he characterised the figure of the intellectual as the embodiment of absolute evil. Intellectualism was everywhere and since the Dreyfus Affair it had reigned as master, thus allowing the 'bureaucrats of thought' surreptitiously to take hold of power. Somewhat like the Jews in the thought of Edouard Drumont, the intellectual was here perceived as the focal point of all the ills that afflicted society, as the location around which crystallised a whole series of anti-values and maladies. Where Berth himself made appeal to vitalism, the intellectual personified immobility; where action was required he embodied sterile abstraction; where, finally, there was need for virility and strength he symbolised femininity and impotence. Overall, for Edouard Berth as for the majority of Sorel's followers, the power of the intellectual was not merely associated with the mechanisms of a bourgeois democracy that they rejected but was also intrinsically bound up with a process that perverted the forces of life. The idea of decadence was not far away.

It is precisely these themes of devitalisation and decadence that serve to give the impression of a possible convergence between the anti-intellectualism of the extreme left and the anti-intellectualism of the nationalist and populist extreme right.[9] Whatever name you choose to give it – the Caesarist right descended from the Bonapartist tradition (R. Rémond), the revolutionary right (Z. Sternhell), the national-populist right (P. A. Taguieff) – the fact is that the body of opinion that came to be associated with Boulangism, with the anti-Dreyfusard cause, with anti-semitic nationalism and with anti-parliamentarianism was heavily impregnated with anti-intellectualist rhetoric. The Barrès of the Boulangist years, for example, began the assault on the republican university system, claiming that its pretentious representatives had as their sole function that of inculcating conformism and mediocrity through the imposition upon the young people of France of abstract systems of thought that 'contradicted their natural sentiments'.[10] A few years later, Barrès the anti-Dreyfusard challenged the notion of an absolute scale of values and in so doing condemned those who believed themselves to be defending principles of universal application. 'There is,' he argued, 'no absolute truth: all truth is relative'[11] and from this he went on to denounce forcibly 'the pathetic wretches who want to teach our children absolute truth' instead of passing on 'French truth, a truth which is by definition the most useful to the nation'.[12]

Within this perspective intellectuals were considered to be the purveyors of false ideas and false values which deluded people by giving them an erroneous view of reality. Such, for example, was the force of the argument deployed by the supporters of social Darwinism and racial determinism. In the eyes of men like Gustave Le Bon, Jules Soury and Georges Vacher de Lapouge,[13] the 'iron laws of universal determinism'[14] inexorably governed the future of man, seen either individually or collectively. For these theorists of anti-intellectualism reason was as nothing when compared to the weight of the hidden forces that controlled man and the world in which he lived. By the same token universal values were adjudged to be both dangerous and illusory. 'In place of the fictions of Justice, Equality and Fraternity,' wrote Vacher de Lapouge in 1899, 'a scientific politics trusts to the reality of Forces, Laws, Races and Evolution. Misfortune awaits those peoples who waste their time with dreams.'[15] Because intellectuals were perceived as the harbingers of this damaging rationalist and universalist discourse that was under attack it followed necessarily that they should find themselves in the first row of the accused, with Barrès happier than anyone to take on the role of principal prosecutor. Responsible for the 'lack of moral unity in France'[16] intellectuals, by dismissing the life-giving forces of instinct and by cutting individuals off from their roots in history, blood and the soil, were the carriers of decadence.

The intellectual was 'an individual who convinces himself that society should be founded on a basis of logic and who fails to see that it rests on past exigencies that are perhaps foreign to individual reason';[17] everything was judged 'in abstract terms' and as a consequence he distanced himself from the people as much as from life. Barrès proclaimed,

> Nothing is worse than this band of semi-intellectuals. Half an education destroys an individual's instinct without putting a sense of moral judgement in its place. This entire aristocracy of thought insists on telling us that it does not think in the same way as the stinking mass. This is all too clear. They no longer have the sense of being spontaneously at one with their natural group but they have not raised themselves to a level of awareness capable of reconstituting a self-conscious understanding of the people. These poor simpletons who are ashamed of thinking like decent Frenchmen.[18]

The modern world of urbanisation and of industrial and financial capitalism, of liberal parliamentary democracy, of emerging mass culture, was heading for disaster and this precisely because it had forgotten the realities of life, overthrown by a series of vague, disembodied abstractions. Intellectuals – amongst others, most notably Jews – figured as obvious scapegoats in this anguished obsession with decadence. They were at fault first because they held a mistaken vision of the world ('Intelligence,' Barrès wrote, 'is a very minor and superficial thing'[19]) and, more seriously, because they took advantage of what was an unwarranted authority to mislead their contemporaries. Amongst the ranks of authoritarian and populist nationalism the 'intellectual' was well and truly equivalent to 'anti-France'.

We can see, then, that on both sides of the political spectrum virtually all the ingredients of the anti-intellectualist position were in place at the exact moment that intellectuals constituted themselves – or were constituted – as a specific group within society. It is for this reason in particular that an analysis of the phenomenon of anti-intellectualism needs to attach careful attention to the conditions of its initial appearance, especially as in subsequent decades the protagonists seemed more often than not content to rely upon minor variations of what was basically an unchanging theme. In essence, it has to be recognised that the strength of anti-intellectualism was a reflection of the place occupied by intellectuals in the imagination of their supporters. In other words – and at risk of stating the obvious – anti-intellectualism was only able to develop in the first place to the

extent that the political culture of the Third Republic was prepared to
grant to intellectuals an all-important symbolic function, that of acting
as the guarantors of universal values, thus turning them into one of the
primary elements in the legitimisation of the State. It was because
French political culture was progressively constructed around a series
of Manichean divisions which invariably entailed the clash of
irreconcilable values (good versus bad, light against darkness, the
future versus the past and so on) and because the accompanying
radicalisation of political discourse became part of what was a
recurring 'internal war between the French',[20] with the Boulanger
crisis and the Dreyfus Affair acting as vital formative elements, that
intellectuals were called upon to assume the role of 'guide' that the
Church's clerics could no longer perform. Even as protesters (above all
as protesters?) they found themselves elevated into the mechanisms of
political and cultural control within the republican system of parliamentary democracy: henceforth any wholesale rejection of the system,
be it the worker-based rejection of the bourgeois model or the national
populist rejection of decadence, had logically to translate itself into an
unequivocal rejection of the world of the intellectual.

In this respect the often witnessed 'guilty conscience' of intellectuals
and the abundant literature that they have produced about themselves
is also indicative of a basic ambiguity that surrounds their role and
status. Polemical memoirs (Péguy's *Notre jeunesse*[21]), reflections upon
the mission of the intellectual (Benda's *La Trahison des clercs*,[22] Sartre's
Plaidoyer pour les intellectuels[23]), attempts at an objective analysis
(Régis Debray's, *Le pouvoir intellectuel en France*[24]), the texts and
styles are as various as they are numerous, but each in their different
ways and at different times illustrates what has been a permanent
uncertainty amongst intellectuals about their own legitimacy. Such an
obvious discomfort and such frequent self-examination is manifestly
the reverse side of the 'hero worship' from which intellectuals have
benefited – or suffered? – as they have been raised up into models by a
society ever eager to see the multiple stresses that run through it
expressed in terms of absolute principles. It is therefore because they
have found themselves (often willingly) at the forefront that intellectuals have been exposed to successive waves of anti-intellectualism.

Viewed from this perspective, the case of Charles Péguy is very
instructive.[25] A pure product of republican meritocracy who threw
himself body and soul into the Dreyfusard cause, his seemingly
paradoxical personal itinerary was such as to lead him little by little
towards a position of radical anti-intellectualism. If, then, from

around 1910 onwards he began a passionate campaign against those
he termed the '*sorbonnards*' and against the 'intellectual party' and if
he also vented his violent and apparently limitless spleen against his
own kind it was because of the lofty conception he had of their
mission.[26] The greater the expectation, in other words, the more
painful was the disappointment in seeing '*mystique*' decline into
'*politique*', and in consequence the more strident were the attacks.
Thus, whether it derived from the feeling that intellectuals had failed
to perform their quasi-sacred role (Péguy's position) or from a refusal
to acknowledge that they were bestowed with a particular function
(the positions of both Berth and Barrès) anti-intellectualism always
gravitated around the idea, either endorsed or denied, that the *clercs*
possessed a role that was specifically theirs and theirs alone and that
this conferred upon them a certain pre-eminence in society and gave
them an element of symbolic, or even effective, power.

It was, then, at the turn of the century that there progressively
emerged what was in effect a well-defined model of anti-intellectualism
in France. Whilst it was undeniably diverse in both intent and form, it
did nevertheless possess a definite structural stability and so much so
that, from the Dreyfus Affair to the 1970s and 1980s, the sources and
mechanisms of anti-intellectualism remained essentially identical.
Obviously this is not to deny that a more detailed analysis would
need to refine this basic postulate or that anti-intellectualism did
subsequently evolve but such at least – given that our aim is not to
provide an exhaustive account but rather to identify certain key
moments and to sketch out the major themes – is the working
hypothesis that allows us to provide an outline typology of the subject.

THE CONTOURS AND DISCOURSE OF ANTI-INTELLECTUALISM IN THE TWENTIETH CENTURY

Anti-intellectualism and Movements of Protest

The first point to note is the extent to which anti-intellectualism has
been associated with wider movements of radical political opposition.
Whether it be the anti-parliamentary *ligues* of the Dreyfus Affair or
the inter-war years, authoritarian veterans' associations (La Rocque's
Croix de Feu), the fascistic movements of the 1930s (Jacques Doriot's
Parti Populaire Français), the collaborators or – better still – the
collaborationists at the time of the Occupation, the Poujadist move-

ment of the 1950s, the nationalist extreme right of the Algerian war and, later, the Fifth Republic (today's *Front national*): each has integrated a pronounced component of anti-intellectualism into its ideology. The hostility directed against the intelligentsia here figures as just one of the multiple facets of what is a much broader discourse of protest and in which to varying degrees are mingled anti-parliamentarism, anti-semitism and xenophobia, anti-modernism (notably, but not exclusively, at the level of society and the economy), anti-individualism, an obsession with decadence and so on. Anti-intellectualism, as we have already established, has, however, not been an exclusive attribute of the extreme right: it has existed, although to a lesser degree and in a less central position, within the ranks of the extreme left, first with revolutionary syndicalism, then in the inter-war period in the shape of the Communist Party's open contempt for intellectuals,[27] and again in the 1960s and 1970s with the grass roots workerism of the various leftist movements and factions.

With each of these examples the positions already identified at the time of the first appearance of anti-intellectualism were again in operation, the denunciation of intellectuals linked systematically to the logic of a wholesale condemnation of both the 'system' and the dominant world view and political culture. Perceived either as the 'watchdogs', in Paul Nizan's phrase, of the existing political, social and cultural order or as those principally responsible for the crisis and disappearance of an idealised society (in this case they are only the watchdogs of a disorder generated by decadence), intellectuals at all events are taken to personify the evil that has to be eradicated. As such the history of anti-intellectualism in France cannot be separated from a history of left-wing and, more frequently, right-wing populist and extremist protest. If therefore for the USA Richard Hofstadter has been able to diagnose anti-intellectualism as a phenomenon that is intrinsically bound up with an existing consensus and with American culture,[28] then in the case of France, by contrast, it has its origins amongst strands of opinion that are situated on the margins of this consensus and which challenge it.

The Intellectuals of Anti-intellectualism: the Example of Drieu la Rochelle

In general a hypothetical sociology of anti-intellectualism would add little to what we already know of the phenomenon, but it would at the least allow us to emphasise – the paradox is only apparent – the decisive role played by a number of intellectuals in the theorisation and formulation of their own rejection. If Barrès in his day had come to constitute the prototype of the anti-intellectual intellectual, in so doing he only initiated what subsequently turned out to be a durable tradition which in turn would be continued by men of very different styles. Amongst the latter, for example, we could cite Drieu la Rochelle, the anti-intellectualism of anguished self-hatred; Péguy and Georges Bernanos, the anti-intellectualism of an integralist Catholicism more open to the impulses of the heart than to the reasoning of the mind; Céline, the anti-intellectualism of despair and misanthropy; and writers such as Jacques Perret, Marcel Aymé or Roger Nimier, the anti-intellectualism of a 'right-wing anarchism' that is as erroneously provocative and truly brilliant as it is difficult to define with precision; and so on.[29]

If, though, it was a matter of choosing only one name from this long list of anti-intellectual intellectuals, then to the extent that he provides an almost complete sample of the various types of anti-intellectualist discourse, without doubt it would be Pierre Drieu la Rochelle who is the most representative figure. Profoundly marked by the experience of the First World War, no one more than Drieu embodied the changing doctrinal uncertainties of the inter-war years, those felt by a whole generation 'dislocated' and disorientated by a wave of modernity that, for want of being able to control, they perceived as a form of decadence.[30] Nothing, in fact, is more striking than the exaggerated ideological versatility of Drieu after 1918, a versatility that derived precisely from his desperate search for values and for doctrinal coherence. Momentarily attracted to Maurras, he subsequently became involved in the early phase of the surrealist movement, before briefly moving towards the Radical Party, associating himself with Gaston Bergery and his calls for a *Front Commun Contre le Fascisme*, only in 1934 to announce his adherence to fascism. After 1936 he became an active supporter of Doriot's PPF, whilst under the Occupation he was to be one of the leading spokesman of intellectual collaboration. Behind this appearance of chaos there lay, in fact, the permanent sense of unease that Drieu felt towards the world of his day and the resulting desire to find radical solutions to what he considered to be a profound decadence. Disorder reigned supreme in a world which had lost the sense of honour, of heroism, of friendship and of virility. But Drieu went further than this. The disorder that he observed around him he also saw within his own person, the 'little' dandy who dreamed only of warlike deeds, the 'little' bourgeois who yearned for revolution, the 'little' intellectual who wanted to be an athlete and a man of action. Such was the tragedy of Drieu la Rochelle, that of a self-disgust that drove him to fascism as an illusory and 'romantic' means of transcending his own contradictions and which, for the same reasons, led him to articulate a particularly acerbic form of anti-intellectualism.

In effect, the intellectual was never more than a mutilated and incomplete individual ('In making use of myself as a character in a novel,' Drieu wrote, 'I in no way console myself for being an imperfect man'[31]). To express his anti-intellectualism he resorted frequently to the theme of impotence, seen normally in spiritual and moral terms but also as a physical and even sexual trait (intellectuals are 'miserable little *clercs*, little monks dressed in their habits'[32]). Seen as veritable sub-humans, intellectuals were moreover adjudged to be responsible for the generalised decline of the French people: they had developed an abstract and disembodied conception of existence, taught the French to cut themselves off from real life, to distance themselves from the realities of the body and to take refuge in the reassuring myths of false, universal values:

A people which has only a sense of confort is not capable of preparing itself for anything to do with life, real life. It is not our school teachers or our university professors who can teach us what life is. They talk to us of progress, of perpetual peace, of permanent well-being for the whole of mankind. But life on this planet is not about that at all. Life is about earthquakes, tidal waves, cyclones, storms, fires, epidemics, social and family problems, etc . . . Life could not be tranquil and confortable from birth to death – or else it would resemble death.[33]

Mutilated, disembodied, weaponless (castrated?), intellectuals were stripping the nation of its spiritual and physical vitality and as such were leading it towards disaster and handing it over to the interests of the world of finance. 'European statistics,' Drieu commented, 'provide a damning condemnation of the way the French nation has been run by the old gaga clique of left-wing intellectuals.'[34] The intellectual epitomised a world dried up by rationalism, the very antithesis of youth, vigour and life. He was 'the big fat intellectual of the past century who watched his 'sick mother' whilst smoking his pipe'.[35] In a way Drieu's anti-intellectualism was a kind of synthesis of that found in Edouard Berth and Barrès.

Against this anti-model represented by the intellectual, Drieu set up the model of the complete man, young, strong, virile, all-conquering: in a word, the model of the fascist:

> He resembles the crusader, the soldier of the One Hundred Years War, the mercenary of the wars of religion, the Spanish conquistador, the puritan pilgrim, the Jacobin volunteer, the member of Napoleon's Old Guard. More than this he is like one of the soldiers of Alexander and of Caesar. They too felt a violent reaction against over-refinement. He is the type of man who rejects culture, who grows strong even though he is surrounded by sexual and alcoholic depravity and who dreams of giving back to the world a physical discipline that will have radical consequences. He is someone who does not believe in ideas and, therefore, who does not believe in doctrines. He believes only in action and locates his own acts within what is a very rudimentary myth.[36]

For a while Drieu believed that he had actually found this new and complete man in the person of Jacques Doriot and it was of him that he provided descriptions that are particularly revealing of his own aversion to intellectuals and, therefore, to himself:

> Doriot is tall, big and strong. He sweats a lot. He wears glasses, which is regrettable [why, we might ask, is it 'regrettable' if not for the fact that, in the imagination of some, glasses represent one of the classic features of the intellectual?], but when he takes them off it is clear that he can see clearly. He has a good head of hair. He is strong and vigorous. He enjoys good health.[37]

Doriot was, then, the antithesis of Drieu himself, the embodiment of everything that Drieu loathed not being, a man of the people, of 'life', of physical strength, of action. The fascination for the leader of the PPF was, in other words, an expression of the same anxieties that were visible in the repulsion he felt towards intellectuals.

It is, therefore, in the writings of Drieu la Rochelle, a pure intellectual, that are concentrated – and with a special intensity – all the multiple components of anti-intellectualism. One, however, merits our special attention: the not infrequent coupling of anti-intellectualism with anti-semitism. In his novel, *Gilles*, for example, Drieu deploys a form of anti-semitism that was, in effect, very typical of the extreme right in France between the wars. 'As for myself,' comments Gilles's mentor Carentan, 'I cannot bear Jews because they are the supreme representatives of the modern world'.[38] Obviously there is nothing very original in this; it is, however, interesting to note the recurring identification of the figure of the Jew, 'as awful as a graduate of the *Ecole Polytechnique* or the *Ecole normale supérieure*',[39] with 'the whole little world of trembling and shaking bourgeois intellectuals'.[40] It is clear that for Drieu all Jews were to an extent intellectuals and that they all shared the latter's vices – 'the most frivolous of Jews stands for the Stock Exchange and the *Sorbonne*'[41] – as in much the same way that all intellectuals were to an extent Jews or at least they all carried the same germs of decadence as Jews.

This particular identification of Jews with intellectuals was not, however, an isolated case. In the 1880s, for example, Drumont discerned in history the working out of an immemorial conflict between two models: that of the Semite and that of the Aryan. The former was 'money-making, greedy, scheming, shrewd, cunning' whilst the latter was 'enthusiastic, heroic, chivalrous, disinterested, candid, trustful to the point of naïvity'.[42] The 'ingenious' Jew was a man of nimble intelligence, the 'chivalrous' Aryan was a man of life: one was an intellectual, the other a non-intellectual. Likewise Céline, when in the 1930s he derided 'hairsplitting' intellectuals, found it natural to equate intellectuals with Jews. 'They take you all,' he proclaimed, 'to be what you are not! Talmudists! complicated people! as worthless as themselves!'.[43] It is precisely this image of the Talmudic intellectual, spawned in the association of intellectuals with the Dreyfusard cause and focused around a whole set of Manichean divisions, that summarises what has been a widely-shared (mis)conception: Jews and intellectuals line up on the side of abstraction, universal values, rationalism, the modern capitalist and liberal world; they embody weakness, lies and decadence, represent a threat to the forces of life. As Régis Debray has vividly expressed it:

A wordsmith, the intellectual, without either faith or quality, disincarnate and rootless, circulates through the world like money, with no idea of a homeland or of the true values of feeling. In a word, he is Jewish – in spirit, if not by birth. And this is the basic affinity between merchants, intellectuals and politicians, grouped together as they are under the auspices of a State which leeches off the people and which is itself the historic creation of the merchant and intellectual bourgeoisie. All the parasites are alike. And where do they come together? In cities, which themselves live off the countryside.[44]

Anti-semitic fantasies and anti-intellectualist fantasies, therefore, originate in broadly similar processes, although the latter are clearly less dangerous than the former and, if it is true to say that anti-intellectualism does not necessarily imply anti-semitism, then by contrast anti-semitism is almost always accompanied by anti-intellectualism.

A Many-sided but Coherent System

Like anti-semitism, therefore, anti-intellectualism has the appearance of being a multifaceted phenomenon, but it is one that is reducible to several unchanging key themes.

(a) Intellectuals are distanced from the concrete and worldly realities of everyday life and action. They have no purchase on reality, they are by nature condemned to sterility. Let us, for example, reflect upon the frequency of the sexual imagery which describes them as either homosexuals or as being impotent (in 1955, Jean-Marie Le Pen had no hesitation in asserting that 'France is governed by pederasts: Sartre, Camus, Mauriac'[45]) and upon the ways in particular in which female intellectuals such as Simone Weil are especially criticised (their 'treason' is two-fold as they have strayed from both real life and their own femininity). Generally speaking intellectuals delude themselves and create dangerous illusions. Men drawn to words and to systems, they participate in a flight from reality via which 'man believes himself to be the master of things simply because he is the master of the abstract linguistic signs which represent them'[46] and all this when, in truth, 'men of letters, it has to be admitted, are not made to speak the truth, especially if it is tiresome, and by that I mean constraining': all of them quite simply must 'strive to be more original than their colleagues, that is conform to current usage and put forward fashionable commodities in the most unusual way'.[47] The conclusion can be taken from the mouth of Jacques Laurent in 1991: 'We must not trust to intellectuals. They live in a shell secreted by a type of thought that goes back to Aristotle. They have no grip on reality, no contact with those that they call the people. It is because of this that in politics they are almost always mistaken'.[48]

(b) They fall back on utopias and on the dream of values that are uniformly rationalist and erroneously universal. This said, they embody a dubious and decadent cosmopolitanism which leads to a dilution of the nation's identity. Let us first of all note in passing the paradox which consists in denying that intellectuals have any impact upon real life whilst nevertheless regarding them as dangerous exemplars. The main point, however, is that they encourage decadence by contributing to the uprooting of individuals. Barrès, for example, in his trilogy, *Le Roman de l'énergie nationale*, lays very heavy emphasis upon the figure of Paul Bouteiller, a philosophy teacher in Nancy whose Kantian ethics incites his disciples to make a break with their past and which leads the most susceptible of them to commit the worst of mistakes (Racadot and Mouchefrin go so far as to become criminals).[49] Gustave Le Bon, writing around the same time, took an identical view: 'Our schools of today,' he argued, 'are producing malcontents and anarchists and are preparing the Latin peoples for a period of decadence.'[50] Very similar complaints were voiced by the defenders of Vichy's National Revolution and then later at the time of the Algerian war when a good few intellectuals were to find themselves cited amongst the leading representatives of what was regarded as 'anti-France'.[51]

(c) They are distinguished by an arrogance that derives from their sense of belonging to a caste, despise the masses yet aspire to lead them without ever accepting the responsibilities involved. In short, they are at one and the same time illegitimate authorities and poor counsellors. Conceited and ridiculous, irresponsible and deceitful, intellectuals make use of a power which they have usurped and which they abuse without the slightest personal risk. Prisoners of their own ideological systems and of their byzantine word-games, trapped by their jargon and their conscience, they profit from the credulity of their victims in order to impose their own vision of the world and to sow error. The 'people', the possessors of a real truth forged in the realities of everyday life, should therefore avoid like the plague these bourgeois who lead them astray. And so, for example, Pierre Poujade, as a typical representative of 1950s popular protest, could boast that he did not use 'a political vocabulary like that of politicians and the *Ecole des Sciences Politiques*' and that he did not speak 'a language that at a minimum you needed a degree or a doctorate in law to understand'.[52]

(d) Thus intellectuals are not only dangerous but also totally useless. According to Céline, for example, academics are 'the very worst parasitic, speechifying, cunning, cut off, manoeuvring, incompetent, eunuch-like, disastrous clique in the universe'.[53] As for Poujade, he was of the opinion that 'France is suffering from an over-abundance of academically qualified people . . . who have lost contact with the real world',[54] whilst today J-M. Le Pen makes use of an argument that is in every way identical. 'I am absolutely convinced,' he has stated, 'that we accord too much importance to university and to school . . . Culture is not an end in itself: it is life that is an end.'[55]

YESTERDAY, TODAY: AND TOMORROW?

Overall, therefore, the phenomenon of anti-intellectualism seems to have constituted one of the constant elements of French political culture since the rise of Boulangism in the late 1880s and especially since the Dreyfus Affair. Ever-present amongst certain sections of the intelligentsia itself, it has found direct political expression especially at those moments when the prevailing political system has been under the severest challenge: the end of the nineteenth century, the crisis of the 1930s, the 'black years' of the Occupation, the epoch of Poujadist protest, the Algerian war, and so on. Moreover, as a history characterised by alternating periods of calm and resurgence, it is clear that anti-intellectualism has been more closely wedded to the rhythm and chronology of political developments than it has been to developments specific to the world of the intellectual.

The mechanisms which permit intellectuals to be vilified and defamed are therefore part of a well-known process through which individuals or groups, confronted by a traumatic present, seek to escape from their feelings of insecurity and anxiety by holding one or several scapegoats responsible for all their misfortunes.[56] However, there are in addition certain elements that are specific to this particular phenomenon. So, for example, if we are right to remain unconvinced when Régis Debray in *Le Scribe*[57] puts forward the argument that anti-intellectualism always begins life on the left, only always to finish up on the right, we would, on the other hand, be inclined to agree when he stresses that 'it is not unimportant that the attempt to denigrate 'politics' proceeds by accusing 'the scholar' '[58] and that 'he who repudiates, diminishes or execrates the intellectual repudiates, diminishes or execrates the rule of law'.[59] Behind anti-intellectualism, in other words, there lies an ideology which stresses eternal immutability and which, in line with this, systematically devalues the idea of culture to the advantage of the idea of nature. We all know the extent to which this ideology does not exactly lead to an endorsement of the values of democracy and the rights of man.

Nevertheless, does it necessarily follow that anti-intellectualism is destined to remain a permanent feature of France's political culture? The product of history, it might be the case that, to the extent that the conditions which gave rise to its birth disappear, it will itself progressively decline or even vanish completely. Those conditions relate above all to two French peculiarities: in the first place, the existence of a form of politics fashioned by a 'culture of conflict' (J. Julliard), replete with a whole procession of Manichean confrontations pursued in the name of absolute values; secondly, and related to this, the special importance attributed in France to the figure of the intellectual.[60] Now it seems that in the last decade or more France has begun the process of breaking with these two peculiarities. Its style of politics is becoming more banal and ordinary, whilst intellectuals – at least in the sense that the term has acquired since the Dreyfus Affair – are becoming ever rarer. It would seem to follow, therefore, that little by little anti-intellectualism should lose its *raison d'être* and, in fact, one might be inclined to think that it has lost something of its virulence and its impact.

To reason in this way would, however, be to risk being too logical. We would in particular be failing to take into account both the weight of the past and the power of the irrational. Is it not the case, for example, that when the occasion arises, the *Front national* does not hesitate to resort to the rhetoric of anti-intellectualism? Admittedly, they are happiest attacking the civil service graduates of the *Ecole Nationale d'Administration* or the media – both of whom embody a more tangible source of power than discredited intellectuals – but they never forget when possible to stigmatise a 'left-wing intelligentsia' which they continue to see as irresponsible and deceitful. By the same token, the last few years have seen the emergence of a fashion whose repetitive quality leads one to doubt its own good intentions and which consists in cataloguing – and with an ill-disguised pleasure – the past errors of intellectuals. By turns the knife has been stuck into the corpses of Sartre, Aragon and so on.[61] Thus, just like anti-semitism which, as we know, can exist without any real Jewish presence, so it would seem that anti-intellectualism still has a brilliant future before it.

Notes

1. P. Desproges, *Manuel de savoir-vivre à l'usage des rustres et des malpolis* (Paris, 1981) pp. 102–3.(Some of the humour of Desproges's diatribe is lost in translation. 'Intel' can be understood as 'Monsieur Un tel' which translates as Mr So-and-so.)
2. F. Brunetière, *Après le procès* (Paris, 1898), p. 73.
3. Ibid., p. 93.
4. See P. Ory and J-F. Sirinelli, *Les Intellectuels en France, de l'Affaire Dreyfus à nos jours* (Paris, 1986) and P. Ory, 'Qu'est-ce qu'un intellectuel?', in P. Ory (ed.), *Dernières questions aux intellectuels* (Paris, 1990) pp. 9–50.
5. See the doctoral thesis of C. Prochasson, *Place et rôle des intellectuels dans le mouvement socialiste français, 1900–1920*, Université de Paris 1, 1989.
6. See S. Sand, *L'Illusion du politique: Georges Sorel et le débat intellectuel 1900* (Paris, 1985) and J. Jennings, *Syndicalism in France: A Study of Ideas* (London, 1990).
7. H. Lagardelle, 'Les intellectuels et le socialisme ouvrier', *Le Mouvement socialiste*, 183, 1907, pp. 105–20.
8. E. Berth, *Les Méfaits des intellectuels* (Paris, 1914). See C. Prochasson, 'Y-a-t-il un âge d'or des intellectuels?', in P. Ory (ed.), *Dernières questions*, pp. 107–54.
9. See Z. Sternhell, *La Droite révolutionnaire, 1885–1914: Les origines françaises du fascisme* (Paris, 1978) pp. 348–400.
10. M. Barrès, *L'Ennemi des lois* (Paris, 1893) p. 6.
11. M. Barrès, *Mes cahiers* (Paris, 1929–38), II, p. 163.
12. Ibid., p. 86.
13. See especially Z. Sternhell, *La Droite revolutionnaire*, pp. 146–76.
14. J. Soury, *Le système nerveux central: structure et fonctions* (Paris, 1897), p. 95.
15. G. Vacher de Lapouge, *L'Aryan, son rôle social* (Paris, 1899) p. IX.
16. M. Barrès, *Scènes et doctrines du nationalisme* (Paris, 1925) I, p. 113.
17. Ibid., p. 280.
18. M. Barrès, 'La protestation des intellectuels', *Le Journal*, 1 February 1898.
19. M. Barrès, *Les Déracinés* (Paris, 1897) p. 318.
20. See 'Les guerres franco-françaises', special number of *Vingtième siècle*, 5, 1985 and M. Winock, *La fièvre hexagonale: les grandes crises politiques de 1871 à 1968* (Paris, 1986).
21. C. Péguy, *Notre jeunesse* (Paris, 1913).
22. J. Benda, *La Trahison des clercs* (Paris, 1927).
23. J-P. Sartre, *Plaidoyer pour les intellectuels* (Paris, 1972): translated as 'A Plea for Intellectuals', in J-P. Sartre, *Between Existentialism and Marxism* (London, 1983) pp. 228–85.
24. R. Debray, *Le pouvoir intellectuel en France* (Paris, 1979): translated as *Teachers, Writers, Celebrities* (London, 1981).
25. See G. Leroy, *Péguy entre l'ordre et la révolution* (Paris, 1981).

26. For example this revealing stanza taken from *Eve* (1913):

> Et ce n'est pas d'un scribe et de ses répertoires
> Que nous nous pourvoirons le jour du jugement.
> Et ce n'est pas des voeux des professeurs d'histoire
> Que nous nous munirons le jour du règlement

27. See for example J-P. Morel, *Le Roman insupportable: L'Internationale littéraire et la France (1920–1932)* (Paris, 1985).
28. R. Hofstadter, *Anti-intellectualism in American Life* (New York, 1963).
29. On Drieu la Rochelle, see especially P. Andreu and F. Grover, *Drieu la Rochelle*, (Paris, 1979) as well as M. Balvet, *Itinéraire d'un intellectuel vers le fascisme: Drieu la Rochelle* (Paris, 1984): on Péguy, see G. Leroy, *Péguy*; on Bernanos, see M. Winock, *Nationalisme, antisémitisme et fascisme en France* (Paris, 1990) pp. 397–415 and J-L. Loubet del Bayle, 'Bernanos, Une crise de civilisation', in his *Politique et civilisation: Essai sur la réflexion politique de Jules Romains, Drieu la Rochelle, Bernanos, Camus, Malraux* (Toulouse, 1981) pp. 149–99.; on Céline, see F. Vitoux, *La Vie de Céline* (Paris, 1988) and F. Gibault, *Céline* (Paris, 1985); on the 'anarchists of the right', see F. Richard, *L'anarchisme de droite dans la littérature contemporaine* (Paris, 1988).
30. M. Simard, 'Intellectuels, fascisme et antimodernité dans la France des années trente', *Vingtième siècle*, 18, 1988, pp. 55–75.
31. P-E. Drieu la Rochelle, *Etat civil* (Paris, 1921) p. 178.
32. P-E. Drieu la Rochelle, *Gilles* (Paris, 1939) p. 338. On *Gilles* as an illustration of Drieu's journey towards fascism, see M. Winock, 'Une parabole fasciste: 'Gilles' de Drieu la Rochelle', *Nationalisme, antisémitisme et fascisme en France*, pp. 346–73.
33. Drieu la Rochelle, *Les chiens de paille* (Paris, 1944) p. 256.
34. Drieu la Rochelle, *Chronique politique* (Paris, 1943) p. 52.
35. Drieu la Rochelle, in the PPF's *L'Emancipation nationale*, 27 August 1937. (Drieu here speaks of the intellectual smoking not his 'pipe' but 'sa bouffarde radicale'. Lost in translation, this is meant to be a reference to the complacent politicians of the Radical Party, for example Edouard Herriot.)
36. Drieu la Rochelle, *Notes pour comprendre le siècle* (Paris, 1941), pp. 159–60.
37. Drieu la Rochelle, *Avec Doriot* (Paris, 1937), p. 20.
38. Drieu la Rochelle, *Gilles* (Paris, 1962), p. 111.
39. Ibid., p. 112.
40. Ibid., p. 336.
41. Ibid., p. 112.
42. E. Drumont, *La France juive: essai d'histoire contemporaine* (Paris, 1885) p. 9.
43. L. F. Céline, *Bagatelles pour un massacre* (Paris, 1937) p. 80.
44. R. Debray, *Le Scribe* (Paris, 1980) p. 300.
45. Cited in S. Hoffman (ed.), *Le Mouvement Poujade* (Paris, 1956) p. 184.
46. Bernanos, 'Conférences à Bruxelles', *Oeuvres Complètes* (Pléïade edition) p. 1075.

176   *Anti-intellectualism in France*

47. M. Aymé, *Le confort intellectuel* (Paris, 1949) pp. 190–1.
48. J. Laurent, *Valeurs actuelles*, 8 April 1991.
49. See J-F. Sirinelli, 'Littérature et politique: le cas Burdeau-Bouteiller', *Revue Historique*, CCLXII, 1985, pp. 99–111.
50. G. Le Bon, *Psychologie des Foules* (Paris, 1895) quotation from Paris, 1983, p. 57.
51. J-F. Sirinelli, 'Les intellectuels dans la mêlée', in J-P. Rioux (ed.), *La Guerre d'Algérie et les Français* (Paris, 1990) pp. 116–30.
52. Cited in S. Hoffman, *Le Movement Poujade*, p. 184. See P. Birnbaum, *Le Peuple et les 'gros': Histoire d'un mythe* (Paris, 1979).
53. Céline, *Bagatelles pour un massacre*, p. 166.
54. *L'Express*, 18 March 1955.
55. Cited by M. Winock, 'L'éternelle décadence', *Lignes*, 4 October 1988, p. 65.
56. See especially T. Parsons, *Essays in sociological theory* (Glencoe, Ill., 1954); L. Poliakov, *La Causalite diabolique: essai sur l'origine des persécutions* (Paris, 1980) and R. Girardet, *Mythes et mythologies politiques* (Paris, 1986).
57. R. Debray, *Le Scribe*.
58. Ibid., p. 25.
59. Ibid., p. 193.
60. D. Lindenberg, 'L'intellectuel est-il une spécialité française?', in P. Ory (ed.), *Dernières questions*, pp. 155–205.
61. Here it would be interesting to analyse the changes that have taken place in the image of intellectuals in the cinema and in 'popular' literature. On this, see P. Ory's essay, *L'Anarchisme de droite* (Paris, 1985).

9 The Intellectual, the Historian and the Journalist
Jacques Julliard

'When in the silence of abjection, only the chains of the slave and the voice of the informer are heard; when everyone trembles before the tyrant and it is as dangerous to court his favour as to merit his anger, the historian appears charged with exacting the vengeance of the people.' This famous invective of Chateaubriand appeared in *Le Mercure de France* on 4 July 1807, some three years after his break with Napoleon. It mattered little that it was written in response to a volume entitled *Voyage pittoresque et historique en Espagne*, published by Alexandre de Laborde, a man who happened to be the brother of Chateaubriand's then mistress, Nathalie de Noailles, and with whom he was madly in love: everyone knew – beginning with the Emperor – that in this review of what was essentially a work of no lasting significance the 'historian charged with exacting the vengeance of the people' was no one else but Chateaubriand and that the tyrant was obviously Napoleon himself. It was also the same Chateaubriand who did not hesitate to describe himself modestly as 'Chateaubriand, journalist'. And a journalist he was, throughout his life fascinated by the events of the day and someone, moreover, who by launching *Le Conservateur* (1818–20) was able to rally the remnants of the French aristocracy, from Mathieu de Montmorency to Louis de Bonald, behind the cause of freedom of the press.

Nevertheless, with the exception of this short period of his life, he was never, in the modern and professional sense of the term, a journalist. And even less was he a historian: he held no academic qualifications, no academic position, and scarcely ever passed any of his time buried in archives. Throughout the greater part of his active life the flamboyant viscount oscillated between two vocations: that of the writer and of the politician. And if for us he remains to this day one of the greatest of French writers, there are numerous passages in his *Mémoires d'outre tombe*[1] which show that, not without an element of ostentation, he was ready to sacrifice his literary reputation for a possible political career.

Historian, journalist, writer, politician – what today we would probably refer to as an intellectual – for Chateaubriand as for many men of his generation, it was all of a piece. Benjamin Constant, François Guizot, Alexis de Tocqueville and Victor Hugo did not think otherwise. In the same way as Chateaubriand, so for example on many occasions Benjamin Constant voiced the opinion that a literary career was not incompatible with the exercise of political power. The Restoration and then the period of the July Monarchy, the golden age of parliamentarianism in France, did in fact establish the reign of the writer–politician, a reign under which we still live today. The stupid modern professional specialisations which stipulate that the historian must be an academic and that the politician is exclusively the man of the ballot-box had yet to be invented.

When, moreover, in the quotation cited above, Chateaubriand declares that it is 'the historian' who appears, it is clear that he had in mind the journalist. The proof is that it was published in *Le Mercure* with all the stir given to an article that has the advantage of being read on the same day and at the same time by a whole social microcosm and of being commented upon that very evening at all the important dinners that are taking place. What a joy it must have been to write at that time and not to care about what pedants and knaves might think!

Not without purpose I have also referred to several other figures. And this for the simple reason that, if the *Mémoires d'outre tombe* remains *the* masterpiece of this type of sublime journalism, then in the same genre we also have de Tocqueville's *Souvenirs*,[2] recounting the events of 1848, Victor Hugo's monumental *Choses vues*,[3] covering the period 1830–85, and even Guizot's *Mémoires pour servir à l'histoire de mon temps*,[4] each one a brilliant work, bristling with life, in turns descriptive and critical, readable as a story or as philosophy, as varied as the events they describe and a lot less dated. To these brilliant pieces of journalism can also be added Marx's pamphlets, *The Class Struggles in France*, *The Eighteenth Brumaire of Louis Bonaparte* and *The Civil War in France*, works recounting specific events, in some cases commissioned by American newspapers, which appeared in the press long before they were reduced by his disciples to mummified doctrinal statements and which serve to disprove the argument that works written in the heat of the moment lack either depth or insight. A great writer, whether he chooses to exercise his talent as a historian or as a journalist, is always able to shed light on his subject: on the other hand, whether in the heat of the moment or in the cold light of day, with or without the passage of time, a mediocrity will always remain a mediocrity, an imbecile always an imbecile.

Let us give a second illustration of this idea. This time it is taken from the other great epoch of parliamentary life in France, the Third Republic before 1914. There again the leading roles were played by men who, to differing degrees, were simultaneously writers, journalists, historians and politicians. Thanks to those such as Rochefort, Maurras, Drumont, Clemenceau, Jaurès and Blum, public life was characterised by an exceptional vigour. Jaurès's *Preuves*,[5] published in 1898, and Léon Blum's *Souvenirs sur l'Affaire*[6] are, for example, amongst the classic texts evoked by the Dreyfus Affair. And what can we say of the articles written by Clemenceau, published for the most part – although not exclusively – in *L'Aurore*, and which, brought together in book form, amount to almost 3000 pages of text? What we have to imagine is the future victor of the First World War, year after year, writing his article on 'the Affair' virtually every evening: sometimes it took the form of a commentary upon events or an article of analysis, at others it was an interview, a story, an attempt at self-justification, or a piece of reporting. Either way, it cannot be denied that within this political marathon – the greatest ever of press campaigns conducted by a single man, to my knowledge – there is to be found Clemenceau the journalist (this is obvious), the historian (his writings on the Dreyfus Affair remain of major importance), the writer (never was he to display greater talent) and the politician (and this because his formidable, almost military-style, campaign was to lead him to the brink of being prime minister, something he was to achieve in 1906).

Admittedly, it is not every day that by the side of our morning croissants we have in our hands a Chateaubriand, a Clemenceau, a Camus or a Mauriac, but the fact of the matter is that France is a country which abounds in people who have pursued multifaceted careers and where the short term jockeys with the long term as a source of inspiration and as the means of establishing someone as a writer or (at least) as a personality.

Where then is the problem? As I have already indicated, it arises out of the recent professionalisation of the various activities associated with public life and the progressive specialisation of those people who were formerly known quite properly as *publicists*. From Michelet, de Tocqueville and Fustel de Coulanges onwards the historian ceased to be the gentleman–scholar who, like Voltaire, was able to write *Le Siècle de Louis XIV* and the *Essais sur les mœurs*, only to become a professional researcher governed by the powerful restraints of his discipline and the often boring and repetitive demands of his work. Following Emile de Girardin, the man who revolutionised newspapers in France during the 1830s, the press became a commercial product, the journalist a full-time investigator.

The division of roles was henceforth to be of Biblical simplicity: to the historian went the past, the long-term, the book, scholarship and the in-depth analysis: to the journalist went the events of the day, the short-term, the article, reporting, the straightforward facts. All well and good. But perhaps not. Things are not quite so simple as that, and for this we should perhaps be grateful. One day, when someone was speaking to him of Raymond Aron, General de Gaulle, with his typical sense of humour, asked: 'Who are you talking about? The professor who writes for *Le Figaro* or the journalist who teaches at the *Collège de France*?' In fact, the best-known person I missed out of my earlier list, a person who was at once a politician, a historian, a writer and even a journalist – of the television rather than the written word, it has to be said – was none other than the General himself!

I have no idea how Raymond Aron responded to this remark, even if he had been aware of it, but I know that for my part I would have been delighted. I remember clearly the comment of the great historian Edouard Perroy when I visited him on the day after I had been awarded the *agrégation*. Talking about my future career I told him: 'What I really want to study is contemporary history.'

'You would do better to forget all about that,' commented the great medievalist. 'After 1789 there is no history, only journalism.'

'Perfect,' I replied. 'That is exactly what suits me.' Ever since I have never ceased to question myself about this, without ever finding a completely satisfactory and definitive answer. Convinced, like the brilliant Italian philosopher of history Benedetto Croce, that 'all history is contemporary history', I have always been interested in the past to the extent that it enables us to understand the present. 'The understanding of the present,' wrote the great German sociologist Ernst Troeltsch, 'is always the ultimate goal of the scientific discipline we call history: it brings together the totality of mankind's lived experience.'[7] If there is no one single historical method – or at least there is not one as far as I am aware – there is, however, a postulate upon which history rests: that of the unity of the human race, through time and through space. Far from leading us to merge together the specific elements of this spatio-temporal nexus, this implies, on the contrary, that we are to attempt to grasp them systematically. And things are comparable to each other: a child's sketch to a painting by Miro, the battle of Agincourt to a football match in South America, Lucky Luke to King Lear. Fernand Braudel had the great merit of making us think about historical facts in the long term, but this does not mean that the former should be identified entirely with the latter. To the extent that history covers periods spanning centuries it becomes one with geography.

By contrast, the closer we approach the present the more is an event a form of condensed experience. 'History of the past, history of the present,' commented Lucien Febvre, for whom the method of history was always more or less regressive. The historian, in the account he gives, pretends to descend through time as one descends a river in a canyon, not knowing the location of the next set of rapids. This is a form of false modesty: in his investigation and in the line he follows, the historian climbs back up the canyon. That is why there is this permanent criss-crossing between the historian and the journalist: the former, if he is curious, will always want to go forward to see where he is being led; the second, if he is serious, will always want to look into the past in order to understand how we have arrived at the point we have reached. But for the one as for the other a fact in its brute state does not exist. It constitutes not a point of departure but a point of arrival, the multifaceted eye which reflects a plurality of worlds, the cigarette end discovered by Sherlock Holmes behind the armchair which reveals the complete history of the crime.

That is why for my own part I have never been interested in the past as anything else but the third dimension of the present, that which gives its depth and contrast, in a word that which enables it to exist as something other than an insignificant and transient object, destined to be forgotten. History, or if you prefer it, the past, is the truth of the present: every journalist who seeks to be truthful must not only submit himself to being impartial but also to the discipline of history.

The point is that the present-day provider of information – put otherwise, the journalist – is more likely than the historian to fall foul of the infantile malady of the investigator: the concentration upon events. Information, in its brute state, whether it concerns the past or the present, says nothing, signifies nothing, and therefore this veritable avalache of news stories of every kind, duration and importance, that we see pass by in Indian file in the course of a television news bulletin is truly equivalent to an attempt to destructure the brain. Take the trouble, for example, to ask yourself at the end of a half-hour news programme how much different information its audience will have retained and the modesty of the result will surprise you. Out of this comes the absolute necessity – to the extent that the sheer volume of available information continues to grow – of re-structuring the system of providing information or, put differently, of putting that information into an intelligible context.

But in all this we have yet to perceive – beyonds the idioms of each craft – the fundamental differences that might exist between history and journalism. In both cases the nature of the work is the same: first of all find the relevant documents, when necessary even bring them into existence, then, in line with methods that have been tried and tested and which have been inherited from the positivist tradition, subject them to internal and external scrutiny in order that, finally, they might be investigated, allowed to speak, compared, connected together via an interpretation or, better still, a particular problem. The actual duration or breadth of the chronological period does not matter, nor does its antiquity in relation to us. It is the nature of the problem that determines the process to be followed and which defines its character. 'The journalistic 'fact',' wrote Paul Nizan, then head of the foreign service at the French communist paper *Le Soir*, just before the Second World War, 'is not subject to any other criterion than those of the historical fact – all the classical rules used to examine evidence apply: the length of time that has occurred between an event and the account of it does not essentially modify the problem. This morning's history is not worthy of any other method than that applied to the eleventh century.'[8]

But reference to the document as the primary material of the historian invites us to go a little further than we have done so far. Up to now we have above all considered those reciprocal aspects of the historian's and the journalist's trade which arise from the fact that, in terms of knowledge, the past and the present constitute an indissoluble unity. We need, however, to go further and to ask ourselves if the traditional barriers that have existed between the two professions are in their turn about to disappear.

If in general there is agreement that the supposed opposition between the past and the present does not constitute a relevant criterion of contrast between history and journalism, then by the same token it is often thought that the form of knowledge pursued or, rather, the nature of the inquiry envisaged does serve to distinguish the two activities. The journalist possesses an immediate knowledge, wheras the historian is the possessor of a form of archeological knowledge that, in some sense, is mediated via the elements of the events that he recounts.

In truth, this is far from always being the case. From the moment that the historian agreed to venture upon the terrain of what is properly contemporary history, to inhabit the world of lived experience as seen by the observer, then his conduct has been subject to exactly the same conditions as that of the journalist. The expression 'immediate history', coined by Jean Lacouture, perfectly summarises the break that is entailed with traditional history, where the emphasis is always on mediated experience.

But has even traditional history always been as suspicious of the present as this would suggest? Here it is sufficient to recall the examples cited above of the writers–historians–journalists–politicians of the nineteenth century. They speak to us of things which they personally lived through and of which they were witnesses. Voltaire did much the same thing, as did the great chroniclers of the Middle Ages and the historians of antiquity from Thucydides through to Tacitus, the very fathers of the discipline of history. Closer to home, the *Annales* school, which admittedly has not born its best fruits in the field of contemporary history, nevertheless is based upon the wish to bring the noise of the streets into the silence of the study.

In the case of France, then, when did the break take place? Undoubtedly with the introduction of compulsory primary education. The policy of secularisation, which in the case of philosophy and religion was such as to make it virtually impossible to assess the impact of Christianity upon Western civilisation, and so much so that in the teaching of philosophy Descartes was treated as the immediate successor to Plotinus, thus leap-frogging in one jump over the Christian Fathers and medieval philosophy, produced a virtual blindness towards a recent history that was thought capable of dividing people in their opinions. Every child in France has experienced the same strange sense of frustration at school or at college: the teaching of history stops at the very moment that it becomes interesting.

Happily, today we have abandoned this reticence. When it comes to the teaching of Russian, then Soviet, and now again Russian history in the twentieth century, the professor of history finds himself in the same position as the journalist. Worse still: he is obliged to rely upon the latter in order to teach his courses whilst he awaits the appearance of the relevant textbooks. Mediated history dies at the doors of the present.

But conversely, is it always true that the journalist is a direct witness of contemporary events? Not at all. Beyond the very best reporters, who are after all the élite of the profession, just how many journalists are really the witnesses to the facts they relate? Not very many, in truth. The star presenters of our television news programmes – who for the general public are the very symbols of journalism – are more often than not obliged to rely upon information from news agencies. What, for example, is the purpose of the various 'press services' – services which are springing up everywhere, in government ministries, administrative offices, private companies, associations, town halls – if not to provide journalists with ready-made information prepared by the institution itself in an attempt to stop journalists putting their noses into matters where they are not wanted? The desire to convey the right 'image' does not explain everything. What is the function of these innumerable 'press conferences', information sheets, publications destined exclusively for the press, pieces of inside information provided by likeable young men, unofficial leaks, receptions, dinners, lunches, all manner of different things, if not to ensure that the journalist is ready to transform what is essentially propaganda produced by the individual or institution concerned into what is supposedly information about that individual or institution?

But there is more to it than this. Despite all the attempts to constrain the journalist, the modern world is the world of the sign. The journalist, like the historian, works with words, documents, reports, statistics, papers. An economics journalist, for example, does not go to the market place in order to establish the increase in the retail price index. He relies upon primary documents which are his real sources. More often than not he has no difficulty understanding the speech of an important political leader because he has been given the text an hour before. It is, in other words, vitally important that he displays the same critical spirit and curiosity towards his sources as the historian does towards his archives.

Nevertheless, I do not want to subscribe to the absurd thesis that the work of the historian is identical to that of the journalist. And this because, amongst the host of differences that are easily visible, one above all is noticeable: their respective publics. The historian speaks first of all to his equals, whom he tries to convince and (sometimes) to seduce. He must always provide proof of the argument he puts forward. No serious piece of work can be exempt from these constraints. The general public, it is true, does not always understand the central place allotted to footnotes in a piece of serious history, but if at times they have more to do with exhibitionism and hypocritical deference towards predecessors in the field than anything else they do nevertheless form an integral part of the argument. By contrast the journalist, whatever he might say, is usually taken at his word. The only risks that he runs are those of being refuted by the interested party or of being contradicted by one of his colleagues. But this is not often the case. The larger the public, the less likely is it that falsehood will be noticed: that is one of the great paradoxes of communication. All the experts know that it is the biggest lies that have the greatest chance of being believed.

It is, in other words, a very different thing to converse at leisure with five hundred readers than it is to address 500 000 in the hope that brevity and lively presentation will be sufficient to retain their attention. Certainly it is true that the historian at times broadens his public, but he does so in concentric circles: he who abandons the inner circle is no longer a historian but a vulgariser and entertainer. If, therefore, I wanted above to emphasise the similarities between history and journalism it was because of the responsibility they share towards the people of our day to communicate what can be regarded as their common patrimony.

History aims to provide men with a cumulative picture of their voyage through time: news serves to make known their diversity and their similarities at a particular moment in space. If, then, the continuing increase in the amount of information about the present available to each individual human being is not accompanied by a recapitulation of the experience of humanity through the centuries, the result will be a fearful loss of identity for both individuals and the groups within which they live. History is thus the indispensable complement to the widening of the space in which we live.

Now if the trade of the historian is one of the oldest in the world, that of the provider of news information and of the journalist in the conditions under which it operates today is one of the most new. The former has hardly changed its methods since the time of Herodotus and Thucydides. The second is being constantly revolutionised by technological innovations, the most recent and spectacular of which is the appearance of television. And so much so – if we are to believe Marshall McLuhan – that the media becomes the message.

In history the rules which govern the discipline were progressively put into place over a period of centuries. The activity of the historian is subject to an element of professional and social control which in principle ensures its quality. In a sense it is a function that is regulated much like the professional bodies of the *ancien régime*. Conversely, the job of the journalist takes shape in what amounts to a veritable cultural desert: it is subject to few laws, little social control and entails a professional training that is either non-existent or, most often, inadequate. And this is why I want to pose the following questions: for how long will our society continue to tolerate a situation in which the education of our children is subject to strict rules and which is undertaken by competent and qualified personnel whilst that of adults is thrown over to anarchy and the vagaries of the market? What, for example, is the use of trying to inculcate our children with the correct use of language if every day television undoes what the teacher has tried hard to do all day? What is the point of the education system's efforts to convey the message of humanism if the media is dominated by deceit and violence? What is the use of understanding a text at school if there is no understanding of the image? What is the purpose of educational responsibility if it is accompanied by irresponsibility in the media? And yes, what in truth is the use of school if television does not change?

Notes

1. A. de Chateaubriand, *Mémoires d'outre tombe* (Paris, 1849–50)
2. A. de Tocqueville, *Souvenirs* (Paris, 1893).
3. V. Hugo, *Choses vues* (Paris, 1888, 1890).
4. F. Guizot, *Mémoires pour servir à l'histoire de mon temps* (Paris, 1858–67).
5. J. Jaurès, *Les Preuves* (Paris, 1898).
6. L. Blum, Souvenirs sur l'Affaire (Paris, 1935).
7. E. Troeltsch, *Protestantisme et modernité* (Paris, 1991) p. 25.
8. P. Nizan, *Chroniques de septembre* (Paris, 1978) p. 13. Quoted in J-P. Rioux, 'Histoire et journalisme, remarques sur une rencontre', *Histoire et medias, journalisme et journalistes français 1950–1990* (Paris, 1991) p. 196.

10 About Intellectuals[1]
Pierre Nora

So there is something like an intellectual power. And I imagine that a magazine that aims at a concourse of intelligences and that places its birth under the zodiac sign would not represent an insignificant part of it. But let us take a closer look.

The word 'power' belongs to the register of politics and to the vocabulary of the State. What relation can there be between the intellectual act and the exercise of authority? The law, if you ignore it, reminds you of its existence, but no one is obliged to become acquainted with the productions of the mind. The world of books is, by its very nature, the realm of liberty; the world of politics, that of constraints. The universe of power is ruled by scarcity; that of letters, sciences and arts by productivity indefinitely open to desires and to talents. The world of power is governed by a visible institutionalised hierarchy defined by progressions, positions, careers, tables of organisation. The world of the mind is constituted by incomparable creations, by reputations that are made and unmade. We cannot compare lectors and electors, an influence to an authority, reception by a public to coercive power, the handling of ideas and words to the manipulation of men and things.

Certainly, there is no shortage of intellectuals ready to place their fame at the service of a political cause or to use their prestige to political ends. The multiplication of the number of students, the favour of the media, may even have created a degree of intellectual stardom that turns certain thinkers into quasi-political personalities. Too bad for the victims of vanity. It is also possible that today, through a complex organisation of the market of symbolic goods and in limited circles, intellectuals and politicians share something of the magic of those few who seem to be able to do anything they want. But it is only the confusion of our time or the jealousy of frustration that opens the way from superficial resemblance to natural identification of one power with the other, that dares to speak of *intellectual* power as an element of *power* as such.

It is easy to see how contemporary intellectuals may withdraw into subjectivity and insist that they speak only for themselves. This retreat reflects their disavowal of a cause that is not (or no longer) their own.

Ever since modern intellectuals came into existance, which really means since the beginnings of representative democracy, political commitment has appeared to them as representing true ambition and ultimate justification. The political disalignment of recent years has withdrawn their political ardour within the sphere of their own peculiar activities, and has increased the care they lavish on its public expression. Those who only yesterday would have placed their talent at the service of the masses devote their militant capacity to the service of their own glory with an assiduity beyond all praise. Whether it concerns the technique of the coup d'état, the infiltration of the media, flanking or outflanking operations, weary Leninists are left aghast and out of breath. The very title of Thinking Masters (or Masters of Thought – *Mâtres Penseurs*) may have officially inaugurated the age of internal politicisation of cultural life. After all, one has to have a little fun; and the preceding generation, my own, did not abstain from 'seizing power' just because it was busy denouncing every kind of power. And since there is nothing left in political life to sustain agitators, there is every reason why they should express themselves elsewhere. A complete democracy, checked and ruled by the regular play of its institutions (like the United States, for example), excludes in a certain fashion the appearance of those unexpected expressions by which men of talent attract to their benefit first attention, then interest, then desire, then the will to servitude of their fellows. The situation controls you, you never completely control the situation. In a democratic regime which prohibits the affirmation of raw power, it is normal that genuine politics should take refuge in intellectual life.

The media have served this tendency. It is less easy to discuss books – which one would have to read first – than to interview their authors. By its very principle, the magic of television brings things closer and distances them at the same time. It distorts the causes and neglects the works for the sake of presences which it prefers. It promotes the producer at the expense of the product. It creates that universe of the elect, of the separated: the precise presence of political personalities, accessible yet inapprehensible. It offers an unequalled sphere of communication to these professionals of communication. And since the elect are few, it replaces discussion between professionals, and the intellectual pluralism of different points of view, with monopolies of monocratic monologues.

The disappearance of a common language would render discussion between professionals awkward in any case. Language was connected with tradition, but tradition has broken. The intellectual alters when the literate world crumbles. There has rarely been a time when there was so little common ground to defend, and so much – everything – to re-invent alone. No more intellectual administrators of tradition. That is finished. No one would dare to bother us unless they had to offer at least a radically fresh start for thought. The civic role of the intellectual, his social function, have been stripped down and revealed. The obliteration of Rome and Athens as models of civilisation, the end of the humanities as mistresses of national education, and, most profound, the disappearance of the rhetorical ideal as backbone of French intellectual tradition – this republican and bourgeois matrix that stretched straight from the elementary school teacher to the greatest writer – have completely subverted the original model. Or, rather, there is no more model. Every intellectual tends to be himself alone, his own beginning, his own end. There used to be places of worship, a language and offices of the creed. No university, no chapel, no academy would, today, pretend to such a role.

The shift from literature to knowledge has done the rest. Until Sartre – who played a crucial role in this respect – French intellectual tradition set itself carefully apart from the university. This was different from what happened in many other countries, especially Germany. Today, the university has absorbed everything, even if it is no longer the same university. In this connection, the influence of the 'human sciences' (or social 'sciences') which began around 1950 and is now treading water, proved capital. It blurred the clear old frontier that distinguished the specialist from the man of letters, the erudite from the inspired, the researcher from the expert, the professor from the writer. It replaced these distinctions with a frontier, internal to a university that is breaking up, more subtle and less visible to the wide public. The contemporary intellectual flourishes over a university in ruins. The old system established a very clear separation between the intellectual who could talk of everything without specific knowledge, and the scholarly professor, prisoner of a narrow domain. Warranted or not, scientific justification and the equally new prestige of nurturing institutions – labs, seminars, centres and institutes – began to alter decisively the definition of the intellectual . . . Positive knowledge as source of legitimacy has radically modified intellectual identity.

The contemporary conjunction of these two poles, university and intelligentsia, has ended a division that illegitimated each somewhat. The prestige of the intellectual has undergone a transformation, reinforced on the personal plane by the sanction of a knowledge that is not him, while diminished on the individual plane by his folkloric charisma. Social function has become the determining factor. It is the end of the leisure class. The intellectual is no longer an idler, a rentier; he has become a functionary, an expert, an administrative potentate (though free not to use his power), rather than lord, master, or good bourgeois. His legitimacy heretofore came from owing nothing to the State; today it is just the opposite . . . The institutional legitimation of competence has become an integral part of the definition of the intellectual.

There is no doubt that what the intellectual has gained on the one hand he has lost on the other. There may be Master Thinkers. There are no more masters of thought. The intellectual oracle has had his day. No one would think of going to ask Michel Foucault, as they once asked Sartre, whether to join the Foreign Legion or to arrange a girl friend's abortion. However great the Master's prestige, it is no longer sacerdotal. . . . In the vast transfer from the 'literary' to the 'scientific', an essential dimension of the intellectuals' magic has disappeared: the ethical function. The human (or social) sciences, psychoanalysis in the lead, but also economics, history and linguistics, have killed duty and introspection, the two pillars of old psychology, on behalf of an allegedly exact science of one's self. The morality of everyday life has ceased to be an intellectual problem.

Politicisation, mass-mediatisation, sociabilisation, bureaucratisation, the condition of the intellectual has certainly changed – to the point where we have to ask whether we face a simple degradation of the traditional image, the forfeiture of intellectual hegemony, or whether the recent evolution has not brought to light a tendency present since our beginnings. Perhaps erasing everything that hitherto concealed the reality of intellectuals may permit us today – and only today – to better understand their original nature. Just as the *ancien régime* was only perceived for what it was at the moment when nobody upheld it any more, it may be only today, for reasons that we have to penetrate, that the intellectual phenomenon appears as a phenomenon, and not a matter of course.

The intellectuals are in an impasse. The only means for them to escape the discredit in which they have enclosed themselves and us with them (since none of us can pretend to be anything else) may be to try to say who we are and what we are. Within this modest servant of the intellect dwells a despot. And nowhere has this despot expressed himself more fully than in the French tradition.

Le me explain myself. The democratic state which, of all old Catholic nations, France was the first to experience, expressed itself by a swift and definitive break between spiritual and temporal power. The temporal power of the classic monarch included the spiritual, even if that was delegated. The order of ultimate ends was, once and for all, inscribed in the order of society; the intellectuals (anachronistic though it be to use the term) defined themselves exclusively within the sphere of power, or else outside the world. Rather, there were no intellectuals. The new fact, radically new in the dynamics of modern societies, is that the democratic power, in its very principle, deprived itself of the ability to express what society should be. 'Ultimate ends': the political power of democracy does not recognize that kind of language. It is not up to a president of the republic to say what French democracy is, or should be. If he says that sort of thing it is only in order to open a discussion in which he does not pretend to have the last word. This democracy, in its functioning, expresses the society. It issues from it, it reflects the general balance of forces at a given moment, but it cannot in any way, without denying itself, without foundering into some form of totalitarianism, impose a doctrinal orientation. The only spiritual elaboration permitted to it is the cult of the nation, because the nation was the ideal and limiting form whose contours democracy adopted, and whose possibilities it exhausted. But the nation has, by its nature, left plenty of scope for the establishment of a spiritual power founded on an appeal to society, and transmitted to the (democratic) mechanism of delegation and representation.

This appeal to society has been made historically and successively in the name of reason, of progress, of science, of liberty, of justice, of the direction of history, and of the interest of the masses. But, contrary to what they pretend, the intellectuals no more stand for what this society thinks of itself than political power represents the general expression of the popular will. That is a role which the church should, normally, have played. But the religious power was, in France, too imbricated in the old political regime for the abolition of the one not to weaken the other. That is not the case in protestant countries, notably in the United States, where the incorporation of religion in the very principles of democracy has prevented the development of what in France are called intellectuals. The only historical comparison, and it is illuminating, is with nineteenth-century Russia, which is precisely the homeland of the 'intelligentsia'.

There was thus in France, as in Russia, a possibility for 'intellectuals' to occupy the terrain. Yet, just as there is a representative *political* power, there has been, since the eighteenth century, a representative *intellectual* power. The intellectual, like the politician, appeals to the people, but he does it to distinguish himself from the people whilst expressing their views. According to the times, and for different reasons, the people is called opinion, readers, colleagues, students, public, all of whom provide instances of consecration. One way or another, the legitimation of the intellectual is always conferred by success. This can be due to praise from a single voice, especially if that voice is itself of recognised authority. The young Mauriac, for example, owed his elevation to praise from Barrès. But it can come from the general public, even if that public is ignorant. Bernard-Henri Lévy, scorned by his peers but endorsed by sales that run into thousands possesses a legitimacy based on a type of suffrage that one can debate but cannot reject. That's the way it is.

One cannot say it too often: the criteria that classical sociology provides for defining intellectuals in France are an aberration. It is the nature of the discourse that makes the intellectual; it is on immanent and representative criteria that the public perceives the justification of the discourse. It is the others who declare you an intellectual, never oneself. One understands the present feverishness of authors. It is not on posterity that they can rely for endorsements, there is no more Posterity than there is Tradition. And the only currency one can draw on in this absence is the capital of notoriety immediately acquired. Hence the jealousy and jockeying within a narrow milieu; hence the harrowing libidinal investment in the least pagelet published: the permanent Opera. Hence also the consoling fact that everybody can always become the intellectual of someone. the consecration descends upon you without having been sought. Brigitte Bardot may some day be elected to the *Collège de France*. Simone Signoret is virtually there already. The intellectual is the one in whose discourse the public hears, directly or indirectly, the echo of its ultimate ends. One is an intellectual only on the basis of elective criteria.

The key of this representative mechanism is opposition. The intellectual is an opposer by nature, even if he is not a political opposer, because he has to extricate his own autonomy from the political sphere. He has to be elsewhere, he has to display a distinctive power. And those whom we see least are those who are in the strongest position. The 'great intellectual' is not the one most frequently displayed on TV screens or invited to the presidential palace, but the personality one dare not invite, who knows how to keep aloof. Stressing one's difference from power feeds one's own power.

The history of intellectuals does not begin when the philosophers of the Enlightenment begin to think *against* the powers that be. It begins when the effective effacement of divine right institutes in society a two-power regime. Tocqueville has explained this in a famous chapter: the power of intellectuals established itself in the void left by the dominant class. So the rise of political democracy went hand in hand with the distinction of intellectuals. On the political plane, whether I am for or against, my intellectual power is nil. But I am the other of the political power, the double it cannot do without. If it becomes me, it is Hitler, Stalin, Mao or Khomeini – all, themselves, authors, poets, thinkers. From Voltaire to Sartre, from Marx to Zola, the political involvement of intellectuals in the democratic battle did not signify the truth of the intellectual. On the contrary, it helped to conceal the internal problem of intellectual democracy. That is why we had to await the vast and recent perturbation of the intelligentsia's political investment in the left which rendered obvious, urgent and explosive the problem that the very existence of intellectuals raised from the very beginning. The Republic *in* the Letters is the order of the day.

For the true paradox of intellectual life, and one that the French case illustrates in an exemplary manner, is that, in its very principle, it seems to postulate a democracy. Yet democracy is precisely what the verity of the intellectual act, imperialist and solitary, tyrannical and jealous, excludes in fact. Intellectuals tend to evoke the most amiable of images: cultivated, playful, *fair play*. Yet there is a profound contradiction between the progressive and moderating role that engagement in the combat for democracy has given intellectuals in the past two centuries and the transcendental carnivorous spirit, which in his profoundest reaches, endows a man with the predatory and anti-natural vocation to think and write. Essentially (that is, in essence), an intellectual does not oppose political power; it is other intellectuals he opposes and, accessorily, his public. A virtual paranoiac lies hidden in the most tranquil of intellectuals, a mixture of the archaic tyrant and Emperor of the late Roman Empire. King Voltaire. Political democracy hems individual ambitions within the limits of its juridical limitations. The intellectual act, on the contrary, knows no limitations. It exists by denying the elementary fact that one thinks in the midst of others. An immense work of political auto-education has exorcised on a narrow strip of an endangered planet the hallucinations of pure power. But this intellectual tradition has also exalted in those who profess to write the murderous narcissism of solitary domination. Today, I can only think by preventing others from thinking. I only speak to you to tell you that you will never know. Every intellectual pursues the death of the other; that's how we have been made . . .

Intellectuals have not accomplished their democratic revolution. There used to be, once, an absolute monarchy and a republic of letters; now, we have a political republic and a despotism of letters. In brief, the progressive democratisation of politics, to which intellectuals contributed their share, went with a progressive despotisation of the intellectual. Not an extraordinary blockage if you think of it, in a society that recognises no divine right. Without divine right, where would worldly tyranny exercise itself, if not on the ultimate realms of the spirit? There is a close link between the status of intellectuals and the imaginary realm of absolute power. This is the link that has to be destroyed.

Such an enterprise would make no sense, were we not carried, all of us, intellectuals or not, by a movement of history that is not ourselves. To understand or to plumb this movement, we must return from the psychology of imagination to the effective exercise of what has been, up to the present, this celebrated 'intellectual power' in relation to 'society'. Two things distinguish secular spiritual power from religious power: on the one hand the disappearance of a final fixed point, the God of Christian theology; on the other hand the absence of homogeneity within the social body that incarnates the secular spirit. Rules of access to political power used to be simpler, because power itself, in its sacred heart and head, lay beyond profane covetousness. Rules of access to the clergy were simpler too. Social order, monarchic order and divine order marched in lockstep under heavens of similarly immutable intelligibility. The effacement of the divine as keystone of the whole hierarchy tore apart temporal and spiritual, political and intellectual. It also opened an endless inquiry about the nature of this new society, and launched the obsession of its future. Indeed, it constituted, established, this nature as an auto-society where it became possible for men to exercise power. Power had been a simple instrument of upkeep. It became an instrument of transformation. But to what end, and to do what? In a nutshell, the birth of modern historical consciousness overturned our investment in time: a history made to last became a history made to change. Those who were called philosophers in the eighteenth century, doctrinaires in the nineteenth century, intellectuals at the dawn of the twentieth century, were simply the interpreters and guides of this change, the guardians of the sense of history.

Yet, unlike the clergy, intellectuals have had neither rules of access nor a source of authority that was given once and for all. And even though in every epoch and despite differing opinions they were able to share a common body of ideas – the 'unsurpassable horizon' of their time – what was it that could be found in history that could ever guarantee their point of view *about* history? This is the ambiguity that rules over intellectuals and that constitutes their essence. The ambiguity is inherent to what they are, and it prohibits any kind of definition, be it ideological, sociological or existential. They exist at one and the same time *within* history and *outside* history. Within history because they are its familiar product and even the inventors of the concept; outside history, whose verbal expression they provide without anyone having given them the right to do so. Consubstantial with history and external to it, secreted by historical sensibility and charged with its expression. Perpetual representatives of something other than themselves, and never representing anything other than themselves. Impressed by a sense that makes sense only when they express it. Here lies the essential ambiguity that allows intellectuals, now at a high price and now free of charge, simultaneously to claim the monopoly of historical truth and escape the sanction of its verification, to claim the privilege of the legislator and the immunities of the law.

The only gangway between the two types of modern power will have been the national formula: synthesis, compromise, reconciliation. The nation looks like a ballet of the spheres: spiritual within the temporal sphere, historical within the geographical, ideological within the fleshly, indefiniteness within delimitation, the universal within the particular, the eternal within the chronological. The nation, that mystery of modern times, is the radically original post-ideological formula that only long-established habit prevents us from questioning with the wonder it deserves. It has represented the only ideology that could engender a political democracy and also the minimal political framework that would not constrain the continuous operation of power bouncing off society. We think of nation (political fact) and society (intellectual construct) as one. Yet this identity is hardly evident. Alone in history, the nation permits the reconciliation of that continuity which the government of men demands with the ever-renewed discontinuity of social perspectives. A fixed, stable, final harmony, risen from the depths of ages, but also a historical category absolutely undefinable except when it becomes immediately palpable to all in its spiritualised form: *the fatherland*. The nation, sole repository of that familiar miracle: the constitution of a history in history.

The formula has worked marvellously well. It reached its golden age in the great republican synthesis achieved on the eve of the First World War. Its expression was found in the struggle for secular power that proved a powerful factor of national integration, both political and spiritual; and in a powerful educational system infused in every part and at every level by the civic imperative. It also expressed itself in the success, at every political crisis, of liberal forms of government, and in the flaring up of every kind of patriotic myth. And it expressed itself in the powerful ideological charge all political parties carried, as in the profound national assimilation of socialist internationalism of the Jaurès school. Intellectuals were never more divided over the concept of the fatherland than they were in those days, but their relation to politics, their relation to history, were never so dependent on national concepts. You might even say that here is where intellectual and national concepts meet: in February 1898, with the Dreyfus Affair in full cry, in the wake of Zola's *J'accuse*. That is when, almost simultaneously under the pen of Barrès and of Clemenceau, the word 'intellectual', used only as an adjective until that time, enters the public vocabulary. And with it, soon after, the term 'avant-garde'.

This solemn date marks one central turning point in a chronology (still to be drawn) of cultural crossroads and junctures of historical sensibility among intellectuals. One would have to establish just how and why displacing the centre of gravity from 'literature' to 'science' (vague and undefinable though the expression be), ushered in a new stage that mutates or ends right now, under our gaze. What did these sciences called human (or social) have in common, when compared to a relatively univocal definition of literature in the singular? What bestows on the declarations of those who profess them, economists or sociologists, historians, psychoanalysts, ethnologists or linguists, that ideological aura which their scientific ambitions should have denied them? Are all ethnologists intellectuals, are all historians or linguists intellectuals, simply because of their discipline, when the peculiarity of a discipline is to parcel out knowledge and to raise doubts about those who claim to master its whole? Finally: what relations of reciprocal jointing or exclusion or of internal dissymetry exist between these 'sciences', between history and the others, or psychoanalysis, each with its hard kernel and its soft frontiers – unless we ought to say the opposite? Vast questions: let us just say, for the moment, that the intellectual pertinence of the 'human sciences', their relation to the ultimate ends of history, appears to be related to the abuse of the word 'science', and that the more scientific the human sciences look to public opinion, the less so they are. . . .

The only basic certitudes these sciences have contributed to the general public is that men spoke a language different from what they thought, acted for motives they ignored, tended towards results they had not wanted, and ignored the history that they made. Something to make you think, in effect. Something to enslave you to the masters of suspicion. Something to endow quaint subjects as exotic as Bororo myth, as microscopic as the use of the ergative in Caucasian languages, with that thrill of interest that colours the uncertain identity of the present. Yet, in the context that interests us, the internal organisation of this anthropology remains to be traced. What, for example, might be the relation of history to History? Or that of biology to History? These are not empty questions, since it is from such relations that the professional of a discipline derives his intellectual authority. It is not indifferent to note that the topic of 'intellectual power' (or authority, or control), so urgent and devastating today, with its train of hierarchic and inequalitarian connotations, with its stock of castrating images, with the visions of domination and perversity it carries, owes its efficacy to the symbolic centrality of psychoanalysis in our culture, and specifically of psychoanalysis in the version of Lacan.

Between the eighteenth century and the dawn of what we might call the age of human sciences, various kinds of historical relations to History have differed from each other. Yet, however much they differed, they shared one fundamental aspect: a fixed point of reference. In the uncertainty of its determinism as in the vast realm of its possibilities, the very notion of history offered one enduring, unfailing vision: the perspective of a *future*. Uncertain future, always under debate, but whose distant certainty began to depend on mankind. Control of the future governed both the analysis of the present and the historical investment of the past. No intellectual without an idea of the future, without a secret of the present, without knowledge of the past.

Since the eighteenth century there have been roughly three models that permitted one to think the future: one could imagine – hence expect and favour – the *restoration* of the old state of things. One could imagine *progress*, technical and scientific, moral or political, and set its limits here or there. One could finally imagine *revolution*, in diverse forms, all of which would constitute a point zero or *omega* of History. These three models are dead; and the future, that future which defined the end of history in both senses of the term, died with them. The counterpoint that accompanies the background noise of the human sciences is the historical liquefaction of those traditional benchmarks which, since the French Revolution, guaranteed the destiny of society, dictating in one infallible continuity the judgement of the present, the imagination of the future and the reconstitution of the past.

History has finally discovered itself, only to deny itself. It had projected its conclusion in the very act of its birth. In the very first of his lessons on *The Philosophy of History*, Hegel announced both the advent of History and the end of universal History. But perspectives of finality are foreign to our day. The future, the thinkable future that had been truly the new idea of revolutionary Europe, lies behind us. It foundered in the calamities of our century, leaving us to face a future without face or name, uncontrollable, undefined.

This is what has abolished the historical figure of the 'despotic' intellectual. A liberating shipwreck which has inaugurated the democratic revolution of spiritual power and summoned intellectuals to a new historical role: *within* history and only within history. Assuming, that is, that we still choose to call them 'history' and 'intellectual'. History, nation, democracy, intellectuals, made up a historical constellation every term of which now drifts to a new re-definition, whose very meaning capsizes in searching for a new meaning. Our only task is to live up to what is happening through us. To understand what is happening: we are living the end of historical finality.

A second age of historical consciousness has begun: an age of exploration.

Note

1. A slightly longer version of this article first appeared as 'Que peuvent les intellectuels?', *Le Débat*, 1, 1980, pp. 1–19. It has been translated by Professor Eugen Weber.

11 Intellectuals in Britain and France in the Twentieth Century: Confusions, Contrasts – and Convergence?
Stefan Collini

I

Cultures, like individuals, can become imprisoned in images of themselves. Any discussion in contemporary Britain of the topic of 'intellectuals' is sooner or later touched by the cliché that the reality of the phenomenon, like the origins of the term, is located in Continental Europe, and that British society, whether for reasons of history, culture or national psychology, is marked by the absence of 'intellectuals'. It is as well to acknowledge the presence and continuing power of this cliché, since, even if not explicitly invoked or endorsed, it will inevitably colour expectations of and responses to an essay which offers to engage in a historical discussion of the topic in the comparative framework provided by a book devoted to the role of intellectuals in twentieth-century France. In fact, as I shall suggest, the most traditional form of the claim about the absence of intellectuals in Britain totters between a semantic confusion, a misleading over-simplification and an outright falsehood. But its repetition has helped to create a consciousness which has itself been one of the main means of making what it describes appear true. Changes in the condition of British culture and politics in the late twentieth century (to which I shall return later) are beginning to strip this cliché even of the appearance of plausibility, so that attempts to insist on its continuing truth in present conditions now reveal themselves to be blatantly ideological exercises.

However, the very durability of this cliché indicates that it fits easily into a larger pattern of British culture's self-understanding. In fact, the persistence and appeal of the hackneyed claim that intellectuals are an alien species not naturally found in Britain becomes more intelligible once we realise that the earliest versions of this claim were grafted on to a *pre-existing* set of ideas about national identity and the peculiarities of British history and politics. More specifically, nearly all the assumptions and prejudices which this claim expresses turn out to have been present in dominant notions of national identity long before the term and the phenomenon it (unsteadily) referred to entered discussion – for example, those self-congratulatory contrasts with less fortunate nations, especially France, which were such a staple of political argument in Britain throughout the nineteenth century, pitting stability and political good sense against revolution and political over-excitability, pragmatic empiricism against abstract rationalism, irony and understatement against rhetoric and exaggeration, and so on. In the negatively characterised half of each of these pairings we can see already the components of what was to become the dominant representation in twentieth-century Britain of (European) intellectuals.

These John Bullish contrasts may no longer occupy the place they once did, but language is an effective preserving medium, and contemporary usage of 'intellectuals' still bears the marks of the confidently dismissive attitudes which informed its earliest uses. Moreover, these have become intertwined with or overlain by meanings and associations derived from other contexts, so that the noun 'intellectual', especially in its plural form, now marks out a force-field of overlapping and partially conflicting senses, deposited by several interconnecting cultural developments. A full mapping of these senses and their evolution would, therefore, require a much more extensive exploration of the cultural history of twentieth-century Britain than space allows, but since cross-cultural comparisons which assume comparable and stable meanings for apparently equivalent terms are a rich source of confusion, it may be helpful to begin with some basic semantic discriminations.[1]

The most general sense of the term is the sociological. Here, 'intellectuals' are defined as a socio-professional category within a comprehensive classification of occupations. The intuitive core of this sense is clear enough. It tries to discriminate those whose occupations involve a *primary* engagement with ideas or culture from those whose orientation and purpose is more directly practical: thus it will tend to include writers and academics, for example, but to exclude businessmen and manual workers. Attempts to agree upon the limits of the range of occupations to be included under this label have not been very successful – not all sociologists want to use the term to apply to journalists or television producers, musicians or dancers, teachers or psychotherapists, and so on – nor has any one attempt to define the term itself met with general endorsement. One of the most frequently cited has been Lipset's 'all those who create, distribute, and apply *culture* – the symbolic world of man, including art, science, and religion'.[2] But in practice this has come to seem too broad to be helpful. All kinds of occupational groups could be said to be involved in 'distributing and applying culture', but classifying librarians and cameramen, let alone paperboys and tee-shirt designers, as 'intellectuals' might seem to strain against acceptable usage. Nonetheless, some variant of this sense has been extensively used in the (predominantly American) social scientific literature in English, and is perhaps the most frequently encountered sense in academic publications.[3] Moreover, all other senses are to some extent parasitic upon the sociological sense, at least in its narrowest interpretation: whatever further attributes the other senses build into the concept, those to whom the term is applied will practically always turn out to include some of those writers, thinkers, artists and scholars who are the core of the sociological definition.

The second sense may be termed the cultural, since it focuses on the exercise of some kind of cultural authority or leadership. Here, not *all* those who engage in 'intellectual activities', even in the narrowest version of that sociological category, are termed 'intellectuals': they must also be recognised as having acquired a certain standing in society which is taken to license them, or even to provide them with opportunities, to address a wider public than that at which their occupational activity is aimed. Closer analysis of this apparently familiar sense raises several tricky issues. To begin with, there is an element of circularity, or at least of definitional parasitism, in that the 'qualifying activity' has to be recognised as one that is 'intellectual' in some sense in the first place. A businessman or sports personality who speaks out on general moral or political issues does not thereby qualify as an intellectual. Moreover, it is essential to have some achievement or proficiency in a sphere of activity loosely recognised as 'intellectual' or perhaps 'cultural' *independently* of the activity of speaking out on public issues. Thus a novelist or academic who writes a regular column in a newspaper is likely to attract the label, but a professional journalist with no independent claim to cultural authority is not. At the same time, the 'speaking out' is crucial: a scholar who only addresses other scholars in the relevant specialism, or the painter who only paints, do not qualify either. Finally, but most elusively, there must seem to be some connection between the intellectual proficiency and the public role: some notion of being 'good at' handling ideas, of being more reflective, of being able to set issues in a wider frame, and so on. Whatever its deeper complexities, this is the sense of the term implicitly appealed to in most discussions of 'leading' or 'prominent' intellectuals in twentieth-century Britain – those who, as a recent analysis puts it, 'were cultural experts or leaders . . . [who] spoke with some authority on that account', and this, it is claimed, 'has unquestionably become the predominant meaning of the word in English'.[4] Bertrand Russell or Stephen Spender or George Orwell or A. J. P. Taylor or Raymond Williams or Harold Pinter or George Steiner are the kinds of people who are unhesitatingly defined as intellectuals in this sense.[5]

The third sense is the political. The defining mark of the intellectual here is one who, from a base in an activity of recognised 'intellectual' standing, attempts to 'intervene' in or act upon the political sphere. This sense, too, is parasitic upon some version of the sociological sense – the individual's primary activity has to be classifiable as 'intellectual' in the first place – and even draws upon some of the cultural sense as well – the individual is at least likely to have already attracted attention beyond his or her professional group, to have already earned some title to be heard. This sense can sound unnatural to English ears, or at least as if it builds into the definition what is only a frequent but not essential part of the role. But in France this has been the predominant sense, and intellectuals are commonly seen as a group, in some respects like workers or industrialists, who act collectively in the political sphere. Thus, Ory and Sirinelli in their recent synthetic account take the Dreyfus Affair to have given the fundamental French sense of the term: 'l'intellectuel ne se définit plus alors par ce qu'il est, une fonction, un statut, mais par ce qu'il fait, son intervention sur le terrain du politique'.[6] Their book and the many other works on the same topic referred to in earlier essays in this volume are seen as contributions to *political* history (and correspondingly, the history of intellectuals in France has, until very recently, been written almost entirely by political historians). In this usage, an intellectual is not regarded as a social type who happens to be particularly prone to intervene in politics; the intervention in politics is constitutive of the definition of the social type.

The fourth sense may be called the normative. This obviously operates at a somewhat different level, since it focuses upon an individual's attitude to and degree of interest in ideas as measured against an implicit standard of reflectiveness and intellectual seriousness, where it emphasizes a particular commitment to truth-seeking, reflection, analysis, argument, often pursued as ends in themselves. This is the sense usually at work in judgements that a particular individual is 'a real intellectual', where there is an implied contrast with those who might at first sight seem to deserve the label according to one of the above senses, especially the sociological or occupational sense, but whose want of the right subjective attitudes and purposes excludes them. This is not merely a conversational sense: we surely see a version of it at work in, for example, Alan Montefiore's stipulative definition at the beginning of his recent essay on 'The political responsibility of intellectuals': 'By 'an intellectual' I mean here to refer to anyone who takes a committed interest in the validity and truth of ideas for their own sake.'[7] This sense tends not to be very useful for historical analysis for obvious reasons, but it can colour such analysis and can sometimes be used to identify a section of society which is narrower than that encompassed by the sociological sense but considerably broader than that designated by the strictest uses of the cultural or political senses, though it is difficult to isolate any external markers of membership of this group.

In addition, there is a hostile or disparaging usage of the term which may perhaps best be seen as the pejorative form of the normative sense. Here, an 'intellectual' is someone distinguished by a particular form of pretentiousness or self-importance, someone who affects what is judged to be an inappropriately abstract or complex vocabulary or who appears to assert an unjustifiable intellectual superiority. This is the sense illustrated in Bertrand Russell's characteristically perverse remark: 'I have never called myself an intellectual, and nobody has ever dared to call me one in my presence. I think an intellectual may be defined as a person who pretends to have more intellect than he has, and I hope this definition does not fit me.'[8] Of course, Russell's response, like this usage more generally, would have no point were there not already at least one of the other senses in circulation. Indeed, in some ways it can be seen simply as the normative sense with the plus sign changed to a minus, and it obviously trades on a wider anti-intellectualism. (A variant of this sense was being identified in an editorial commentary in *Encounter* in 1955 which began: 'What is it about the English language that gives to the word 'intellectual' an ever so fine, an ever so indelible, ironic complexion?')[9] It sometimes surprises observers from other European countries that the word can still have this derisive sense among highly educated English people,[10] but it is important to realise that some of the associations of this sense are subliminally at work affecting understanding and response even when another sense is the one explicitly being used. The entry for the term in Raymond Williams's (admittedly highly impressionistic) survey concludes that up to at least the middle of the twentieth century 'unfavourable uses of 'intellectuals' . . . were dominant in English, and it is clear that such uses persist'.[11]

II

The historical development of the several senses of the word in twentieth-century English usage is revealing. When the Fowler brothers produced their standard-setting *The King's English* in 1906, they discussed those neologisms 'which come into existence as the crystallization of a political tendency or movement in ideas'. One such example was 'intellectuals':

> 'Intellectuals' is still apologized for in 1905 by *The Spectator* as 'a convenient neologism'. It is already familiar to all who give any time to observing continental politics, though the index to the *Encyclopaedia* (1903) knows it not. A use has not yet been found for the word in home politics, as far as we have observed; but the fact that intellect in any country is recognized as a definite political factor is noteworthy; and we should hail 'intellectuals' as a good omen for the progress of the world.[12]

It is interesting to note, first, that this early usage is in the plural, and, second, that the context is political, suggesting very clearly the importing (shortly after the Dreyfus Affair) of the European 'political' sense of the term discriminated above. At the same time, the final sentence expresses a curiously pious form of Edwardian optimism, deliberately at odds with the more familiar attitude of aggressively hard-headed 'realism'. The entry in Fowler's later *Modern English Usage* (1926) catches another dimension of the dominant tone. Discussing 'intellectual' as an adjective, he observed: 'An intellectual person is one in whom the part played by the mind as distinguished from the emotions and perceptions is greater than in the average man. . . . "Intelligent" is usually a patronizing epithet, while "intellectual" is a respectful one, seldom untinged with suspicion or dislike.' Revising this entry for the new edition in 1965, Sir Ernest Gowers modified this comparison to end:

> 'Intelligent' is always a commendatory though sometimes a patron-
> ising epithet; 'intellectual', though implying the possession of
> qualities we should all like to have, is tainted in the communist
> ideology by its use in disparaging contrast to 'workers'; elsewhere
> too it is seldom untinged by suspicion or dislike – called by a leader-
> writer in the *TLS* 'a rather fly-blown word beloved only of
> sociologists'.[13]

The quoted phrase is a neat example of the *TLS*'s perennial tendency
to kill two birds with one sneer, and that tone is maintained in the
further observation that the sense of 'intellectual' is 'not unlike the
definition given by the *OED* Supplement of the colloquial equivalent
'highbrow' (US 'egghead') as 'a person of superior intellectual
attainments or interests: always with derisive implications of conscious superiority to ordinary human standards''. Interestingly,
although the proposed equivalent registers the negative force of
English usage at this point, this entry does not introduce the political
dimension which references to the Dreyfus Affair, in particular, had
accentuated in the early plural uses of the noun.

In the first decades of the century, the milieu in which the term had
the greatest currency seems to have been that of Socialist theory and
discussion.[14] Here, it tended to be used in the extended sociological
sense, to designate 'workers by brain' as opposed to 'workers by
hand', though there was, of course, frequently a polemical edge to
comments about the role of largely 'middle-class intellectuals' in an
assertively 'working-class' movement. The association with Socialism
no doubt also encouraged that anyway powerful tendency in British
attitudes which assumed that 'doctrinaire' (again, the foreign word for
the foreign thing) positions in politics were exclusively the property of
the left; in domestic political debate, 'left-wing intellectuals' has long
had a familiar cadence to it, while 'right-wing intellectuals' only
emerged from the ghetto of Marxist usage fairly recently. The
linguistic situation was further complicated by the importing of
'intelligentsia', initially from Russia. Frequently used in English as a
collective term for 'intellectuals', 'intelligentsia' heightened both the
negative force and the oppositional political identity. By 1965, Gowers
could suggest, not altogether persuasively, that it was 'now an
outmoded word with its leftist colouring washed out of it'.[15]

The 1930s witnessed a marked increase in the use of 'intellectuals', in part because in that decade issues thrown up by the political life of Continental Europe played such a powerful role in structuring domestic political divisions. In some ways, this made the perpetuation of the 'foreign' connotations of the term even easier, as in Orwell's gibes against those English intellectuals who 'take their cookery from Paris and their opinions from Moscow'.[16] Orwell's remark, and indeed his sustained campaign against the mixture of pretension, dishonesty and lack of patriotism which he claimed characterised the English 'left-wing intelligentsia', points to the continuing difficulty experienced by those who wished to represent their identity as unproblematically combining the positive features of being both English and an intellectual. Orwell was referring particularly to writers – the 'Auden gang' were his chief target – and subsequent accounts of intellectuals in the 1930s nearly always refer, explicitly or implicitly, to a rather small number of poets and novelists.

In retrospect, the 1930s was seen as the period during which Britain came closest to what had by then established itself as the classic French model of the oppositional intellectual. For example, writing in the late 1960s (perhaps the latest moment at which this view could confidently be held), T. R. Fyvel observed: 'The novel feature of the thirties was that for the first time English intellectuals reacted as a class to political events. . . . (F)or the first time in England something like a dissident intelligentsia had been formed.'[17] Those in subsequent decades who bemoaned the absence of just such a 'dissident intelligentsia' in Britain frequently evinced nostalgia for what they had come to see as the enviably 'committed' ideological politics of those years, an attitude which has fuelled much of the scholarly interest in 'writers of the 1930s'. The pessimistic premise of such nostalgia is displayed in Swingewood's claim that 'the left-wing intellectuals who emerged during the 1930s left no discernible intellectual and cultural legacy'.[18]

Whether or not this interpretation has tended to exaggerate the number, significance and degree of 'dissidence' of British intellectuals in the 1930s, it is undeniable that the experience, and still more the victorious outcome, of the Second World War has come to seem to have played a crucial role in integrating potentially dissident intellectuals into official institutions and in making a version of patriotism seem the natural expression of their intellectual commitments.[19] Perhaps one hardly needs to underline the importance for subsequent forms of national self-definition of the very different ways in which Britain and France experienced the war. In France (as the essays by

Lindenberg and others above indicate), the Vichy episode re-animated memories of the Dreyfus Affair, and kept that founding division of French intellectual life at the heart of contemporary consciousness in a way which was ultimately to confer valuable moral capital on the *résistants* and thereafter the Communist Party. In Britain, by contrast, the war and what it stood for in the post-war era effectively gave a new lease of life to a late variant of the old Whig interpretation of English history, where the national character had again displayed its sterling qualities in the defence of liberty.[20] Rather than the Sartrean existential dilemmas involved in choosing between betraying one's comrades or seeing one's mother tortured by the Gestapo, the cultural legacy of the war was a rejuvenated conception of 'the nation as pastoral' and the representative status accorded the down-to-earth decencies of J. B. Priestley.[21]

In the post-war period, the usage of the term 'intellectuals', and the assumptions it embodied, continued to be governed by this familiar Anglo-French contrast. In this as in other matters, the mid-1950s represented a minor peak of self-satisfaction. In 1955 the (anonymous) reviewer in the *TLS* of Raymond Aron's *L'Opium des Intellectuels* seized on Aron's account of French intellectuals' self-intoxication and utopianism as providing fresh illustration of a well-worn contrast: 'We can reasonably congratulate ourselves that our intellectuals either have more sense or are not encouraged to be so silly, but it is an ominous fact that the world is full of intellectuals of the French type.' Aron had, of course, been using the term in the French 'political' sense, but the *TLS* reviewer's usage slides between senses without acknowledgement (in the sentence quoted above, for example, silliness and political intervention are more or less equated, but he still uses the term 'our intellectuals'). The reviewer endorsed the Tocquevillian contention, elaborated by Aron, that in Britain academics and men of letters had traditionally been sobered by intimate involvement in practical affairs, a situation that brought rewards as well as responsibilities: intellectuals in France may get a lot of public attention, but they are 'not nearly as much in contact with reality as they are, if they want to be, in the much more closely integrated English society'. Similarly, the reviewer hints at the way in which authority would be less readily granted to a potential intellectual in the 'cultural' sense in Britain, where, in dismissive contrast to France, 'the fact that a man has written a good novel means simply that he is a man who has written a good novel'. Throughout, Sartre, predictably, figures as the antitype, and subsequent attitudes towards 'intellectuals' in Britain were much shaped by the attention, some favourable but mostly hostile, stirred by Sartre and his associates in a period when the contrasts between Britain and France in these matters seemed particularly marked.[22]

In the same year Edward Shils published in *Encounter* an article on intellectuals in Britain that was to be widely referred to in the subsequent literature. Shils's article was a classic case of a polemic masquerading as a piece of objective description. The core of his argument was that the period between the wars when the English intelligentsia had affected to be 'alienated' from British society was a brief deviation from an otherwise uninterrupted pattern of healthy integration, to which they had returned emphatically in the post-war world. 'The cranky antinomianism of the twenty years between the wars was more like a digression from the main course of the British intellectual class in its relations with British institutions.' Contemplating the deep normality of the mid-1950s, he was evidently pleased to be able to report that 'never has an intellectual class found its society and its culture so much to its satisfaction'.[23] As his usage of 'intellectual class' suggests, Shils was on the whole using the sociological sense in this celebrated essay, as for example in his observation that 'The pattern of alienation [between the wars] by no means covered all parts of the intellectual class' since many in the universities, journalism, and the Civil Service did not conform to it. But while his generalisations tend in this way to refer to the sociological sense, it is noticeable that his examples are always well-known figures, most often writers. Shils's own conservatism has become more explicit with time, and it is now perhaps easier than it was in 1955 to see his essay less as an illuminating analysis of the role of the intellectuals in either the sociological or cultural senses in Britain, and more as an Anglophile American's enthusiasm for what he perceived as a society where 'civility' outranked 'commitment' and where as a result intellectuals in the political sense were practically unknown.

The 1960s marked the beginning of a major change in the perception of the place of intellectuals in British culture. The most striking feature of the change was the abundance of laments about the absence of 'real' intellectuals in Britain. The increased size of the category of 'intellectuals' in the sociological sense was one important pre-condition for this development, an increase that was itself dependent upon the expansion of higher education: in 1960 there were approximately 100 000 students in higher education in Britain; by 1988 this had reached 580 000. The exploration and dissemination of ideas derived from the European Marxist tradition was the most obvious intellectual component of this development. It had, of course, been something of a commonplace that Marxist theory had never really flourished in Britain,[24] but reviewing the changes that had taken place in the 1970s and 1980s, Perry Anderson has recently remarked upon the growth of a new 'radical public sphere' whose 'dominant temper was pervasively, if never rigidly or exclusively, Marxist; and whose influence stretched from slowly increasing positions in colleges and universities and an intermittent presence in the national media, through a numerous undergrowth of its own periodicals and associations, across to allied strands in the performing arts and metropolitan counter-culture.'[25] The wider reception of diluted versions of this body of thought helped to domesticate the notion of 'the intellectuals' in the political sense, even when the analyses within which such usages appeared continued to report the rarity of the species in Britain.[26]

The impact of *marxisant* history and social theory also promoted one form of comparative analysis, largely devoted to explaining Britain's 'deviation' from some presumed norm of capitalist development, which has in turn made the role of that congeries of attitudes, values, symbols and practices referred to as 'Englishness' a subject for critical scrutiny. There has been a minor boom in publications exploring the ways in which the constituent elements of this 'Englishness' have been cultivated and deployed, and even where such analyses have appeared reductively functionalist or historically insensitive, they have stimulated reflection upon the ways in which the different strands in still-enduring images of 'national identity' have been formed and perpetuated.[27] As a result, various frequently-repeated claims about the nature of English culture are coming to be seen less as objective descriptions and more as elements in the tangled historical growth of those stories it has proved useful for a society to tell itself about itself. One reason why an analysis within a comparative framework of the place of intellectuals in Britain now appears so inviting is precisely that it has become easier in recent years to see the cliché about the absence of intellectuals in Britain as a part of this construction of 'Englishness'.

III

Identifying differences between British and French culture, and speculating on their causes, is a familiar and seductive activity. Readers of this volume will doubtless already have begun to play the game for themselves by this point. But even if some of the grosser semantic confusions or misleading preconceptions can be set aside, such cross-cultural comparisons are, notoriously, plagued with difficulty. And, of course, the more one attempts to cope with these difficulties by attending to the specificity and cultural density of each of the societies involved, the more the particular feature one originally set out to explore comes to seem to be so deeply embedded in a given history and institutional framework as to be, strictly, incomparable. By the time, in the present case, one has been led back to, say, the contrasting legacies of Locke and of Descartes, or to the different social patterns of the English gentry and the French court, or to divergent development in the late Middle Ages of the English ancient universities and the Sorbonne, then the differences between intellectuals in the two societies in the twentieth century come to seem inevitable and, therefore, relatively uninteresting.

But the enterprise seems a good deal less dispiriting if one does not begin by asking, as so much writing on this subject has implicitly done, 'why weren't British intellectuals more like the norm as illustrated by the French case?'[28] The comparisons can be more open-textured, and hence revealing, if each case is recognised as but one possibility on a spectrum of possibilities. The discrimination of the different senses of the term can particularly help here. It is the 'political' sense which has dominated French reflection on the subject, and since several of the most politically active French intellectuals have also been internationally known as intellectuals in the 'cultural' sense, this has reinforced the image of France as the true home of the species. Britain has, by and large, not known such a tradition of political intervention by intellectuals conscious of their collective role, and since, as we have seen, the deep strains of anti-intellectualism in British life have for long given the term itself a pejorative or dismissive edge, it has been possible to maintain that there have been no 'real' intellectuals in Britain.

Obviously, in the sociological sense Britain, like any other complex modern society, has long had a substantial stratum of people in this category, but the more interesting questions arise with the cultural sense. To proceed for a moment by enumeration, there would be no difficulty in assembling an extended list of twentieth-century figures here, beginning with George Bernard Shaw, Beatrice Webb, H. G. Wells, T. E. Hulme, Hilaire Belloc, Bertrand Russell, G. M. Trevelyan, Leonard Woolf, J. M. Keynes, T. S. Eliot, F. R. Leavis, R. H. Tawney, A. D. Lindsay, Harold Laski, A. J. Toynbee, Richard Titmuss,

Stephen Spender, George Orwell, Cyril Connolly, Lewis Namier, Karl Popper, Michael Oakeshott, A. J. Ayer, A. J. P. Taylor, Lionel Robbins, Isaiah Berlin, Stuart Hampshire, R. D. Laing, Peter Medawar, Raymond Williams, E. P. Thompson, W G. Runciman, Harold Pinter, George Steiner, and so on. Indeed, one can round out the list nicely by adding the name of the author of one of the most influential recent laments about the absence of indigenous intellectuals in Britain: Perry Anderson is only the most recent of a long line of British intellectuals.

The interesting question that arises in considering the role of such figures concerns the nature and sources of the cultural authority they are able to invoke, explicitly or implicitly, in addressing a general (if still not necessarily terribly wide) audience. Indeed, since everyone who writes about intellectuals should be allowed at some point to reveal their own favourite persuasive definition of their chosen sense of the term, I should declare my own candidate at this point: in the cultural sense, an intellectual is someone of acknowledged standing in a creative or scholarly activity *who also speaks with authority on matters on which there can be no experts*. Putting it in this way emphasises that the mere deployment of expertise or the 'application' of a body of technical knowledge to social questions does not constitute the defining activity at the heart of the puzzle of the role of the successful intellectual. In the matter of deciding which values a society should seek to uphold or what goals individuals should pursue there can be no experts.

Looked at in this way, especially with the benefit of a little cultivated distance, one is bound to wonder at the immense confidence manifested by those who have most prominently and successfully played the role of intellectual. Why have they been so confident that anyone will listen, that anyone ought to listen? Taking up the matter from, as it were, the opposite end, one can similarly ask what kinds of contribution do the dominant concerns and register of public debate invite or allow room for? Approached with these questions in mind, Anglo-French comparisons may yield more fruit. In this vein, I propose to sketch two contrasts between the historical place of intellectuals in Britain and France that I find illuminating. Condensed into a phrase, the first is a contrast between types of confidence which may be termed 'social connections versus intellectual prestige'; and the second is between styles of political language which may be represented as 'the Condition of England versus the Rights of Man'.

The question of the intellectuals' relation to their audience inescapably involves the question of confidence. In Victorian Britain, as I have remarked elsewhere, leading intellectuals enjoyed an intimacy with the governing élite which is evident in their characteristically confident tone – they were 'confident of having the ear of the important audience, confident of addressing concerns and invoking values which were largely shared with that audience, confident of an easy, intimate, even conversable, relationship with both Reason and History'.[29] This description refers to a particular period, the mid- and late Victorian years, but despite many changes the same pattern is recognisable deep into the twentieth century, perhaps in some ways right up to the present.[30] Throughout the intervening century, leading members of the educated class have exhibited a social confidence that has not derived from their intellectual activities – indeed, it has sometimes even seemed to survive in spite of rather than because of such activities. It has essentially been a consciousness of social links with the traditional élite. A common public school or Oxbridge education has contributed to this even when social origins have been fairly far apart; a consequent sense of access to the wielders of power has reinforced it. The seduction of exercising influence from the 'inside' has been powerful – a discreet note to a man one knew at university, a word in the ear of a fellow-member of one's club (the maleness of this world is again very striking), the opportunity of a place on a Royal Commission, perhaps even eventually a seat in the House of Lords. The source of the confidence is social, but the mode of action envisaged has remained individual, a sense of exploiting one's *personal* connections rather than acting collectively with other members of the intellectual class.

The confidence characteristically exhibited by leading French intellectuals has been of a different sort. It has been a confidence, first, that intellectual activity was highly regarded by the society in general, and, second, that there existed within that society a smaller, but still substantial, audience responsive to one's public statements and disposed to try to exercise some collective impact on the nation's political life.[31] These conditions were first clearly exposed in the Dreyfus Affair, which represented, as Ory and Sirinelli observe, the intellectual class's 'imposition' of an issue on the political class.[32] Since then, the relevant audience has never been a purely academic one – else the title of 'intellectuel' would have been forfeited and replaced simply by 'érudit' – but it has been to some extent conscious of a degree of insulation from society at large, constituting a sub-culture with its own institutions and forms of life.[33] There have certainly been changes in the composition and role of this audience in the twentieth century, but, once again, a pattern established in the late nineteenth century has proved remarkably durable. At least until recent years, these conditions have allowed a confidence that, if one signed a manifesto or wrote an article or addressed a public meeting, one could expect support and perhaps even success.

These two brief characterizations already bring in their train dozens of other questions clamouring to be answered, but for the moment I shall confine myself to the second contrast, itself half suggested by the first, that of 'the Condition of England versus the Rights of Man'. In Britain throughout the nineteenth century and the greater part of the twentieth, the nature and legitimacy of 'the State' was not really an issue – indeed, the question was thought to have had something of a foreign ring to it. The agenda of public discussion, in the broadest sense, was dominated far more by the social consequences of industrialism, by questions of poverty, of cultural and aesthetic deformation, of the loss of 'community'. (This helps explain, incidentally, why so many of the leading social critics in Britain, from Carlyle, Arnold and Ruskin to Eliot, Leavis and Williams, have worked from a base in literature.[34]) Moreover, the parochial and, more obliquely, nostalgic connotations of the phrase 'the Condition of England' accurately represent the range of reference and preoccupation found in so much of the writing of British intellectuals in this period. The legacy of Protestantism, filtered through the narrow social assumptions encouraged by the educational pattern mentioned above, also helped foster a moralising discourse involving more talk of 'duty' than of 'rights', more attention to the building of 'character' than the building of constitutions.[35]

In France, the Revolution set the political agenda for at least the next 150 years; perhaps only with the kind of 'consensus' about the basic legitimacy of republican political institutions which has developed under the Fifth Republic have these old fault-lines ceased to be the structuring cleavages of French public life. Moreover, the enduring Enlightenment legacy, which was given fresh vitality by the Third Republic's ambitious educational project, encouraged French politicians and publicists to assume they were on first-name terms with Reason. Where 'the Condition of England' points towards concerns that are local, historical and qualitative, 'the Rights of Man' calls up a perspective that is universal, abstract and programmatic.[36] Obviously, in a fuller account one would have to say more about the ways in which the right have attempted to counter this kind of political rationalism by celebrating the 'nation', the 'race' and the 'soil', though even this involved a kind of theorising, and a degree of explicitness, that was less marked in Britain. An education system that has accorded pride of place to philosophy and a public life so largely constituted by the exchange of abstractions are obviously mutually nourishing, and it is hardly surprising that so many French intellectuals, in contrast to the situation in Britain, have had philosophy as their primary academic identity.[37]

This contrast in styles of political language is linked to at least one other feature of the political culture which it may be worth isolating here. The greater stability and structural importance of political parties in Britain has encouraged intellectuals in search of political effectiveness to work through them. The Fabians, for example, discovered that their influence was immensely increased by becoming more intimately involved in the structure of the Labour Party rather than pursuing their earlier role of an external pressure-group willing to work through whatever party would respond to their ideas. In their different ways and for their different generations, Sidney Webb, Harold Laski and Richard Crossman are emblematic figures of left intellectuals whose public activity was largely channelled through the Labour Party. But in France political parties have arguably been less important and have certainly been less continuous. New groupings have tended, at least until very recently, to form around ideological nodes, and this has naturally given the shapers and exponents of ideas a correspondingly more prominent role in the political culture. The Communist Party, to be sure, is, or was, something of a special case, but hardly one that diminishes the role of ideologies and their exponents.

However, even here, where the contrasts might seem at their most marked and incontestable, over-simplification lurks. It is too simple, for instance, to think that the lack of regular overt appeals to Reason or the Rights of Man in British public debate indicates that there are no 'universals' in play. As with the parent question about intellectuals, the road to wisdom here lies not in assuming there were no universals but rather in enquiring about the different forms under which they appeared. Some illumination may be provided by the example of just that figure quoted earlier saying he hoped he would never be called an intellectual, since in some ways he neatly reverses the two contrasts I have just offered. Bertrand Russell is quite properly associated with the founding of analytical philosophy, which has itself long been regarded as one expression or even source of the particularising, low-key, atheoretical quality alleged to be characteristic of public debate in Britain. At first sight, Russell's own political views, too, seem ill-adapted to furnish later generations with any kind of universals in that he remained stuck in a recognisably Edwardian version of English Liberalism throughout his long life (he died in 1970).[38] Politically, he belonged in the company of his actual as well as metaphorical godfather, John Stuart Mill, and his closest intellectual links seem to to be with those late Victorian agnostics like W. K. Clifford or Leslie Stephen who wrote impassioned defences of 'free thought', sermons on the obligation of truthtelling and the duty not to be deceived, including, above all, self-deceived. But we need to realise that this precisely *was* the content of 'the universal' in Russell's social thought: he was in this sense a dogmatic Liberal for whom the values signalled by the slogans about 'freedom of thought' were beyond compromise or even, it sometimes seemed, adaptation. Russell could, in his own way, be as doctrinaire as Sartre.

Moreover, Russell is a particularly interesting case here because he combined social and intellectual authority. Certainly, his titles, family connections and even (once the day of radio and television arrived) his accent all gave him a claim on the attention of a wider public in the deeply deferential society of Britain of the first half of the twentieth century. Interestingly, Russell managed to augment this social capital by displaying some of the identifying marks of the species *homo intellectualis* in its familiar continental form: he exhibited the right degree of bohemianism socially and sexually, and he was for most of his life a freelance, supporting himself by his pen and his personality, and only rarely holding full-time academic posts. But it is clear all this rested upon his standing as a philosopher: presumably the majority of those who responded to his pronouncements on peace and war or on love and marriage were not deep students of the three volumes of his *Principia Mathematica*, but his authority would have been the less had the professional philosophical community not taken these and other works as seriously as it did. (And of course some of his philosophical writing was widely read: there is abundant testimony to the influence of his *History of Western Philosophy*, and it was so successful that it eventually brought him a form of financial security.) But Russell also illustrates that the connection between the intellectual achievements and the public pronouncements does not have to be that the latter are simply 'derived from' or 'applications' of the former. This is most obviously the case with his work in logic and the philosophy of mathematics, but Alan Ryan argues further that 'Russell's strictly philosophical views on ethics made no difference to his moral and political commitments.'[39] In studying the history of intellectuals, it can be a mistake (one often committed) to attempt to analyse their contributions to public debate in terms of the 'ism' with which their name is linked in the relevant theoretical or technical domain. In my view, it is generally likely to be fruitful to recognise the role of their intellectual achievement in winning them a kind of authority, but then to explore the ways their actual performance in public debate has more to do with articulating and deploying values which they and their audience already largely share.

IV

One of the many dangers even of such quick brush-stroke contrasts as was attempted in the previous section is that one tends to represent the two terms of the comparison as static. This would be particularly unfortunate in the present case, since the last decade has seen probably the most significant shift in the position of intellectuals in these two societies to have happened since the beginning of the century. The unacknowledged presence of the familiar stereotypes may particularly obstruct our view at this point. I would suggest, though it is not a claim that can be adequately substantiated here, that the tendency of these changes has been to narrow the gap between the situation, and even to some extent the perception, of intellectuals in Britain and France. Certainly, in France their nature and role, in the 'political' but also the overlapping 'cultural' senses discussed earlier, have changed considerably in the last decade or so, as the essays in this volume amply demonstrate: the familiar model of the 'general intellectual', with a hot-line to the universals of Reason and History, dictating ideological fashions to Left-Bank *enragés* and heading a force of some consequence in political debate, has passed. Since 1983 the theme of 'the silence of the *intellos*' has caused a lot of noise, though it should be clear that this represents a mutation of, rather than a close to, a tradition of self-reflection. But undoubtedly, by comparison to the Sartrean apogee – and his performance in the role is still looked back to as the epitome of the notion of the 'general intellectual', whether its alleged passing is regarded with regret or relief – intellectuals in contemporary France tend to be regarded as more specialised and less significant, as more remote from effective political action and less able to exert a general cultural authority. As Pascal Balmand puts it in his essay: in France, 'Its style of politics is becoming more banal and ordinary, whilst intellectuals – at least in the sense that the term has acquired since the Dreyfus Affair – are becoming ever rarer'.[40]

In Britain the changes have been less remarked, but there are certainly signs of a move in the opposite direction, producing, given the contrasting standpoints, a kind of convergence. As remarked above, changes since the 1960s in both the size and social composition, and to some extent in the favoured styles and themes (at least in the humanities and social sciences) of the academic sub-culture have been important. Moreover, there are signs that this sub-culture is becoming more self-contained, with its own internal preoccupations and reference-points, and with a feeling of being increasingly at odds with the dominant cultural and political attitudes of the most influential sections of society. This may have contributed to a further change, briefly touched on above, namely a modest internationalization of British intellectual life, initially in the form of following or importing trends from America, but increasingly revealing itself in a greater responsiveness to European developments. The more prominent part played by theoretical discussion in a whole range of areas of intellectual enquiry, not least the flourishing of different styles of academic Marxism, has been a notable expression of this, since a body of theory is more readily translatable, both literally and metaphorically, than the substantive observations and insights from which it originally derives.

But in the 1980s the greatest disruption to British intellectuals' traditionally cosy sense of their role has come from the right. In national politics this period has seen the end of that broad governing-class consensus which had obtained since 1945, but it is worth remarking that it is the right which has emphasised the role of ideas here. Those overlapping groups of academics, journalists and policy advisers who formed what was dubbed the 'New Right' argued that what they diagnosed as Britain's malaise was primarily attributable to the dominance of certain liberal–collectivist orthodoxies. The creators and disseminators of ideas were thereby given new prominence, albeit usually as targets.[41] It was representative of the emphasis on the *intellectual* roots of larger social developments, as well as of the ill-judged partisan opportunism characteristic of this strategy, that a junior education minister should have used the occasion of the death of the eminent philosopher A. J. Ayer to mount yet another attack on the 'dethroned hegemony' Ayer was said to have helped to sustain.[42]

But 'the Thatcher years' have fostered a self-conscious sense of identity among intellectuals in a more general way. Despite the pap of official pronouncements, it cannot be denied that Thatcherite Toryism has expressed a very deep hostility to the values embodied in the notions of liberal culture, artistic integrity and disinterested scholarship. These values had previously enjoyed considerable support, even if of a largely habitual and unconsidered kind, from those overlapping social and political groups which had for so long set the tone of public life in Britain. The Thatcher Governments' violent disruption of that cosy relationship (which has been part, of course, of a broader assault on many of the established social institutions of the country) has forced those primarily engaged in intellectual activity to reflect more anxiously upon their place in the wider society. Faced with narrow-minded commercialism in policies for the arts, with deliberate vandalism in the treatment of universities, and with official encouragement to a newly aggressive populist *ressentiment* of cultivation or free enquiry in general, an unprecedentedly large number of the country's intellectuals have come to feel a greater sense of common cause, a greater distance from political power and a greater need to generalise the case for their activities. It would be absurd to think that even the petty-bourgeois destructiveness of Thatcherism could cause a complete rupture with long-cherished cultural attitudes, but it has undeniably brought about a change. We have to recognise that the gap between our world as we near the end of the century and that in which intellectuals like Ayer grew up sixty years ago is at least as great as that which divided the England of the young Ayer from the England of the ageing John Stuart Mill sixty years before that.

Moreover, changes in the agenda and to some extent the style of national politics inevitably shape the size of the space in which intellectuals in the 'political' sense can operate. Whereas in France the development under the Fifth Republic, and especially since the election of a Socialist President in 1981, of a kind of constitutional consensus has reduced the room available for fruitfully challenging the legitimacy of the Republic as such, in Britain the trend has rather been in the opposite direction. The complacent belief in the fundamental health of British political institutions, which had for so long made argued discussion about constitutional and legal principles appear optional or of merely 'academic' interest, has been considerably eroded by the pressure of events in the last decade. In a society in which there is now serious debate about both the possibility of the dissolution of the so-called 'United Kingdom' and the need for a written constitution and/or a Bill of Rights, and at a time when its economic, social and legal arrangements have more and more to be discussed in the context of the principles acknowledged in other European countries, the always wilful commitment to an untheorised 'muddling through' has come to seem less and less persuasive. Political and moral fundamentals have been increasingly pushed to the centre of public attention, thereby creating one of the necessary conditions for a more intellectuals-friendly environment.

It would be silly, of course, to exaggerate the scale of these signs of increasing convergence. Though the two forms of confidence contrasted earlier have each waned somewhat, that contrast still expresses a real difference. After all (to take a minor, but not entirely trivial, illustration), in France the philosophy questions from the *baccalauréat* are still reprinted in *Le Monde*, while in England *The Times* publishes lists of the names of successful final degree candidates together with the names of the schools they used to attend. Furthermore, although it is a valuable corrective to glib generalisations to have a well-documented essay on some of the manifestations of anti-intellectualism in twentieth-century France, the English reader cannot but be struck by the enduring prestige of ideas, literature and the life of the mind in modern France,[43] and can only envy the public attitudes expressed in the French state's greater willingness to use resources imaginatively to further a variety of cultural and scholarly projects. Anti-intellectualism in Britain still has deeper roots and is sanctioned by more central, even official, forces in British life.

This point can be made more concretely by comparing the nature and reception of two ostensibly similar popular books on intellectuals published in recent years. The fact that both are nigh-on worthless productions in their own right only makes them more revealing as symptoms. Bernard-Henri Lévy's *Les Aventures de la liberté* certainly displays all the tendentiousness, selectiveness and sheer silliness that its numerous critics among French reviewers complained of. But for all his posturing, Lévy's book does idealise something about the notion of a 'true' intellectual, albeit denying the title to large numbers of those normally so described on the grounds of their alleged 'betrayal' of the pure type (especially their 'uncritical' endorsement of the Soviet Union).[44] Moreover, although Lévy's place in the media world meant that the book was not short of brazen puffs and factitious 'reviews', several of the more serious French newspapers and periodicals chose recognised students of the subject to scrutinise its pretensions.[45] To both author and audience, the topic was manifestly deserving of sustained attention.

The awfulness of Paul Johnson's *Intellectuals*, the nearest British equivalent to Lévy's book, is of a different order of magnitude. It is simply one long gossipy sneer at the vanity, self-importance, financial dishonesty, and sexual and alcoholic degeneracy of a random selection of figures from Rousseau to Lillian Hellman, designed to demonstrate the monstrousness of the intellectual's claim to speak with moral authority. Johnson takes the defining characteristic of 'the secular intellectual' as the belief that 'the world and humanity could be transformed by ideas coming out of nothing'; that 'nothing' sufficiently indicates the book's regard for reasoned argument.[46] Johnson's publisher was presumably right to assume there was a market for such literary sewage; the book largely received respectful or admiring reviews, including several by eminent public figures.[47] The anti-intellectualism all this represents would appear to be alive and depressingly well in contemporary Britain, despite the changes in usage, attitude and conditions discussed above.[48]

But it would be misleading to end on that pessimistic note. As Jeremy Jennings points out in the Introduction to the present volume, a further sign of the changes in the position of intellectuals in France is the spurt of historiographical interest in the subject there in recent years, which may indicate the Owl of Minerva following its usual flight schedule. Not surprisingly, given the predominance of the 'political' sense of the term in France, the greater part of this recent work has originated from among political historians. By contrast, in Britain and the United States, it has tended to be from within intellectual history, and especially the history of disciplines, that the beginnings of a serious interest in the history of intellectuals has emerged, reflecting the importance of the 'cultural' sense and its problematic relation to a period which has seen a marked increase in the academic specialisation of intellectual life.[49] In both places, more detailed, sceptical and comparative studies may perform one of the most valuable of history's traditional tasks by challenging stereotypes and eroding certainties, especially those long cherished as part of the nation's image of itself. It has been an immensely slow and painful business for Britain to come to realise, in so far as it yet has, that it is one medium-sized European country among others, with similar interests and problems. It may be some small contribution to the successful resolution of this protracted identity crisis if the cliché of the 'absence of intellectuals in Britain' comes itself to be seen as an idea with a particular and limited history within British culture, thus enabling the reality it has helped to mask to be analysed as no more than one distinctive variant of a larger international pattern.

Notes

1. As an example of the potential misunderstandings, consider Peter Allen's comment in a recent survey of uses of the term in English: 'Antonio Gramsci's immensely influential comments on intellectuals . . . deal specifically with those people who owe their social position to higher education, but it would not be surprising to find him approvingly quoted by modern writers in English whose real interest is with the cultural élite and who would not for a moment think of the average Italian priest as an intellectual, as does Gramsci.' Peter Allen, 'The meanings of 'an intellectual': nineteenth- and twentieth-century English usage', *University of Toronto Quarterly*, 55 (1986), p. 350. Arguably, Allen's comment does not altogether do justice to Gramsci's characterisation of 'organic' intellectuals.
2. Seymour Martin Lipset, 'American intellectuals: their politics and their status', *Daedalus*, 88 (1959), p. 460. Lipset continued: 'Within this group, two main levels may be discerned: the hard core, who are creators of culture – scholars, artists, philosophers, authors, some editors, and some journalists; and second, those who distribute what others create – performers in the various arts, most teachers, most reporters. A peripheral group are those who apply culture as part of their jobs – professionals such as physicians and lawyers.'
3. See, for a recent survey, Alain Gagnon (ed.), *Intellectuals in Liberal Democracies: Political Influence and Social Involvement* (New York, 1987). The classificatory impulse of such literature does not always lead to the most nuanced characterisations of other dimensions of the topic. For example, the editor's 'Introduction' to the above volume declares: 'While all the contributors to this volume concur that intellectuals are involved in the production of ideas and the manipulation of cultural symbols, a clear demarcation is made between intellectuals as legitimators and servants of the prevailing order in society and critical intellectuals as forces for changing the status quo' (p. 5).
4. Allen, 'Meanings of 'an intellectual'', pp. 347, 349.
5. For a fuller list, see p. 210–11 below. There are, of course, important questions about why so few women would figure in most such lists, and whether the disparity has been more marked in Britain than elsewhere. Certainly, the criteria mentioned above do not readily apply even to prominent female novelists like Virginia Woolf or Iris Murdoch. Whether the criteria themselves reflect a 'masculinist' bias is a question which would involve an extended discussion of a quite different kind.

6. Pascal Ory and Jean-François Sirinelli, *Les Intellectuels en France, de l'Affaire Dreyfus à nos jours* (Paris, 1986) p. 9. Or again, 'Dans notre ouvrage, l'intellectuel sera donc un homme du culturel, créateur ou médiateur, mis en situation d'homme du politique' (p. 10).
7. Alan Montefiore, 'The political responsibility of intellectuals', in Ian Maclean, Alan Montefiore and Peter Winch (eds), *The Political Responsibility of Intellectuals* (Cambridge, 1990) p. 201.
8. Quoted in H. W. Fowler, *A Dictionary of Modern English Usage*, 2nd edn., rev. by Ernest Gowers (Oxford 1965 [1st edn., 1926]) p. 289.
9. *Encounter*, IV (1955) iv, 2.
10. When, on a committee composed entirely of university teachers, the views of one member were dismissed, to general laughter, with the remark: 'the trouble with Dr X is that he's an intellectual', there was a revealing play between the normative and derisive sense. This vignette comes from Cambridge in the late 1980s. It is not a surprise to find that there are still circles in Britain in which to be manifestly serious about ideas is taken to reveal a disqualifying lack of 'soundness'; it is dispiriting to think that universities should be among them.
11. Raymond Williams, *Keywords: A Vocabulary of Culture and Society* (London, 1976) p. 142.
12. H. W. Fowler and F. G. Fowler, *The King's English* (Oxford, 1906 [2nd edn 1919]) p. 22.
13. H. W. Fowler, *A Dictionary of Modern English Usage* (Oxford, 1926) p. 278; 2nd edn revised by Sir Ernest Gowers (Oxford, 1965) p. 289.
14. See the examples quoted, largely from American Socialist sources, in Lewis S. Feuer, 'The political linguistics of 'intellectuals' 1898–1918', *Survey*, I (1971) pp. 156–83.
15. *Modern English Usage* (1965 edn) p. 290.
16. George Orwell, 'The Lion and the Unicorn' (1941) in *The Collected Essays, Journalism, and Letters of George Orwell*, ed. Sonia Orwell and Ian Angus, 4 vols (Harmondsworth, 1970) II, p. 95. Orwell further emphasised what he liked to present as the inherent tension between the intellectuals' sense of their role and their nationality when he remarked: 'England is perhaps the only great country whose intellectuals are ashamed of their own nationality' (ibid., p. 95).
17. T. R. Fyvel, *Intellectuals Today: Problems in a Changing Society* (London, 1968) pp. 41, 49.
18. Alan Swingewood, 'Intellectuals and the construction of consensus in postwar England', in Gagnon (ed.), *Intellectuals and Liberal Democracies*, p. 89.
19. Orwell provides one of the best-known illustrations of this process; see Bernard Crick, *George Orwell: A Life* (London, 1980) esp. pp. 403–8, and, for a more hostile view, Raymond Williams, *Orwell* (London, 1971; rev. edn 1984) ch.2.
20. One figure who benefited from as well as contributed to this development was G. M. Trevelyan: see Joseph M. Hernon, 'The last Whig historian and consensus history: George Macaulay Trevelyan 1876–1962', *American Historical Review*, LXXXI (1976) pp. 66–97. The war also provided the occasion for the most famous critic of the 'Whig

interpretation' to discover new kinds of relevance in it: Herbert Butterfield, *The Englishman and His History* (Cambridge, 1944).

21. See Simon Featherstone, 'The nation as pastoral in British literature of the Second World War', *Journal of European Studies*, XVI (1986) pp. 155–68; and Eric Homberger, 'Intellectuals, Englishness, and the 'myths' of Dunkirk', *Revue Française de Civilization Britannique*, 4 (1986) pp. 82–100.

22. [Anon], 'The role of the intellectuals', *Times Literary Supplement*, 16 September 1955, pp. 533–4. The article provoked one correspondent to complain of the 'insularity and daftness' of its discussion of French intellectuals, but the reviewer in reply re-stated his points in ever more disdainful tones; 'The role of the intellectuals', ibid, 30 September 1955, p. 573.

23. Edward Shils, 'The intellectuals: (1) Great Britain', *Encounter*, IV (1955) pp. iv, 7.

24. Perry Anderson, 'Components of the national culture', *New Left Review*, 50 (1968), pp. 1–57.

25. Perry Anderson, 'A culture in contra-flow I', *New Left Review*, 180 (1990) p. 45. Less optimistically, Swingewood, too, comments on the existence by the 1980s of a 'shallow' Marxist sub-culture in Britain, not organically connected to working-class culture or the political expressions of organised labour, but confined to academics, students 'and a marginalized radical intelligentsia working within state institutions, local government and the mass media'; Swingewood, 'Intellectuals and the construction of consensus', p. 89.

26. For example, Tom Nairn, 'The English literary intelligentsia', in Emma Tennant (ed.), *Bananas* (London, 1977) pp. 57–83.

27. See, for examples, R. Colls and P. Dodd (eds), *Englishness: Politics and Culture 1880–1920* (Beckenham, 1986); Brian Doyle, *English and Englishness* (London, 1989).

28. Two recent television documentaries displayed the enduring power of these stereotypes. The French director of a programme on British intellectuals went in search of figures who corresponded to one traditional view of the French model: his programme concentrated almost entirely on the group around Harold Pinter and Salman Rushdie as providing the only examples of intellectuals making an impact on public political debate. The English director of the corresponding programme on French intellectuals was no freer of preconceptions: the first shot of Bernard-Henry Lévy showed him being made up for the cameras. 'Océaniques', broadcast on FR3 27 May and 3 June 1991.

29. Stefan Collini, *Public Moralists: Political Thought and Intellectual Life in Britain 1850–1930* (Oxford, 1991) p. 58.

30. The most striking illustration of this continuity is furnished, not always wittingly, by Noel Annan, *Our Age: Portrait of a Generation* (London, 1990). For reservations, of different sorts, about Annan's account, see Christopher Hitchens, 'Annan's unacknowledged legislators', *New Left Review*, 185 (1991), pp. 184–92; and Stefan Collini, 'The thoughts of Chairman Noel: Annan's *Our Age*', *Cambridge Review*, 113 (1992) pp. 18–21.

31. In 1979, Régis Debray estimated that the 'haute intelligentsia', those who are 'socially authorized to express individual opinions on public affairs' beyond what any citizen is expected to do, numbered about 4000, while the 'basse intelligentsia', who constituted the bulk of the audience for such opinions, amounted to perhaps 140 000 people. Régis Debray, *Le Pouvoir intellectuel en France* (Paris, 1979) pp. 50–1.

32. Ory and Sirinelli, *Intellectuels en France*, p. 15. For a more detailed discussion, see Christophe Charle, *Naissance des 'Intellectuels' 1880–1900* (Paris, 1990).

33. See Jennings, 'Introduction' above (pp. 23–5), and for a detailed prosopographical analysis of an increasingly self-sustaining 'caste' of the academic élite, see Christophe Charle, *Les Elites de la République 1880–1900* (Paris, 1987).

34. Raymond Williams, *Culture and Society* (London, 1958) remains a classic discussion of this tradition, as well as being a late example of it.

35. I have tried to explore this moralistic discourse more fully in *Public Moralists*, Part I 'Governing Values'.

36. Among many possible symbolic expressions of the contrast, one may remark that the centenary of the Revolution was also the year which saw the first recorded use of 'English' to refer to the new academic subject.

37. For the place of philosophy in the education system, see J-L. Fabiani, *Les Philosophes de la République* (Paris, 1988).

38. See Philip Ironside, 'The Development of Bertrand Russell's Social Thought', D.Phil. dissertation, University of Sussex, 1987; Alan Ryan, *Bertrand Russell, A Political Life* (London, 1988); Peter Clarke, 'Bertrand Russell and the Dimensions of Edwardian Liberalism', in Margaret Moran and Carl Spadoni (eds), *Intellect and Social Conscience: Essays on Bertrand Russell's Early Work* (Hamilton, Ont., 1984) pp. 207–21.

39. Ryan, *Russell*, p. x.

40. Balmand essay above, p. 173. Of course, to English ears, the very prominence of the dismissive term 'se banaliser' in French discussions of these matters may suggest a certain lingering affection for more exciting times.

41. The irritable, cranky quality of these polemical forays into intellectual history is most revealingly exhibited in Maurice Cowling's 'Introduction' to the second edition of his hatchet-job on one of those held to blame for the triumph of secular liberalism, *Mill and Liberalism* (2nd edn Cambridge, 1990 [1st ed., 1963]). The volumes which have so far appeared of Cowling's massive *Religion and Public Doctrine in Britain* are further backhanded testimony to the significance attached to the power of ideas even by writers of this professedly anti-intellectual stamp.

42. Robert Jackson, Letter to the Editor, *The Independent*, 30 June 1989, p. 21: 'His [Ayer's] is the voice of a dethroned hegemony – dethroned largely because of the poverty and superficiality of its thinking'.

43. See Priscilla P. Clark, *Literary France: the Making of a Culture* (Berkeley, Calif., 1987).

44. Bernard-Henri Lévy, *Les Aventures de la liberté: Une histoire subjective des intellectuels* (Paris, 1991).

45. For example, J-F. Sirinelli's review in *Libération*, 3, March 1991.

46. The quotation occurs in the following tendentious passage in which he is distinguishing between 'the traditional man of letters' and the 'secular intellectual', taking Henry James as an example of the former: 'He rejected with disdain the notion of the secular intellectual that the world and humanity could be transformed by ideas coming out of nothing. For him, history, tradition, precedence and established forms constituted the inherited wisdom of civilization and the only reliable guides to human behaviour'. Paul Johnson, *Intellectuals* (London, 1988, p. 252).

47. For example, Lord Quinton in *The Sunday Times* (2 October 1988, G5), in the course of a generally sympathetic review, praised its 'force, lucidity, and eloquence', and so on. In the *TLS* it received a brief, judicious, though not particularly critical notice, but there was an admirably unimpressed assessment of it by Bernard Williams in *The New York Review of Books*, 36 (1989), p. 11.

48. *The Independent* is undeniably a serious newspaper, but it is still capable of making the following kind of remark in its leading articles: 'It can safely be said that intelligence is more highly prized in France than in Britain; in France they even admire intellectuals.' Whatever allowance one makes for the clumsy attempt at irony, the 'even' here is dispiriting.

49. For further references, see Collini, *Public Moralists*, chs 1 and 6, and T. W. Heyck, *The Transformation of Intellectual Life in Victorian England* (Beckenham, 1982) ch 1. For the United States, see the essay (first published in 1978) by David Hollinger, 'Intellectual history and the discourse of intellectuals', now collected in his *In the American Province: Studies in the History and Historiography of Ideas* (Bloomington, Ind., 1985).

Index